D0870187

ABOUT ISLAND PRESS

Island Press is the only nonprofit organization in the United States whose principal purpose is the publication of books on environmental issues and natural resource management. We provide solutions-oriented information to professionals, public officials, business and community leaders, and concerned citizens who are shaping responses to environmental problems.

In 2004, Island Press celebrates its twentieth anniversary as the leading provider of timely and practical books that take a multidisciplinary approach to critical environmental concerns. Our growing list of titles reflects our commitment to bringing the best of an expanding body of literature to the environmental community throughout North America and the world.

Support for Island Press is provided by the Agua Fund, Brainerd Foundation, Geraldine R. Dodge Foundation, Doris Duke Charitable Foundation, Educational Foundation of America, The Ford Foundation, The George Gund Foundation, The William and Flora Hewlett Foundation, Henry Luce Foundation, The John D. and Catherine T. MacArthur Foundation, The Andrew W. Mellon Foundation, The Curtis and Edith Munson Foundation, National Environmental Trust, The New-Land Foundation, Oak Foundation, The Overbrook Foundation, The David and Lucile Packard Foundation, The Pew Charitable Trusts, The Rockefeller Foundation, The Winslow Foundation, and other generous donors.

The opinions expressed in this book are those of the author(s) and do not necessarily reflect the views of these foundations.

Correction Lines

Correction Lines

Essays on Land, Leopold, and Conservation

Curt Meine

RECEIVED

DEC 2 0 2007

MINNESOTA STATE UNIVERSITY
MANKATO, MN 56002-8419

WASHINGTON COVELO LONDON | Island Press

QH
76
.M45
2004

Copyright © 2004 Curt Meine

All rights reserved under International and Pan-American Copyright Conventions. No part of this book may be reproduced in any form or by any means without permission in writing from the publisher: Island Press, 1718 Connecticut Ave., Suite 300, NW, Washington, DC 20009.

ISLAND PRESS is a trademark of The Center for Resource Economics.

Acknowledgment of Sources appears on page 283.

Library of Congress Cataloging-in-Publication data.

Meine, Curt.
  Correction lines : essays on land, Leopold, and conservation / Curt Meine.
    p. cm.
  Includes bibliographical references and index.
  ISBN 1-55963-731-5 (cloth : alk. paper) —
  ISBN 1-55963-732-3 (pbk. : alk. paper)
  1. Nature conservation—United States.
  2. Leopold, Aldo, 1887-1948—Influence.
  3. Nature conservation—Philosophy. I. Title.
  QH76.M45 2004
  333.72—dc22

                    2004004035

British Cataloguing-in-Publication data available.

Printed on recycled, acid-free paper ♻

Design by Teresa Bonner

Manufactured in the United States of America
10 9 8 7 6 5 4 3 2 1

6517201

For

Evelyn De Vivo Meine

To change ideas about what land is for
is to change ideas about what anything is for.
——ALDO LEOPOLD

ACKNOWLEDGMENTS

Earlier versions of the essays in this book appeared in publications edited by Sarah Bates, Steve Branca, James Deane, Michael Dombeck, Theresa Henige, Rick Knight, Peter Landres, Robert Manning, Ben Minteer, Faith Miracle, Joan Nassauer, Max Oelschlaeger, Suzanne Reidel, Bill Urbrock, Jack Williams, and Chris Wood. I am grateful to all of these colleagues for their prompting and patience, their advice and wisdom, and, especially, the passion they bring to their work.

It is simply impossible to thank all the family, friends, and colleagues who have contributed in one way or another to the making of this book, and to the work behind them, over many years. For all the cups of coffee and glasses of beer, expeditions and explorations, recommended readings and conference conversations, arguments and meetings, stories and songs, and even the e-mail messages—thanks to all.

For particular contributions during the original preparation and revision of these essays, I am indebted to George Archibald, Jeb Barzen, Rich Beilfuss, Chuck Benbrook, Dan Binkley, David Blockstein, Jim Bohnsack, Jeff Burley, Baird Callicott, Bill Conway, Allen Cooperrider, Bill Cronon,

Kenneth Dahlberg, Susan Flader, John Francis, Francesca Grifo, Jim Harris, Mark Harvey, Jack Holzhueter, Buddy Huffaker, Randy Hunt, Wes Jackson, Paul Johnson, Deborah Karasov, Rick and Heather Knight, Sherri Kuhl, Gail Lamberty, the Leopold family, Charlie Luthin, Allen Mazur, Gary and Nancy Meffe, Ramona Montoya, Milford Muskett, Reed Noss, Rob Nurre, Peter Onuf, David Orr, Phil Pister, Mike Putnam, George Rabb, Kenneth Robertson, John Ross, Carl Safina, Eduardo Santana, Lauret Savoy, Simon Stuart, Stan Temple, and Donald Worster.

I have had opportunities to work with many conservation groups, agencies, and other organizations during the years these essays were composed. I appreciate beyond measure the quietly heroic efforts of my colleagues in all these organizations. Among these, I especially thank the Aldo Leopold Foundation; the Biodiversity Support Program (comprising The Nature Conservancy, the World Wide Fund for Nature, the World Resources Institute, and the U.S. Agency for International Development); Defenders of Wildlife; the Center for Humans and Nature; the International Crane Foundation; the Mesa Refuge; the National Academy of Sciences/National Research Council; the Sauk Prairie Conservation Alliance; the Town Creek Foundation; the Society for Conservation Biology; the U.S. Bureau of Land Management, USDA Forest Service, USDA Natural Resources Conservation Service, and U.S. Fish and Wildlife Service; the Wisconsin Department of Natural Resources; the Wisconsin Academy of Sciences, Arts and Letters; and the World Conservation Union (IUCN). Thanks also to my good neighbors in Sauk County and at the Village Booksmith.

Thanks to Miss Fitch, wherever you are.

This book owes its existence to the thoughtful prodding and wise counsel of Eric Freyfogle.

And as anyone who has worked with them knows, Jonathan Cobb and Barbara Dean at Island Press do more than create books; they steward their authors' spirits.

Introduction: Turning the Corner

ACROSS MOST of the continental United States west of the Appalachians, federal land surveyors laid out the original grid of township and range lines that have so profoundly shaped American history and the American landscape. The land survey was the brainchild of Thomas Jefferson and his fellow framers of a series of land laws adopted in the 1780s and 1790s. They aimed to bring order to the land, to apply geometric logic to the earth. The surveyors divided the land into the six-mile-square townships and 640-acre parcels of land ("sections") that are so familiar to us now. The resulting patterns on the ground are easily seen: the straight roads, rectangular properties, and city blocks that define our lives; the Midwest's characteristic quilt of pastures and cropfields; the Great Plains' green poker chips of irrigated land; the Northwest's checkerboard of logged and unlogged forest.

If you have lived within or visited these three million square miles of surveyed American land, you have at one point or another come upon a correction line.

In running the original survey lines, the surveyors faced a dilemma: *the earth is round*. Flat squares can't be consistently fitted onto a spherical globe, because the north-south meridian lines converge as they move away from the equator and toward the poles. To address the problem, the surveyors placed an east-west line in the grid at regular intervals (in much of the country, every twenty-four miles) to compensate for the curvature of the earth's surface. Along this "correction line" they reoriented themselves, shifting the entire grid slightly to the east or west. It was at the correction line, as one observer has succinctly noted, that "theory butted up against reality."[1] This "makeshift" did not solve the problem, but it allowed the survey to continue.

And continue the survey did, all the way to the Pacific. As European settlement proceeded, the strips of land along the main survey lines were often designated as road rights-of-way. Hence, modern roads often follow the old survey lines. Inevitably, north-south-running roads meet the east-west-running correction lines. Where they do, the result is often an abrupt corner, and an awkward ninety-degree turn to the right or left along an otherwise straight thoroughfare. At such points, the traveler must either make the turn or leave the road.

We all come upon correction lines from time to time—places where theory and reality meet. They meet all the time, of course. But at the correction line their intersection is plain, and the need to shift one's orientation unavoidable. Such places give us pause to look both backward and forward. History brings communities and societies up to correction lines as well. I believe we have reached one. In these essays, I try to walk that line.

◄ ►

These essays were written and published over the last fifteen years. This has been a period of dramatic change in the world and in our thinking about the relationship between people and nature. Amid the major events and trends of the times—the collapse of communism and the lifting of the iron curtain; the bubble economy, culture wars, and venal politics of the 1990s; the digitizing of our lives and the rise of the Internet; the turning of the millennial clock; corporate scandals and globalizing economies; the shock of terrorism and the still-unfolding response—ecology, conservation, and environmentalism have also changed. The trends are many, but it is useful to identify a few at the outset.

Ecologists have set aside notions that nature exists in a static, balanced state, and they now call attention to the dynamism of ecosystems. Paleontologists, paleoecologists, and paleoclimatologists have significantly expanded our understanding of ancient extinctions and long-term human environmental impacts. Environmental ethicists and historians have reexamined assumptions about the idea and meaning of wilderness, the human–nature relationship and, in the western hemisphere, the effects of people on the pre-Columbian landscape. Conservationists have de-emphasized approaches that focus on separate resources, isolated properties, and single species; they have adopted approaches that recognize relationships among all the parts and players in ecosystems, including people. They have placed greater emphasis on the conservation of private lands, on community participation in decision making, and on the complex connections between cultural diversity and conservation. Environmentalists have realized important successes in safeguarding environmental quality at the local, national, and global levels, even while being buffeted by strong and constant political winds.[2]

These changes and trends raise many questions about the past, present, and future of conservation. Each of the essays in this volume, when originally written, gave me an opportunity to pause and ask them of myself (the reader will notice a lot of question marks here). Through these years I have worked on conservation projects as a biologist, writer, advisor, teacher, and advocate. In all these activities, I have drawn upon my background in the history of conservation for insight and guidance, criticism and hope. I have found history to be essential in understanding conservation's many challenges and, I hope, making a difference on the ground. As noted above, these have been years of expansive scholarship in environmental history, yielding new ways of understanding our past, our places, our work, ourselves.[3] And our view of history, of course, also shapes our sense of what lies ahead.

And so I think of these as "speculative essays." I have also thought of them as "stimulative essays," hoping that they might spur others on to ask questions and offer their own interpretations. I have no illusion about their conclusiveness. They reflect my own experience in trying to tie the history of conservation science, policy, and philosophy to current conditions and future needs. Many good friends, colleagues, and reviewers have contributed to the shape and substance of these essays, but they ought not to be held accountable for them!

In preparing the essays for this volume, I have revised them to varying degrees to reflect more recent scholarship, to minimize overlap, and to correct (for now!) my own past miscalculations.

◄◄ ►►

The essays are organized into three parts.

The essays in Part 1 look back on conservation's history and development. In them I suggest that we are still struggling to find a coherent and comprehensive narrative of conservation's past. That is a large project, much beyond the scope of these essays. They do, however, seek to provide some useful leads and connections.

"The Oldest Task in Human History" first appeared in a volume titled *A New Century for Natural Resources Management*.[4] The editors of that book asked if I could provide a history of natural resource management ... in twenty-five pages or less. The result, which was aimed primarily at students, was an overview of conservation history, with patterns of change painted in broad brushstrokes. It serves here as something of an overture, introducing and framing themes explored in greater detail in the essays that follow: changes in the sciences underlying conservation; the interplay of conservation science, policy, and politics; the complex relationship between social and environmental change; the consequences of specialization on the land; the impact of world events on the course of conservation history.

The second essay, "Conservation and the Progressive Movement," is more in the middle ground of history, focusing on the rise of the conservation movement in the Progressive Era and the later emergence of environmentalism.[5] Revisiting the progressive tradition in conservation—its premises and flaws, achievements and shortcomings—seems to me essential if we are to get our heads and hearts around our current situation. A century has passed since the Progressive movement transformed America's political and actual landscape. Much has changed since then, in American society, in the body politic, in the economy, and on the land. Much has changed, too, in the way we understand how nature works. It is easy to gloss over these changes, to take refuge in ideology, and to either celebrate or condemn the achievements of the Progressive Era. This essay aspires to a more critical view.

"Conservation Biology and Sustainable Societies" examines more recent history.[6] The editor of the volume where it first appeared asked me to prepare a compact history of the concept of sustainability and the then-new field of conservation biology (lesson: friends just shouldn't let friends edit books). Fortunately, I had stimulus for the task. The assignment coincided with the twentieth anniversary, in 1990, of the first Earth Day. I was working at the time with the National Research Council in Washington, D.C., on a series of reports on sustainable agriculture, international development, and biodiversity conservation. This coincided, too, with the run-up to the 1992 United Nations Conference on Environment and Development in Rio de Janeiro (the "Earth Summit"). Official Washington was awash in draft reports, preparatory meetings, and policy briefings. The original essay was written in a fit of irrational optimism. My main task in revising it for this volume was to tamp it down. Somewhat.

Taken together, then, these three essays offer a long-, middle-, and short-term view of the history of conservation and environmentalism.

·◄· ·➤·

The name Aldo Leopold appears prominently in any effort to link conservation's past and present. As much as any figure in the twentieth century, Leopold (1887–1948) anticipated and stimulated fundamental changes in conservation thinking and practice. Leopold's understanding of the significance of evolutionary biology and ecology, his integration of science and ethics, his sensitivity to the cultural context of conservation, and his personal example as a pragmatic manager and healer of land, changed the direction of the conservation movement. The essays in Part 2 reflect upon Leopold's life and legacy.

In 1988, I published a biography of Leopold that coincided with the centennial of his birth.[7] Interest in Leopold has only expanded in the years since, as his writings have become more available to the public and as scholars have continued to explore his life and work.[8] This, however, is not just a publishing phenomenon. Leopold's ideas and example have informed many of the developments in conservation in the last decade. In his own generation, Leopold was not alone in driving such innovation. However, he was unusually broad in his interests, creative in his synthesis, and gifted in communicating essential lessons. Those at work in conservation continue to find Leopold a valuable source and reference point.

The job of the biographer requires one to draw close to one's subject; in the essays in this section, the biographer steps back and takes another look. My biography of Leopold could not contain all of his life. It could not explore in detail his lasting influence, or foresee which aspects of his legacy would emerge in higher relief. The five essays in this section consider current themes in conservation through the prism of Leopold's experience.

The first two essays may be thought of as extended conversations with Aldo Leopold on two key themes: the historic tension between utilitarian and preservationist approaches in conservation, and the evolution of thinking on the importance of biological diversity.

A reviewer of Leopold's life noted that "he had a practical understanding of conservation as wise use as well as a sense of the aesthetic and idealistic; his evolving ecological reasoning bound these strains. His life is evidence that the traditional division between aesthetic preservationists and utilitarian conservationists is not as clear as historians have often portrayed it."[9] "Leopold's Fine Line" takes a closer look at this proposition.[10] Since this essay was first published, scholars and advocates have engaged in intense deliberations over the very definition and meaning of wilderness.[11] This "great new wilderness debate" has sometimes obscured the fact that important progress has been made over the last century in reconciling these views of conservation. Leopold's experience reflected this trend. Leopold's efforts to resolve tensions without sacrificing essential conservation values remain relevant to conservationists worldwide today.

"Emergence of an Idea" examines in greater detail a theme introduced in the earlier essays: the emergence and development, since the mid-1980s, of biological diversity as a core concept in conservation.[12] This essay makes the case that this represents not a wholly new or radical shift in conservation, but a culmination of long-term trends in conservation science and practice. I believe we need a more detailed understanding of these trends in order to put our recent history into broader context. This essay reviews Leopold's role as an early leader in these transitions.

During the time that most of these essays were written, I have worked on conservation projects with the International Crane Foundation and the Aldo Leopold Foundation (both of which make their home in Baraboo, Wisconsin) and with the Wisconsin Academy of Sciences, Arts and Letters in Madison, Wisconsin. "Giving Voice to Concern" was first published as a joint project of these organizations.[13] Cranes provided an important focal point for Aldo Leopold at a critical moment in his career, as his concerns expanded to include the full breadth of biological diversity, and especially rare and threatened species. In Leopold's day both of North America's cranes, the whooping crane and sandhill crane, *were* rare and threatened species. This essay traces the commingling of Leopold's story and the story of the cranes' survival. It is best read in conjunction with Leopold's own "Marshland Elegy," his haunting ode to cranes and their wetland homes.[14]

"Marshland Elegy" was among the first essays Leopold wrote in the poetic voice that would soon become familiar to readers of his classic *A Sand County Almanac* (1949). The last two essays in this section were both published around the fiftieth anniversary of the *Almanac*'s publication. "Moving Mountains" describes how and why Leopold pulled together the *Almanac* in the final years of his life.[15] The remarkable thing, in retrospect, is that Leopold was able to do so, despite heavy personal and professional burdens. In fact, though, Leopold did not see his forays into literature and philosophy as a distraction or sideline. They were essential to his work, and to the development of the fledgling field of wildlife ecology and management. In the decades since, conservationists have come to appreciate how essential cultural expression is to their work. It is tempting to consider Leopold prescient in this understanding; but for him, it was just second nature.

"The *Secret* Leopold" examines, not Aldo Leopold per se, but the varied views of him that have arisen in the decades since his death.[16] Leopold has served as an important link across three generations of readers, conservationists, and environmentalists. Along the way, for better or worse, he has become an icon. This essay was my own attempt, after many years of interest in Leopold, to cleanse the scholarly palate. It samples the vast secondary literature on Leopold in an effort to gain a clearer sense of the fellow and to see what we have made of him. Leopold will no doubt remain an important source of insight and inspiration into the future. It behooves us, I think, to maintain as critical an attitude toward Leopold as Leopold maintained in his own work.

⋘ ⋙

The essays in Part 3 peer down the path ahead.

But not as something disconnected from the path behind us. As William Faulkner famously observed, "The past is not dead. In fact, it's not even past." "Inherit the Grid" was first published in a book that was in turn the product of a seminar exploring connections among landscape ecology and architecture, land-use planning, conservation biology, restoration ecology, and the visual arts.[17] My contribution was to consider the literal and historical background against which we make such connections: the land survey system and its resulting grid. As such it has particular grounding in the Midwest, where the grid is on such prominent display—and where correction lines are hard to miss.

An abridged version of "The Once and Future Land Ethic" was published in the aftermath of the fiftieth anniversary of *A Sand County Almanac*.[18] The anniversary was marked by a series of special conferences, publications, and commemorative events. Because of their timing, these also served as opportunities to examine the state of conservation and the land ethic on the brink of the new century and millennium. In the midst of these events, I tried from time to time to step back and ask, what trends and needs will determine the fate of Leopold's land ethic over the next century? What questions do we need to ask if the land ethic is to remain vital? This essay is a summary report from one fly on the wall.

"Home, Land, Security" appears in its present form for the first time. The first section of the essay was published in 1998.[19] The core theme was *security*, and its meaning for conservationists trying to protect threatened wild things and places over the long run. That theme, of course, assumed entirely new dimensions with the events of September 11, 2001. The terrorist attacks changed the context of conservation, as it changed so much else. But it did *not* change the thread that connects our sense of security to the land, and to our history, and to conservation. We ignore those connections, I believe, at our own risk. And we strengthen those connections by telling our stories. I have updated this first section of the essay and added a second section recalling my own experience on September 11. The third section of the essay addresses the fracturing of the public interest, and the need for renewed consensus, in conservation.[20] This concern, or course, transcends conservation. Conservation, however, can and must play a role in revitalizing our commitment to the common good and to our communities—where security ultimately resides.

⊸+ +⊱

During the time that most of these essays were written I have lived in Sauk County, Wisconsin, just north of Madison. The native Sauk, Fox, and Ho-Chunk were dispossessed of the land in this region in the 1820s and 1830s. The first federal land surveyors came to Wisconsin in 1833, starting their work in the southwestern part of the state, in the old lead mining district along the border with Illinois. They reached present-day Sauk County just a few years later, in the early 1840s.

It was not until I had been living here for several years that I realized just how close I was to a correction line. Wisconsin's first correction line crosses the state from near Port Washington on Lake Michigan to near Ferryville on the Mississippi River. It cuts across Sauk County, just six miles and a hair north of where I sit and write these words.

On the other side of the correction line, just south of Aldo Leopold's farm and his famous shack, there is a quiet rural route called Man Mound Road. It runs east to west through small farms and woodlots. It is so named because it goes to the Man Mound.

Man Mound is an effigy mound, one of thousands built by the region's prehistoric Woodland Indians between about AD 700 and AD 1200. Throughout the upper Mississippi River basin, effigy mounds were widely despoiled or completely destroyed as Europeans settled the land in the 1800s and early 1900s. Most effigy mounds were shaped like creatures of the water, the sky, and the land. Man Mound is one of the very few extant mounds shaped like a human being.

In 1859 a land surveyor, William Canfield, reported the existence of Man Mound. He described it with great care and precision. The mound was then 214 feet long. It rises subtly above the surrounding soil, just three feet or so. It lies along a north-south axis. Its head (which sports horns, or a horned headdress, or elongated ears) rests on the south. The legs stretch northward.

Man Mound Road was constructed straight along the quarter-section line, cutting the man of the mound off at the knees.

The state archeological society and the county historical society purchased the property in 1907 and established a park in order to prevent any further damage.

Along the correction lines, theory meets reality. When theory and reality collide, painful things can happen. When they correspond, and we respect connections, we can heal.

Conservation's Usable Past | PART ONE

1

The Oldest Task in Human History

The whole world is coming,
A nation is coming, a nation is coming.
The Eagle has brought the message to the tribe.
The father says so, the father says so.
Over the whole earth they are coming.
The buffalo are coming, the buffalo are coming,
The Crow has brought the message to the tribe,
The father says so, the father says so.
    —LAKOTA GHOST DANCE SONG (1890)

We end, I think, at what might be called the
standard paradox of the twentieth century: our
tools are better than we are, and grow better faster
than we do. They suffice to crack the atom, to
command the tides. But they do not suffice for
the oldest task in human history: to live on a
piece of land without spoiling it.
    —ALDO LEOPOLD (1938)

ONE WAY to understand the roots of conservation in the United States is to examine documents from official meetings, policy decisions, and legislative actions that occurred as the movement coalesced in the late 1800s and early 1900s. Another way is to examine the evidence outdoors, *in situ*, in the landscapes we inhabit, in the places we are.

Most of the tangible links to conservation's origins have disappeared. The hooves, horns, and bones of the myriad bison were long ago hauled off the Great Plains to meet their end in glue pots and gardens. The remains of the last passenger pigeons roost beneath bell jars, growing fustier with each passing decade. The hats that sported snow-white plumes from Florida's egrets have gone the way of all fashion. Topsoils from the Midwest's prairies rest in downstream mucks; the plants that made them— and that they made—have lost their claim on the horizon, and do well to hold on in their graveyard, railway, and roadside refugia.

Some objects, however, remain to bear witness. Walk among the aspen, balsam fir, birch, and bracken fern forests of the upper Great Lakes and you will find them: the moldering stumps of fallen white pines. They hunker down in the shade of the second-growth forest (to become, with a minor leap of imagination, bears). Others stand out, weathered gray, in dry openings. Their insides have rotted away, rain, lichen, moss, and insects doing the work of the ages. Only the outermost annual rings of punky wood remain, disintegrating easily in the human hand. Many of the stumps are charred, reminders upon reminders, signs of the fire last time.

The epoch of white pine logging reached its climax in Michigan, Wisconsin, Minnesota, and Ontario in the 1880s and 1890s. The seeds from which those old-growth trees grew had sifted to earth two, three, even four centuries before. Who knows how far and deep their roots went. Sometimes white pine followed white pine on the same site, the roots following tried-and-true pathways carved by patient ancestors through glacial soil, boulder fields, and bedrock.

An early forester, writing in 1898, described the effects of one brief generation of lumbering on northern Wisconsin:

> Nearly the entire territory has been logged over. The pine has disappeared from most of the mixed forests and the greater portion of pineries proper has been cut. . . . Nearly half of this territory has been burned over at least once, about three million acres are without any forest cover whatever, and several million more are but partly covered by the dead and dying remnants of the former forest. . . . Here are large tracts of bare wastes, "stump prairies," where the ground is sparsely covered with weeds and grass, sweet fern, and a few scattering runty bushes of scrub oak, aspen, and white birch.[1]

By the time those words were written, the smart lumbermen of the upper Great Lakes and Mississippi River basins had already shifted their attention, equipment, and capital to the piney woods of the South and the astonishing conifer forests of the Pacific Northwest.

From the viewpoint of the culture whose three centuries of expansion brought them down, the extensive stands of *Pinus strobus*, from New-foundland to Minnesota, were in exactly the right place at exactly the right time, providing a raw material it desired most ardently, insatiably, and *finally*. From the white pine's perspective—if we may grant a perspective to another species—its distribution placed it in the worst possible place at the worst possible time, directly in the path of a gathering force with little inclination to pause, even to consider the conditions conducive to its self-perpetuation. As the "inexhaustible" pineries were, in due course, exhausted, pause came of necessity, at least for some people and some forests.[2]

The decaying stumps will not endure much longer. In a few more years, they will have melted back into the soil, reabsorbed by the medium, returned fully to the flow of time and nutrients. For a little while yet, they will record the extreme to which a narrow concept of social and economic development was taken, and the moment when a new commitment to "the oldest task in human history" took root.

→→ ←←

The delirious climax of white pine logging coincided with other indicators of changing times, landscapes, and social conditions across the continent. In 1889, weary remnants of Indian nations throughout the West undertook the Ghost Dance in a desperate effort to revive their lost world. The dance and the dream ended on December 19, 1890, at the Battle of Wounded Knee.[3] The report of the 1890 census, noting that the "unsettled" area of the United States had dwindled to isolated fragments, declared the "fron-tier of settlement" closed. Three years later, at the Columbian Exposition in Chicago, historian Frederick Jackson Turner built on this finding in his seminal discussion of "The Significance of the Frontier in American His-tory."[4] In the fall of 1890, Congress acted to protect lands now included within Yosemite, Sequoia, and Kings Canyon National Parks.[5] And on March 3, 1891, Congress passed the Forest Reserve Act; later that month, President Benjamin Harrison proclaimed the Yellowstone Park Timber Land Reserve, the nation's first forest reserve and the germ of the national forest system.[6]

At the time, some of these "current events" were widely reported; others passed with little notice. Now they appear as transition points in a broad pattern of cultural and environmental change. The pattern is still emerging, and ever-evolving. There is no definitive agreement on its past development or its implications for the future, and there is much room for debate, varied emphases, and alternative visions. But the changes initiated in the 1890s were fundamental. The basic and tacit assumptions of the post–Civil War boom years would no longer go unchallenged. Few citizens of that era saw the lumber barons' "large tracts of bare waste" as anything but evidence of the latest welcome advance of civilization. Deforestation continued (and continues still) to be visited upon other lands. The rationale, attitudes, and incentives behind deforestation persist. By the turn of the twentieth century, however, stumpfields were no longer what they had been just a few short years before: a universal emblem of human progress.

The changes of the 1890s did not arrive unanticipated. Although belief in the creed the stump symbolized had long dominated American society, undercurrents of reaction against it welled up intermittently, emerging through various cultural, legal, and professional channels. Explorers and naturalists, including John and William Bartram, Meriwether Lewis and William Clark, and John James Audubon, described and documented the astounding diversity of the continent. Early and mid-nineteenth century thinkers, writers, and poets—from Thomas Jefferson and Ralph Waldo Emerson to Henry David Thoreau and William Cullen Bryant—articulated an alternative view of the natural world, as a source not merely of material goods, but of intellectual enlightenment, aesthetic satisfaction, philosophical insight, and spiritual solace. Landscape artists of the 1800s, including Thomas Cole, Asher Durand, Frederic Edwin Church, Albert Bierstadt, and Thomas Moran, conveyed a similar view in their light-suffused canvasses. Other adventuring artists—Karl Bodmer and George Catlin prominent among them—gave real faces and lives to the generic "savages" that existed beyond the ken of "civilization."

In the latter half of the century, proto-conservationists, including George Perkins Marsh, Frederick Law Olmsted, John Wesley Powell, C. Hart Merriam, Carl Schurz, and George Bird Grinnell, insisted that the attitudes and policies that had until then dominated the settlement and development of the American landscape required adjustment. Since the colonial era, local communities and the states had sporadically adopted ordinances and regulations to protect water, forests, game and fish populations, and other resources. At the national level, the post–Civil War years saw the establishment of Yellowstone National Park (1872) and the Adirondack Forest Preserve (1885); organization of the American Fish Culturists' Association (1870) and the American Forestry Association (1875); and the founding of the original Audubon Society and the Boone and Crockett Club (1886 and 1887, respectively).

As of 1890, however, there was no coherent body of beliefs, philosophy, literature, history, science, economics, policy, and law through which the American people could understand and better guide their long-term relationship with the natural world, and scant evidence that such was regarded as an important societal or national goal. There was no U.S. Forest Service; there was, for that matter, no effective profession of forestry as yet in the United States. Nor were there professions tending to the stewardship of soils or waters, rangelands or wildlife. There was little public discussion of the responsibility of private citizens and private industry for the natural objects, processes, and conditions upon which their livelihoods and communities depended. By 1890, however, the doctrine of conquest and the undercurrents of opposition to it had begun to precipitate out the social and political movement that would come to be called *conservation*.[7]

No one person can be said to have ushered in the new movement. Three figures, however, have come to exemplify the impulses that drove it and the tensions that divided it in its early years: John Muir, Gifford Pinchot, and Theodore Roosevelt.

In 1890, fifty-two-year-old John Muir was focused on gaining federal protection for the lands surrounding his beloved Yosemite Valley. His success in this led to the creation of the Sierra Club in 1892 and established Muir as the country's leading voice for the protection and preservation of wild nature, a role he occupied until his death in 1914. Building on foundations provided by Emerson, Thoreau, and Marsh, but bringing to his arguments a lifetime of experience in wild country, Muir made the public case for preservation on several grounds. Like many who agitated on behalf of forests, Muir (building especially on the work of Marsh) could cite the benefits of forest cover in regulating water flows and protecting soils. But the protection of forests, and wildlands in general, involved a broader spectrum of values. Muir strongly emphasized the restorative powers of "long-drawn breaths of pure wilderness." Exposure to wild country provided aesthetic, psychological, and spiritual benefits that could not be gained in urban or even pastoral landscapes. There was in Muir's outlook, too, an abiding sense of the intrinsic beauty and worth of all things within the "one great unit of creation." The plunder and waste that had gone by the name of progress, and that Muir had witnessed in America's eastern forests, constituted nothing less than acts of desecration, attributable ultimately to the hubris of "Lord Man."[8]

As the embodiment of the "romantic-transcendental preservation ethic," Muir defined one wing of the nascent conservation movement.[9] What guidance did this ethic offer in the effort to "live on a piece of land without spoiling it"? It said, in effect, that for those remnants of yet "unspoiled" land, one succeeds in the task by not living on them at all but by setting them aside as places where, in the words of the 1964 Wilderness Act, "man . . . is a visitor who does not remain."

At the end of 1890, Gifford Pinchot was twenty-five years old and returning to the United States, having spent the previous year studying forest management in France, Switzerland, and Germany. Although interest in forestry had been growing (primarily among scientists) in the United States through the 1870s and 1880s, Pinchot was the first American to receive formal training in the field. He returned determined to bring professional forestry to a country where, as he later put it, "the most rapid and extensive forest destruction ever known was in full swing."[10] Within fifteen years Pinchot, riding the wave of the Progressive movement alongside his friend and political patron Roosevelt, would succeed. With the creation of the Forest Service in the U.S. Department of Agriculture in 1905, Pinchot established forestry as the locus of conservation within the government and in the public mind.

And what was forestry? Forestry aimed "to make the forest produce the largest possible amount of whatever crop or service will be most useful, and keep on producing it for generation after generation of men and trees."[11] This utilitarian mission lay at the heart of the "resource conservation ethic" that defined the other wing of the conservation movement, and that Pinchot more than any other individual promulgated. "The forest," Pinchot stated, "rightly handled—given the chance—is, next to the earth itself, the most useful servant of man."[12] The utilitarian ethic stood in contrast to the epic wastefulness that had marked the era of rampant forest exploitation. It stood in contrast, as well, to the preservationist ethic. Where Muir saw "one great unit of creation," Pinchot found "just two things on this material earth—people and natural resources."[13] Taken to its extreme, this view led to a particular conception of forests and of forestry. "Forestry," Pinchot maintained until the end of his life, "is Tree Farming."[14]

The guiding principle of Progressive Era utilitarian conservation was to manage natural resources so as to produce commodities and services "for the greatest good to the greatest number for the longest time." To this end, nature was not to be preserved, but actively manipulated by scientifically trained experts to improve and sustain yields. Those yields were to be harvested and processed efficiently, and the economic gains allocated equitably. How then to live on a piece of land without spoiling it? By strengthening the oversight role of government, enacting science-based regulations, adopting rational resource management practices, developing resources with a minimum of waste, and distributing the benefits of development fairly among all users.

As the conservation movement gained definition in the 1890s and the first decade of the 1900s, Muir and Pinchot and their respective followers jostled for primacy and influence, with the overarching figure of the day—Theodore Roosevelt—maintaining a precarious position between them. In his presidential addresses, congressional messages, public speeches, and administrative actions, Roosevelt could and did advocate both development and protection, maintaining the forest reserves "in proper shape" and protecting native flora, fauna, and landscapes.[15] To a degree, the sheer amount of energy and action invested in conservation during Roosevelt's presidential years diverted attention from the movement's internal tensions. However, the rival approaches to conservation could not and would not coexist for long.

The tension surfaced most visibly and vitriolically in the celebrated battle over the damming of the Tuolumne River in Yosemite's Hetch Hetchy valley.[16] The battle, playing out over a twenty-year period, reaching its denouement in 1913, drew the lines uncompromisingly: Hetch Hetchy could not be both preserved as parkland and used to store water. The struggle begged the ultimate question: what was it to *conserve* this place—or any place? Was there *a* conservation movement, or were there in fact *two* movements, born of related concerns but moving toward radically different ends?

The dam at Hetch Hetchy was built, but the question remained unresolved. Muir fought against destruction of wild nature and the attitude that had allowed legitimate use to be perverted into rampant abuse. Pinchot fought against inefficient development of natural resources, the political corruption that such development so often entailed, and the inequitable distribution of wealth and power that both allowed and followed unrestrained exploitation. The preservationists and utilitarians both opposed the destructive forces of the day, and their goals often overlapped. But their worldviews could not be accommodated—much less reconciled—until conservation itself was redefined, its scientific underpinnings reformulated, and its social dimensions reconsidered.

That process would gain momentum in the 1930s. In the meantime, advocacy metamorphosed into administration. The political movement for conservation reform shifted in the interwar years toward the more mundane execution of conservation policy. As that transformation occurred, renewed efforts to protect wild lands intensified. In general, however, the principles of utilitarian resource conservation held sway and by the mid-1930s would be applied not only to forests, but to other "useful" components of the landscape: river systems, agricultural soils, rangelands, sport and commercial fisheries, game animals, scenic areas. As new laws, policies, and bureaucracies were created to promote sustained yields of, and from, these components of the landscape, resource management became institutionalized and professionalized.

The late 1930s stand out as an especially dynamic period in conservation history, as new resource problems arose, new scientific concepts emerged, and new thoughts on the social and economic context of conservation took hold. In retrospect, World War II and its aftermath profoundly altered the roles and relationships among the different resource management professions. The war stands as a sharp horizon line in the history of resource management. For these reasons, it is worth reviewing the origins and development of the various conservation fields and their status on the eve of the war.[17]

Forestry

Forestry continued to serve as the lead conservation profession in the three decades following Pinchot's early campaign. Its role expanded as the Weeks Law (1911) and the Clarke-McNary Act (1924) extended the national forest system to the eastern states, strengthened forestry research, promoted watershed protection, and supported increased forestry activity at the state and local level. Training opportunities also expanded. Led by Yale's Pinchot-endowed Forest School, colleges and universities throughout the country formed forestry departments to stock the Forest Service and state agencies, as well as the timber industry. As the most solidly established and, in many ways, broadest of the resource management professions, forestry also tended to attract those whose interests lay in related fields (such as game conservation, recreation, soil conservation, and range management) that as yet lacked similar training and employment opportunities.

One result of this breadth was that the Forest Service—a young agency with diverse responsibilities (and a relatively flexible structure of administrative authority)—became a proving ground for new ideas in conservation. Through the 1910s and 1920s, many of the founding principles in range and game management, soil conservation, recreation, and wilderness protection derived from work on the national forests. Many leading innovators in conservation—including Aldo Leopold and Robert Marshall—came from the ranks of the Forest Service.

Forestry's adaptability in these years is best appreciated against the background of the nation's changing timber supply and demand. The goals of the Forest Service in managing the national forests (as rather modestly stated in the 1905 *Use Book*, the governing manual of the Forest Service) were to "[preserve] a perpetual supply of timber for home industries, [prevent] destruction of the forest cover which regulates the flow of streams, and [protect] local residents from unfair competition in the use of forest and range."[18] While the emphasis within the Forest Service gradually shifted over the next two decades toward silviculture, fire suppression, and increased timber harvest, there remained much room to consider alternative uses and diverse approaches to forest management. Indeed, timber companies actually urged the Forest Service to limit production from the national forests as a means of propping up prices for timber taken off private holdings. As a result, recreation remained a (if not *the*) leading use of the national forests until World War II.[19]

These trends would have longer-term consequences for the forestry profession. As the cut of timber on private lands continued apace, the threat of depletion began to loom. By the early 1930s, many foresters, foreseeing the inevitable pressure this would bring to bear on public forests, began to argue for much stronger federal control of private forestlands. Pinchot himself inveighed against the "forest butchery" on private lands, calling on the government to exercise its "right to prevent forest destruction by private owners."[20] The warnings went largely unheeded. As the supply of private timber tightened, the Forest Service and the profession of forestry as a whole would have less room politically and philosophically in which to maneuver. Even as forestry came to define itself ever more narrowly by its emphasis on timber production, the conditions under which the profession operated were constricting.

Agriculture

The erosion and exhaustion of agricultural soils had been a concern among conscientious landholders since the earliest days of the republic.[21] Thomas Jefferson, to cite one notable example, conducted early experiments in crop rotation and contour plowing. However, as long as new farmland remained cheap and readily available, farmers had little incentive to follow Jefferson's lead. National movements to protect soil and other farm resources would remain limited in their effectiveness until expansion into new arable lands was economically prohibitive or geographically infeasible. In 1909 the U.S. Bureau of Soils could announce, with full confidence, that "the soil is the one indestructible, immutable asset that the nation possesses. It is the one resource that cannot be exhausted; that cannot be used up."[22]

Over the next three decades, trends in agriculture placed unprecedented emphasis on the conservation of soil, water, and game on the farm. Industrialization was rapidly altering farm landscapes through mechanization and intensification of agricultural production. These transformations affected soils and waters, native ecosystems, and wildlife populations, not only by encouraging agricultural expansion, but by changing the nature of farm inputs, outputs, cropping practices, and pricing, marketing, and processing networks. At the same time, the draining of wetlands and appropriation of surface waters for irrigation altered hydrological functions and aquatic ecosystems over large portions of the Midwest, Great Plains, and the intermountain and far West.[23]

Agricultural expansion and the availability of new farm machinery allowed the number of farms to increase to a high of 6.8 million in the early 1930s, even as rural people moved into cities and towns and the availability of farm labor declined. Intensified agricultural practices took their toll in the form of extensive soil erosion (and associated problems with siltation and flooding), accelerated losses of wildlife habitat, and increasing social and economic instability and dislocation. These forces played out in different ways in different regions of the country but culminated in the mid-1930s with the disaster of the dust bowl in the southern Plains.[24]

In 1928, the U.S. Department of Agriculture published "Soil Erosion: A National Menace," its first advisory bulletin on soil erosion. The bulletin's coauthor, Hugh Hammond Bennett, emerged as the leading public advocate on the issue, proselytizing among farmers and politicians alike, pressing the federal government to assume a more active role. In 1933, Congress created the Soil Erosion Service within the Department of the Interior. In 1935, with the problem literally looming in the air of Washington, the agency was moved into the Department of Agriculture and its functions broadened within the new Soil Conservation Service (SCS). Significantly, the hallmark of the SCS was its promotion of watershed-wide approaches that combined soil conservation measures with other resource management practices.[25]

As the countervailing forces of industrialization and conservation played out on the agricultural landscape, science assumed a growing but dichotomous role. Operating through state land grant colleges and extension services, agricultural scientists increasingly found themselves drawn into two camps. On one side were those who, adopting industrial systems as their model, focused on increasing production through the development of new crop varieties, fertilizers, and other purchased inputs. On the other side were those who, adopting natural systems as their model, focused on maintaining fertility and productivity using agronomic methods and materials, while selectively incorporating new technologies into their operations. At the end of the 1930s, the schism between these two approaches was not yet as wide as it would later become; the dust bowl years had given everyone a sober lesson in the pitfalls and promises of modern agriculture.

Range Management and Conservation

Range management, like forestry and soil conservation, arose in response to the depletion of a resource once regarded as inexhaustible. By 1900, overstocking with cattle and sheep had degraded forage resources throughout the vast arid and semiarid grasslands of the trans-Mississippi West. The number of livestock on the western ranges rose dramatically in the thirty years following the Civil War as the bison herds were exterminated and the Plains Indians subdued, and as new railroad lines connected livestock producers, processors, and markets. But in the late 1880s, a combination of overstocking, hard winters, low rainfall, and financial jitters among distant speculators brought an end to the livestock boom—though not before damaging grasslands throughout the West.[26]

Cattlemen themselves were among the first to draw attention to the situation. By the turn of the century, a series of official surveys and reports confirmed their observations of deteriorating range conditions and prompted development of the first range experiment stations and programs. By 1910 the Forest Service and eight states had established experiment stations devoted to research on grazing practices and forage resources, while state universities throughout the West began to offer coursework in range management.[27] More conservative use of range resources, however, was slow in coming. In many parts of the West (especially the Southwest) ranges were once again overstocked (mainly with cattle) in anticipation of higher demands during World War I—demands that failed to materialize before the war ended. The result in many areas was further deterioration of the range and accelerated soil erosion.[28]

Federal land policies had for decades abetted the decline of rangeland through ill-conceived programs for parceling out the public domain and through lax administration of grazing on those lands that remained publicly owned. Beginning in the 1890s, the government initiated a series of land policy changes to improve conditions for settlers while providing protection for the public lands. These policy changes included, prominently, establishment of grazing regulations on the newly created national forests. The Forest Service thus assumed a key role in the development of range management.

Meanwhile, there remained the vast unreserved rangelands outside the national parks and forests—lands that, after their appropriation from the native inhabitants, had been used freely by both small ranchers and large livestock interests and that had continually been the object of intense turf battles and political dispute. The battle for control of the public rangelands led to passage in 1934 of the Taylor Grazing Act, which withdrew these lands from further disposition, established the federal Grazing Service to administer them, and provided for a system of land leasing through local grazing districts.[29] In 1946 the Grazing Service was combined with the old General Land Office to form the Bureau of Land Management (BLM). Much as the creation of the Forest Service had stimulated the development of forestry as a profession, the establishment of the BLM would prompt the rise of range management as a discrete field.

Wildlife Management and Conservation

Although concerns about the decline of wild animal populations had long fueled the conservation movement, wildlife management did not emerge as a separate profession until the 1930s. Through the 1800s, overexploitation, market hunting, and habitat loss had resulted in the depletion and, in some cases, extirpation of many important game species—most visibly the bison and passenger pigeon, but also the black bear, white-tailed deer, pronghorn, elk, turkey, prairie chicken, beaver and other furbearers, and many waterfowl and wading birds. Efforts to respond to the trend were often initiated at the state level, since states retained jurisdiction over what was then termed "wild life." Meanwhile, sportsmen's organizations and other citizen groups had formed around the issue and pressed for reforms.[30]

In most regions the movement for wildlife conservation focused initially on the protection of game species through stronger law enforcement, tighter restrictions on hunting, and occasional designation of refuges—as well as the persecution of large predators (which were by common consent regarded as "vermin" rather than legitimate "wild life"). By the beginning of the new century, most states had established fish and game agencies, out-lawed market hunting, and enacted fishing and hunting regulations. The new agencies, however, were often ineffective in enforcing regulations.

While states often took the lead in protecting game, many of the most important reforms occurred at the federal level. The U.S. Bureau of Bio-logical Survey was established in 1896 (having originated as the Division of Economic Ornithology and Mammalogy in the Department of Agri-culture). Though lacking enforcement powers, the Bureau provided a focus for the growing interest in wildlife protection. The Lacey Act (1900) strengthened the states' hands by prohibiting interstate transportation of game killed in violation of state laws. Through the national forests and parks, the federal government assumed a larger role in protecting some of the nation's most important and visible wildlife populations and habitats. (And in suppressing others: in 1914 Congress allocated the first federal funds for predator control on the nation's public lands.) Theodore Roo-sevelt had also created, by presidential proclamation, the earliest federal refuges and sanctuaries—the cornerstones of the later system of national wildlife refuges. And in 1916, the United States and Canada signed the landmark Migratory Bird Treaty, providing both governments with new authority to protect waterfowl and other migratory birds.[31]

By the mid-1920s, the movement for game *protection* had begun to evolve into the field of game *management*.[32] The need was self-evident. Many game species—including even small game species whose popula-tions had initially benefited from the expansion of agriculture—had declined due to intensified habitat loss and hunting pressures following World War I. Responses to the situation within the conservation commu-nity varied. Some argued for outright bans on hunting. Others argued for rebuilding game populations through predator control, artificial propaga-tion (especially of waterfowl and upland game birds), and introduction of exotic game species. A new school of thought, however, had begun to emerge, focused on protecting and restoring habitat so that populations of native species could sustain themselves. Aldo Leopold, the leading propo-nent of this approach, summarized his views in *Game Management* (1933), the first text in the field.[33] By applying concepts from the emerging science of ecology to the conservation of wild animal populations and their habitats, Leopold's work revolutionized the field, with repercussions that would extend far beyond the management of game species.

The field evolved rapidly in the crucial decade of the 1930s.[34] Under the energetic leadership of Jay N. "Ding" Darling, the U.S. Bureau of Biological Survey broadened its mission and its budget. The Migratory Bird Hunting Stamp ("Duck Stamp") Act (1934) and the Pittman-Robertson Federal Aid to Wildlife Restoration Act (1937) provided new funds for research, habitat protection, and other management activities. Universities opened research and training programs throughout the country.

The conceptual foundations of the field also broadened during these years. Ingrained anti-predator attitudes began to shift as the ecological functions of predators became better understood and more widely appreciated. The idea of management itself began to extend beyond game species to include "nongame" animals and plants. Rare and endangered species began to receive increased attention. The clearest indication of these trends was the adoption, in the mid-1930s, of the one word term "wildlife," which for at least some wildlife managers included all forms of wild plants and animals.[35] By 1940, wildlife management was established as a distinct field with its own professional society, journal, textbook, and educational programs, more effective state agencies, and a strengthened federal agency, the U.S. Fish and Wildlife Service.

Fisheries Management and Conservation

The early development of fisheries management in the United States paralleled that of wildlife management.[36] By the late nineteenth century, populations of many economically important freshwater, anadromous, and marine fish species were depleted due to overharvesting, habitat loss, dam construction and water diversion, and water pollution from urban, industrial, and agricultural sources. In response, states initiated efforts to place the exploitation of fisheries on a sustained yield basis, establishing fish commissions and enacting regulations or prohibitions on commercial fishing in inland waters. Private fish hatcheries began to supplement natural reproduction as early as the 1850s. Along with law enforcement, the development of hatcheries soon became the primary activity of state fishery agencies. The decline of fisheries and rise of fish culturing led to formation in 1870 of the American Fish Culturists' Association (renamed in 1884 the American Fisheries Society). In 1871, Congress established the U.S. Commission of Fish and Fisheries (the "Fish Commission") to assess the status of fisheries and to promote the artificial propagation and introduction of game and food fishes.

Fish culture came to dominate the field so completely that, by the early decades of the twentieth century, "fishery management" was already essentially synonymous with "hatchery management." The well-established fisheries profession found a ready home in the new utility-minded and efficiency-driven conservation movement. Advances in the study of fish biology, behavior, and ecology were applied quickly to the operation of hatcheries to improve productivity. But while money and hopes were increasingly invested in hatcheries as the key to sustained fish yields, there was scant evidence of their effectiveness in actually increasing or maintaining catches. Meanwhile, relatively little attention was being given to other aspects of fishery conservation: the size, methods, and timing of harvesting; the genetic and behavioral impacts of artificially propagated fish (especially nonnative species and strains) on native wild populations; the status of nongame fish and other organisms within the aquatic community; the effects of surrounding land uses on water and habitat quality; or the hydrological and biological impacts of large-scale irrigation systems, dams, and other engineering projects (especially on the large midwestern and western river systems).

In the marine realm, fisheries biology and management emerged as a separate discipline in the 1890s in response to the decline and depletion of fish stocks.[37] By the 1920s, the focus in marine fisheries science had shifted from studies of individual fish to population biology, and from enthusiasm for fish hatcheries to more careful monitoring of populations and adjustment of the catch. This led in turn to the emergence of the concept of "maximum sustained yield" in fisheries management: the theoretical high point at which a given population could be perpetually exploited.[38] It was a doctrine that would prove problematic in the decades to follow.

From the earliest days of fisheries management, a persistent minority of biologists and fishery managers had questioned the prevailing management approaches, especially the heavy emphasis on artificial fish stocking. This was due in part to the concurrent development of the science of limnology, which had an impact on fisheries management analogous to that of animal ecology on wildlife management.[39] In addition, biologically informed anglers—of whom there were increasing numbers—began to question the authority of fishery managers. By the 1930s, an alternative school had arisen that gave greater attention to the management of habitat for both coldwater and warm-water fish species.[40] According to fisheries biologist J. T. Bowen, "During the 1930s . . . fish culture assumed a less important role in the [American Fisheries] Society, and by 1936 the membership reflected a completely new outlook."[41] Although fish culture would remain dominant, the "new outlook" would begin to address previously neglected aspects of fishery management, including research on fish populations (both game and nongame species) and their aquatic environment, protection and restoration of fish habitat, and development of more effective fishing regulations.

Outdoor Recreation

Camping, hiking, hunting, fishing, and other forms of outdoor recreation were important but nonetheless secondary conservation concerns during the Progressive Era. And in the case of Hetch Hetchy, where recreational values were wedded to the preservationist ethic, they could be considered actual impediments to development by utilitarian resource managers. An important exception, however, was the movement to enhance parks, playgrounds, and other outdoor spaces in the nation's crowded cities. Inspired especially by the works of Frederick Law Olmsted, a new generation of landscape architects began in the late 1800s to experiment with naturalistic designs that provided urban dwellers with greater access to outdoor amenities.[42]

The status of recreation changed with the establishment of the National Park Service in 1916 and the early manifestations of automobile culture in the 1920s. Congress created the Park Service to bring order to management of the nation's thirteen existing national parks (and, in part, to bind political wounds following the Hetch Hetchy dispute). Many of the parks, including Yellowstone, Yosemite, Grand Canyon, and Glacier, were conceived and developed with the support, if not the outright lobbying, of the railroad lines that served them. As the private automobile and new highways provided the public with even greater mobility, areas of important aesthetic and recreational value (at both the state and federal level) were subject to increasing use. Accordingly, conservation agencies and organizations began to devote greater attention to them.

The prosperity of the 1920s, the advent of two enthusiastic fishermen-presidents (Coolidge and Hoover), and the rise (beginning in 1921) of the Izaak Walton League as an important force in national conservation politics all fed the trend. Coolidge convened two National Conferences on Outdoor Recreation (in 1924 and 1926), firmly establishing recreation as a basic conservation concern. This momentum carried over into the New Deal years, especially as the Civilian Conservation Corps channeled labor into the development of park facilities. The heightened visibility of recreational values also raised the status of wilderness protection within the Forest Service, ratcheting up the level of competition between the Forest Service and Park Service over control of potential park and recreation lands.

An important aspect of national park management in the early 1930s was the increasing interest in scientific research and management of wildlife in the parks. In 1931, a Wild Life Division was created within the Park Service and placed under the directorship of George Wright, a young biologist at the forefront of the contemporary advances in ecology and wildlife management. Over the next five years, Wright led a team of like-minded scientists who sought "to plan for orderly development of wild-life management" in the parks.[43] Their efforts to promote ecologically sound and scientifically informed park management suffered a crucial setback, however, when Wright was killed in a car accident in 1936.

Wilderness

The preservationist impulse in conservation had not dissipated after Hetch Hetchy. To a degree, its energies were diverted into the work of the

National Park Service, but a small minority of dedicated wilderness enthusiasts continued to struggle against the tide of development from within the federal agencies, while citizen advocates pushed from outside the agencies. In particular their efforts reflected the growing impact of the automobile, and hence of roads, on the American landscape during these years.[44]

After Hetch Hetchy, the movement to protect wilderness on public lands shifted to the Forest Service. In 1919 and the early 1920s, landscape architect Arthur Carhart persuaded his Forest Service supervisors to limit local resort development at Trappers Lake on Colorado's White River National Forest and in the boundary waters of northern Minnesota's Superior National Forest. In 1924, Aldo Leopold and several of his Forest Service colleagues succeeded in reserving a large portion of New Mexico's Gila National Forest as the Gila Wilderness Area—the first such area to be so designated. Through the mid-1920s, Leopold led a faction of foresters who supported the "preservation of a system of wilderness remnants in the National Forests."[45] In response, the Forest Service gave increasing support to wilderness protection, culminating in adoption of the "L-20" rules in 1929, which formally established wilderness protection as a Forest Service responsibility.[46]

During the 1930s wilderness advocates, led by Robert Marshall, pressed for the inventory and protection of roadless areas on public lands. Opposition to wilderness protection had hardly subsided. Pressures to intensively manage and exploit public lands mounted both within and beyond the federal agencies, often abetted by New Deal conservation programs that stressed intrusive development to provide employment. These threats led Marshall and other wilderness activists to form The Wilderness Society in 1935. Its goal, in part, was to secure statutory support for the administratively vulnerable wilderness areas. Progress toward this goal would prove to be slow, but wilderness protection continued to gain support in the federal agencies in the late 1930s. In 1939, the Forest Service issued updated "U" rules that gave greater protection to some fourteen million acres of roadless land within the national forests.

Through this whole period recreation continued to provide the dominant rationale for protection of wild lands, and public lands continued to be the primary battleground. However, it was during these years too that scientists and conservationists began to appreciate their shared interest in the unique ecological conditions that wild lands, of whatever scale and tenure, harbored. A new view of the wild—its value, its scarcity, and its vulnerability—was taking hold within the conservation world.[47]

Where, then, was conservation *as a movement* at the end of the 1930s? It was broader and deeper than it had been three decades before. It was more urgent, more fully appreciated by the general public, and more thoroughly woven into the public discourse and public institutions. It had gained greater professional definition—and bureaucratic bulk—but it was also more actively promoted by dedicated nonprofessionals and citizen organizations.

Yet for all the strides taken, the recurring challenge of conservation that Aldo Leopold noted had not been satisfactorily addressed: amid the rolling dust storms of the 1930s, neither the utilitarian nor the preservationist philosophy seemed up to the "oldest task." Conservationists began to search for a new approach to the challenge. They would draw upon elements of both older schools of thought. They decried the faulty policies and wasteful practices that had degraded so much of the American landscape and resource base. They embraced the preservationist critique of human hubris and greed, while carrying forward the high regard for and aesthetic appreciation of wild nature. And they accepted and relied upon the authority of science—a legacy of their training as resource managers in the progressive utilitarian mode. But they also had begun to draw upon a new and different kind of science.

◄◆ ◆►

At the conclusion of *Breaking New Ground*, his 1947 autobiographical account of the rise of forestry and conservation, Gifford Pinchot laid out his vision of a future in which injustice, inordinate profit, and concentrated wealth would cease to determine the social order of humanity. "When it comes," he wrote, "I hope and believe the new order will be based on cooperation instead of monopoly, on sharing instead of grasping, and that mutual helpfulness will replace the *law of the jungle.*"[48] Notwithstanding the legitimacy of the ideal that Pinchot hoped to communicate, his choice of metaphors (which he repeated several lines later) revealed much about

the worldview upon which he—and much of the conservation establishment—had built their policies and their professions. The implication?
Unmanaged nature was ruled by unbridled tooth-and-claw competition. It
was a world, in the end, of constant struggle for existence, a world that
could, should, and would be civilized through the application of human
reason and managerial skill.

Pinchot was writing in the mid-1940s, near the end of his life. His
metaphor had sure resonance in the aftermath of World War II, but for a
growing number of conservationists and scientists, the view it implied was
already outmoded.[49] Ecology had begun to revolutionize the scientific
view of "the jungle" and of the natural systems within which human society operated. As philosopher Baird Callicott writes, ecology was revealing
the natural world as "more than a collection of externally-related useful,
useless, and noxious species arrayed upon an elemental landscape of soils
and waters. Rather it is a vast, intricately organized and tightly integrated
system of complex *processes.*"[50]

The workings of human society, it followed, could not be understood
apart from its geographical and evolutionary background and its ecological foundations. Writing in 1933, Leopold suggested that "civilization is
not, as [the historians of its progress] often assume, the enslavement of a
stable and constant earth. It is a state of *mutual and interdependent cooperation* between human animals, other animals, plants, and soils, which may be
disrupted at any moment by the failure of any of them."[51] Conservation,
its scientific and historical context thus recast, could no longer be defined
in either pure utilitarian or preservationist terms. Utility was a far more
complicated matter than even the most ardent utilitarians realized. "Usefulness" was a property not simply *of* discrete parts of nature, but derived
from the entire ecological community.

Moreover, a broad range of factors determined the quantity and quality of any given service, resource, or commodity that nature might provide. "Yields" could be sustained only if economic forces and resource
management practices did not undermine what Leopold termed "land
health"—the evolutionary coadaptations and ecological interactions that
allowed natural systems to function smoothly and renew themselves.
Wilderness, by the same token, had more than aesthetic or recreational

value. It stood at one end of a land use *continuum*. It served as a "land laboratory"—a place against which to compare landscapes subject to more intensive human use and manipulation. Preservation of wildlands afforded protection (or so it was assumed) to their diverse parts and their ecological processes, which had much to offer in the effort to understand "how healthy land maintains itself."[52]

Seeking a more comprehensive ethic to guide conservation, Leopold and a minority of like-minded individuals stressed the need to combine conservative use *and* preservation, based on an appreciation of ecological processes and the diversity, integrity, stability, and beauty of the biotic community. Conservation could then strive for more than just sustained yields of particular resources or commodities, and more than preservation of the nation's dwindling and increasingly isolated remnants of wilderness.

How then to live on a piece of land without spoiling it? The answer turned out to be much more delicate and complex than either the utilitarian or preservationist schools had suggested. Begin with a basic appreciation of the entire biotic community, its composition, structure, and functions, and the evolutionary and historical forces that have changed it. Protect samples, at least, of each different kind of community (and not just the "scenic" and spectacular). Use the resources of the land and waters conservatively, with high regard for native diversity and the fullest possible awareness of the ecological processes that maintain the system's health. Develop and revise management strategies based on the best information that the *integrated* natural sciences can provide. Actively restore, wherever feasible, that which has been lost, degraded, or unwisely altered. Identify and work to change the social and economic forces that constrain such actions. Be active, since time is short; but be patient, since success is by definition incremental and long term.

And something more. In "The Land Ethic," Leopold's final expression of his long-evolving philosophy, he calmly prodded conservation forward with these words: "The land ethic . . . enlarges the boundaries of the community to include soils, waters, plants, and animals, or collectively: the land. . . . A land ethic of course cannot prevent the alteration, management, and use of these 'resources,' but it does affirm their right to continued existence, and, at least in spots, their continued existence in a natural state." [53]

Of the many messages embedded within this passage, the most important may be the most subtle: Leopold's deliberate placement of the term "resources" within quotation marks—perhaps the only time he ever did so. With that slightest of gestures, Leopold simultaneously acknowledged the reality of human resource use and the limits of utilitarian conservation philosophy, even as he confirmed the inherent worth and dignity of "things natural, wild, and free."[54] Conservation could not succeed if people regarded, valued, and managed nature merely as a disaggregated assortment of "natural resources." Success in the oldest task in human history could not be gained simply by developing ever more powerful and sophisticated tools to extract ever more goods and services from the natural world. Success required more comprehensive ways of perceiving, understanding, and appreciating the relationship between people and nature. Success, in other words, required that we not simply change the land, but that we change *ourselves*.

This redefinition of conservation had enormous implications for the various resource management fields. For one thing, it raised fundamental questions about the validity and viability of separate professions, disciplines, and departments. Within his area of special expertise—wildlife management—Leopold tried to push those who "[saw] utility and beauty only in pheasants and trout" to see more fully the "utility and beauty of the biota as a whole."[55] By the early 1940s, all the conservation fields had "dissenters" (to use Leopold's term) who had come to similar conclusions: in trying to understand natural systems and human activity within them, the assumptions and approaches of reductionist science (valid knowledge is best gained by dividing reality into ever-smaller parts), utilitarian philosophy (this knowledge achieves its highest end when used to meet strictly human needs), and conventional economics (human needs are always served through increases in raw productivity) were inadequate. In the view of the "dissenters," attention had to be given to connections, relationships, and changes in nature. One could not simply manage soils, or waters, or trees, or game populations, or fish stocks, or scenic vistas, or any other resource, as isolated entities; one had to consider the diverse components of the entire system or landscape and their interactions over time. Professional labels notwithstanding, conservation implied—demanded—integration.

◂◂ ▸▸

World War II changed everything. The promising synthesis that had begun to emerge within conservation was overwhelmed by the war and inundated by social changes in its aftermath. Even as Leopold put the finishing touches on "The Land Ethic," the resource management professions had begun to move in other directions—indeed, each in its own direction. Instead of growing more flexible, boundaries between scientific disciplines, departments, and agencies became more rigid. Instead of converging on a shared vision of ecological health and integrity, resource managers became more specialized and focused on increasing the output of their particular commodities. Instead of narrowing, gaps in understanding only widened—gaps between various fields of sciences, between basic and applied sciences, between science and other fields of human knowledge, between academic departments and conservation agencies, between different professions, between professionals and the public.

Writing in 1945, Paul Sears traced much of the problem "back to college class-rooms, where a type of fragmental teaching has been going on that breaks the world of human experience up into air-tight compartments." He insisted that "this sort of piecemeal teaching and learning simply has to be stopped. It is getting to be too costly to our modern society."[56] For most, however, those costs—if they were admitted at all—were too far removed to be of much immediate concern. The new generation of postwar resource managers (and their consumers) slipped easily, and for the most part unknowingly, into a disciplinary framework to which there were few alternatives.

The ramifications were, and remain, far-reaching. As Reed Noss and Allen Cooperrider have observed, such strict adherence to disciplines "resulted in a pattern of natural resource management that is fragmented and inefficient. Individuals trained in one discipline work on problems in isolation from other specialists, even within the same agency. Agency land-use plans are often written as if there are separate landscapes to provide for timber, wildlife, livestock forage, clean water, and recreation."[57] The forces of technological innovation, economic expansion, population growth, and rising consumption reinforced the trend. The demand for all natural resources increased dramatically during the postwar boom years.

As pressure to increase production—of crops, lumber, livestock forage, fish catches, game animals, visitor days—grew, so did the faith that all conservation problems had technological solutions. At a point in history when conservation dilemmas were becoming more complex, clear communication more valuable, and unity of purpose more necessary, the counterforces seemed inexorable.

The development of forest management in the postwar years serves as a useful case study. While "dissenting" foresters had argued for a broader view of the composition, function, and management of forests, the profession as a whole drifted in the other direction. Historian Samuel Hays notes, "As early as the 1920s, the dendrology textbooks and courses in forestry schools that described forest species and their distribution became restricted to commercial types. The texts explained that foresters need not know all forest species—foresters were not botanists—but only those that were useful for wood production. This narrowed their conception of a forest considerably."[58]

As forestry's conception of the "resource" tightened in the postwar years, the demand for forest products rose rapidly, especially in response to the housing and construction boom. The effects were most apparent in, though not confined to, the national forests. The means to the all-but-universally accepted end of sustained timber yields began to shift. The selective-cutting methods that foresters began to adopt in the 1930s gave way to even-aged management of larger-scale forest units. Productivity gains were sought through increased inputs in the form of fertilizers and genetically "improved" tree stocks. Pest management was sought through increased applications of synthetic pesticides and intensified control of competing vegetation. Clearcutting became the preferred method of harvest, replanting with trees of the same age and species the preferred method of reforestation. Hays notes that "by the 1960s the elements of this technical system had been worked out in great detail."[59]

As economies of scale and economic incentives reinforced the shifts in forest practices, the *subculture* of the forestry profession also changed. Private timber interests played an ever-growing role is setting the education, research, and policy agenda. Foresters grew further away from the vision of unified conservation that was in many ways their own professional legacy.

Even when, for example, the Multiple-Use Sustained-Yield Act of 1960 directed the Forest Service to balance timber production with other uses, the underlying idea—wiser coordination of forest management's means and ends—remained essentially dormant. Timber production remained the primary use, within the subculture if not the law. There was simply too little integration of thought or action among the managers—much less among the users—much less within society—to give "multiple use" meaningful expression, or meaningful criticism.[60]

The same general pattern played out in other fields of resource management during the postwar years. Hence: to improve agricultural productivity, expand and intensify farm operations using artificial fertilizers and synthetic pesticides, a limited number of "modern" (or, now, bioengineered) seed varieties, and an ever-growing array of "labor-saving" technologies; to improve forage range production, remove woody vegetation, apply herbicides, and seed with more "desirable" forage species; to build up stocks of fish and game, introduce exotic species and expand artificial propagation programs; to prevent floods and manage water resources, dam the headwaters, drain the wetlands, straighten the channels, channelize the streambeds, and raise the levees.

The same forces were at work behind the pattern: primary, if not exclusive, focus on the few commercially valuable components of the ecosystem; adoption of increasingly sophisticated management technologies, input-intensive practices, and systems; increasing economies of scale; standardized planning and production methods; simplification of natural systems and processes; development of an insular professional priesthood; increasingly close ties between resource management agencies and politically and financially influential user groups and industries. The various fields also shared derelictions: a lack of attention to the particular features of places, to the complexity and diversity of ecosystems, to externalized social and environmental costs, to the harmful effects of fragmented thought on both natural and human communities.[61]

◂─┤ ├─▸

There was, however, a counter-counterforce. World War II had had other, more positive impacts on conservation. It gave a generation international experience and increased the availability of information, transforming conservation into a global concern. It tempered the near-religious faith in science as the font of all progress, and in technological change as the ultimate solution to human problems. Yet it spawned technologies that would revolutionize human understanding of natural systems and their evolution. It galvanized those who saw, not specialization, but synthesis of knowledge as the essential requirement in the modern age.

These factors coalesced around particular issues—loss of wilderness, the nuclear arms race, rampant pollution—in the 1950s, then surfaced dramatically in 1962 when Rachel Carson's book *Silent Spring* inaugurated the modern environmental movement. The new generation of "environmentalists" and the older resource managers were far from unified in their motivations, their experience, or their approaches. There was, however, common ground. Starting from it, those within both the natural resource management professions and the environmental movement could begin to revive the integrated understanding that Leopold and his generation had first tried to articulate thirty years earlier.

If increasing specialization marked the years 1945–1965, the remainder of the 1960s and 1970s saw increasing acceptance of environmental values and goals within the resource professions and within society at large. The translation of these values into effective conservation action, however, proved to be slow and fitful. Political and economic obstacles to reform (both within and beyond the professions) remained formidable. Specialization continued to exercise its drag; even in pursuing broader environmental goals, conservationists of all sorts still tended to focus on single species, single resources, single parts of the landscape—single aspects of complex conservation dilemmas. But younger resource managers, users, and scientists, trained after the first Earth Day, had begun to enter and rise through the professional ranks. They carried with them a stronger sense that, to conserve anything, various disciplines and ways of knowing had to be brought together in the human mind and in the landscape.

By the end of the 1970s, the consequences of *disintegrated* conservation could no longer be avoided or misinterpreted. The effects were evident across the landscape, from the innermost city to the outermost wildland: in widespread pollution of air, soils, and waters; in the decline of urban neighborhoods and infrastructure; in the frenetic spread of suburbia and the rise of "edge cities"; in increased stress on agricultural soils and waters, and on farm families, rural communities, and agricultural economies; in the clearing and fragmentation of forests under intensified logging pressures; in the continued loss and degradation of native grasslands, wetlands, deserts, open spaces, and wildlands; in the inability to insulate national parks and other protected areas from air- and waterborne pollutants and other transboundary threats; in the decline of once-vital fisheries due to overharvest and disruption of aquatic ecosystems; in the impairment of life's genetic, species, and ecosystem variety to such a degree that a new term, "biodiversity," had to be coined to comprehend the situation; in the incurring of long-term social and environmental costs under so many different ecological circumstances that a new term, "sustainability," had to be coined to communicate the dilemma.

The systemic nature of these by-now familiar problems became steadily more apparent, as did the limits of the traditional conservation professions, acting separately, to address them. Beginning especially in the 1980s, the need for interdisciplinary approaches became more formally accepted within the established professions. The problems themselves defined new fields of scientific research and application, including conservation biology, restoration ecology, landscape ecology, and sustainable agriculture. Concepts that had hovered around the margins of resource management—sustainability, ecological health, ecosystem management, environmental justice, comanagement, community-based conservation—moved closer to the core of the discussion. The social sciences and humanities reentered that discussion as ecological economics, environmental history, and environmental ethics became established fields of study.

At the turn of the millennium, a century after it first took form, conservation was again reinventing itself, evolving in response to internal tensions and external demands.[62] Behind these adaptations is the tenacious idea that conservation is more than a mere matter of long-term economic self-interest and clever resource management. It entails moral choices and responsibilities involving our fellow citizens and neighbors, future generations, and the community of life in which we evolved and to which we belong. Like conservation itself, this ethic has emerged fitfully over the last century and is only now growing into the role that it must play in human affairs in the future. Ignored by those "[for] whom education and culture have become almost synonymous with landlessness,"[63] muted by a generation of cornucopian dreams and Cold War fears, overshadowed now by the specter of international terrorism—and sometimes invoked by those disinclined to confront the dilemmas it suggests—the ethic rings with greater definition and urgency as conservation enters its second century. But it remains, as Wallace Stegner noted, "not a fact, but a task."[64]

➻ ➻

Conservation is, and always has been, a radical endeavor—"radical" in the first and literal sense of the word: pertaining to, and proceeding from, *roots*. Conservation pertains to and proceeds from the roots of experience; of knowledge, values, and wealth; of needs and dreams and the divine. We who now confront the sobering realities of this brave new century can sense only with difficulty the historical roots of conservation. For now, we can still find them hidden deep in the shade of the recovering north woods, where crumbling stumps of white pines mark the reckless and restless path behind us.

In the world the Ghost Dancers tried to dance back into existence, a kind of wildness had free reign. Its loss resonates in the words of their songs chanted, in dire need, on the Great Plains a century ago. That world will not be regained, but the loss has been at least partially redeemed. Perhaps, after all, a nation is coming—a world is coming—to recognize that wildness, properly known, is not the antithesis of civilization, but its complement and its context, essential to its vitality, inherent in its definition. The revival of the white pine and the northwoods forest, the restoration of the bison and prairie, the building of healthy human communities able to coexist with and within nature—these may yet signify the return of wildness, not as an enemy but as a guide, as another generation prepares to take on the newest, oldest task in human history.

2

Conservation and the Progressive Movement

You shall look and listen for the welfare of
the whole people, and have always in view
not only the present but also the coming
generations, even those whose faces are yet
beneath the surface of the ground—the unborn
of the future Nation.
  —CONSTITUTION OF THE IROQUOIS
  CONFEDERACY (15TH CENTURY)

What government is best? That which teaches
us to govern ourselves.
  —JOHANN WOLFGANG VON GOETHE
  (1826)

TWO THOUSAND AND ONE marked the hundredth anniversary of two signal events in the annals of American government and conservation. On January 1, 1901, Robert M. "Fighting Bob" La Follette was inaugurated as the governor of Wisconsin. Later that year, on September 14, Theodore Roosevelt assumed the U.S. presidency following the assassination of William McKinley. These events marked the arrival of the Progressive Era, during which conservation emerged as a coherent movement. For several decades, the voices of reform had been swelling: Grangers, Greenbackers, and Populists across the rural Midwest; socially conscious urbanites and antimonopolist businessmen; civil service crusaders and progressive educators; suffragists and settlement workers; forest advocates, wilderness preservationists, concerned scientists, and conscientious sportsmen.[1] With the rise of Roosevelt and La Follette, reformists moved to the center stage of politics. In the decade that ensued, conservation flourished.

Roosevelt's immense conservation legacy is well known: proclamation of more than two hundred million acres of national forests, monuments, parks, and wildlife refuges on the public domain; appointment of high-level commissions through which his administration shaped the nation's first concerted conservation policy; enforcement of laws intended "to preserve from destruction beautiful and wonderful creatures whose existence was threatened by greed and wantonness"; the bolstering of agencies to carry out these policies and enforce these laws. We have never had, before nor since, a president more knowledgeable in the natural sciences or one who took closer to heart the conviction that, as concerns conservation, "the Executive is the steward of the public welfare."[2]

La Follette's conservation legacy is more diffuse. A committed supporter of conservation measures throughout his career, La Follette is nonetheless identified primarily with his uncompromising dedication to political reform. To appreciate his contribution to conservation, one must read it in the broader context of the times. Wisconsin's timber barons, who by 1901 were stripping off the last of the white pine, had dominated state politics for three decades. La Follette's rise to the governorship and later (in 1906) to the U.S. Senate marked the end of the pine-logging era, with its attendant political corruption, as plainly as did the vast stump fields of the cutover North.[3]

Under La Follette and his followers, Wisconsin became a leader in policy innovation in fields from education and labor law to public health and electoral reform. Roosevelt and La Follette clashed regularly as their political fortunes intersected—an ongoing battle of progressive titans. During a moment of détente, Roosevelt praised "the movement for genuinely democratic popular government which Senator La Follette led to overwhelming victory in Wisconsin," and recognized Wisconsin as "literally a laboratory for wise experimental legislation aiming to secure the social and political betterment of the people as a whole."[4] For his part, La Follette judged the president's leadership in conservation as "probably the greatest thing Roosevelt did . . . inspiring and actually beginning a world movement for staying terrestrial waste and saving for the human race the things upon which, and upon which alone, a great and peaceful and progressive and happy . . . life can be founded."[5]

The Roosevelt and La Follette anniversaries passed by with no fanfare, no high oratory. It is no surprise, given the lineup of contemporary political constituencies. Few Republicans seem interested in emulating their party's progressive forebears—Roosevelt and La Follette, of course, were both Republicans—and are content merely to invoke TR's legacy in sure-fire applause lines. Few Democrats, who rely on urban and suburban environmentalists as sure votes, even seem aware that there was once a broad-based conservation movement that came out of rural America, without which environmentalism as we know it today would simply not exist. Few of the contemporary heirs to progressivism seem to envision their place in politics as anything but pushing and pulling Democrats further toward the traditional left. Few libertarians seem to care as much about their public responsibilities as their private rights. All are bound by the tired mental image of a one-dimensional left-to-center-to-right political spectrum. All are inclined to render environmental issues into predictable politics.

By contrast, consider Wendell Berry's careful words: "Our environmental problems . . . are not, at root, political; they are cultural. . . . Our country is not being destroyed by bad politics; it is being destroyed by a bad way of life. Bad politics is merely another result. To see that the problem is far more than political is to return to reality."[6] The Progressive movement was indeed an intensely political response to a cultural problem. Roosevelt did not dither in describing the problem: a century-long "riot of individualistic materialism, under which complete freedom for the individual . . . turned out in practice to mean perfect freedom for the strong to wrong the weak."[7] In the arena of resource development, it meant unrestrained power to plunder a continent's natural wealth.

But, however political its means, the Progressive movement did not arise from within a single political party and was not identified with one (not, at least, until the tumultuous presidential election of 1912). Progressive forces fought within and between and outside the Republican and Democratic parties. Difficult as it may be, we must somehow try to imagine a time when the spirit of reform, fairness, public service, and the primacy of the public good defined and pervaded civic life.

The conservation movement was among the fruits of the time and spirit. The twentieth century would see fundamental changes in our understanding of ecosystems, the ethical foundations of conservation, and the social and economic connections between our lives and landscapes. These changes would call into question the scientific assumptions and utilitarian slant of Progressive Era policies regarding conservation and development of the nation's forests, rangelands, minerals, wildlife, and waterways. Nonetheless, the actions undertaken in the first decade of the 1900s ensured that there would in fact *be* a movement capable of evolving with time.

The Roosevelt and La Follette anniversaries did not pass without at least a modest nod. On September 21, 2001, on an evening somber with recent events, citizens in Wisconsin's Sauk County gathered to hear voices from the Progressive tradition. It was a fit setting. Sauk County, in the south-central part of the state, was a historic hotbed of Progressivism and gave the world Fighting Bob's remarkable wife Belle Case La Follette. Sauk County later became the home place for Aldo Leopold's essays in *A Sand County Almanac*. That September night we recited the words of Roosevelt:

> Reformers, if they are to do well, must look both backward and forward; must be bold and yet must exercise prudence and caution in all they do. They must never fear to advance, and yet they must carefully plan how to advance, before they make the effort.[8]

Of Gifford Pinchot:

> Conservation is a moral issue because it involves the rights and the duties of our people—their rights to prosperity and happiness, and their duties to themselves, to their descendants, and to the whole future progress and welfare of this Nation.[9]

Of Wisconsin's own Charles Van Hise:

> The paramount duty remains to us to transmit to our descendants the resources which nature has bequeathed to us as nearly undiminished in amount as possible, consistent with living a rational and frugal life. Now that we have imposed upon us the responsibility of knowledge, to do less than this would be a base communal crime.[10]

We stayed late into the evening, finding solace in the words of those from an earlier generation who worked, each in their own manner, for a robust body politic and a healthier land.[11] In 1901, a revolution dawned in the United States of America. Among its other contributions, that revolution challenged the assumption that had dominated national development for generations: that the American land was a mere storehouse of inexhaustible resources, existing solely for the indulgence of the present generation of its most privileged species. We are still reeling from the revolution.

◂◂ ▸▸

There is much confusion and debate over the way that revolution has played out in the decades since. How did we get from 1910's "conservation as wise use" to the antienvironmental opportunism of the Wise Use Movement in the 1990s? From "sustained yield" to "multiple use" to "ecosystem management"? From "fish and game" to "wildlife" to "biodiversity"? The answers are murky, even for careful observers of the history of conservation and environmentalism.

Take, for example, Peter Sauer's 1999 lament in *Orion* magazine that the environmental movement had deteriorated into "a cacophony of bickering ideologies." "What happened to its unity and idealism," he wondered, "and when did it fall into disarray?" In Sauer's experience, the movement was once characterized by seamless connections between our concern for human rights and for nature. Sauer recalled a golden moment in the late 1940s when, in war's aftermath, we began to realize our joint obligations to the human community and the biotic community. He cast a worried (and nostalgic) look upon a movement that had "[lost] its grip on the principles declared by [Rachel] Carson and Aldo Leopold." That hold, he suggested, had begun to slip with the death of Carson in 1964—two years before *A Sand County Almanac* became available in paperback, six years before Earth Day put environmentalism on the political map. Younger generations, Sauer feared, would never really know what the environmental movement "once stood for."[12]

Take, too, the caricature of environmentalists, popular in postmodernist critiques, as deluded naïfs, dismissive of human concerns, neglectful of local landscapes, seeking escape from history, denying people a place in nature, and waxing sentimental for a North American wilderness that never existed in the first place. This view, rising through the 1990s, under-lay the "great new wilderness debate," at the core of which rests the con-tention that environmentalism, to right itself, must be purged of its false and romantic fixation on an unpeopled wilderness.[13] Proponents of this view posit (in a too typical statement) "an emerging environmentalism that moves beyond merely preserving pristine wilderness and also calls for clean air and water as human rights as well as environmental necessities."[14] By this reading, the environmental movement never "stood for" any kind of broad conception of social obligation or justice. It never had anything like a unifying ideology, except perhaps a shallow one premised on secur-ing opportunities for privileged white folks to contemplate and recreate in the great outdoors. It implies that protectors of the wild and defenders of human justice have never had, and could not have had, much of anything to say to one another.

These opposing takes reflect a broader confusion. They indicate that something is amiss in our reading of conservation and environmental his-tory. We can lay out evidence both for and against their interpretations. We can point out the lax and often anachronistic use of the terms "conserva-tion" and "environmentalism."[15] (Neither Carson nor Leopold, for exam-ple, would have recognized the modern usage of "environmentalism." Leopold used the word "environment" no more than a dozen times in his entire corpus.) We could note that neither position adequately accounts for the complex interplay between social justice and conservation concerns through the twentieth century. We could cite lesser-known verses from conservation's texts to both prove and disprove their premises—and to enrich the dialogue. (One of my favorites: the 1954 statement by the great wildlife biologist and wilderness defender Olaus Murie, comparing con-servation's modest ethical development to "our heavy-footed progress in toleration of 'other' races of men," and calling for "tolerance for the views and desires of many people.")[16]

The point is that, in the rush to criticize, deconstruct, salvage, advance, and reform "the movement," those who care about such things have not yet achieved a satisfactory story. For all the work and writings of a generation of environmental scientists, historians, journalists, advocates, and critics, our narrative still has major holes, still misses the mark. The difficulty derives in part from the massive challenge of covering all the relevant bases. We have no comprehensive history of conservation—much less one that captures both the continuity and disparity between conservation and environmentalism.

Ironically, this may reflect the fact that environmental history as a field achieved definition even as the baby-boomer, Earth Day–inspired, counterculture-tinted, increasingly politicized, ever more globalized environmental movement grew through the 1970s, 1980s, and 1990s. Historians and other observers in this generation could be expected to view the past through the lens of the environmentalism they grew up in and with, to overlook or underemphasize important aspects of earlier conservation history, and to see plainly the conspicuous flaws in their own generation's environmental worldview. The effect, moreover, is not confined to environmentalists per se; "conservative" skeptics and outright antienvironmentalists see through the same lens, just from the other side.

In short, before we can "reconstruct" conservation, we need to lift the lens and see conservation and environmentalism with fresh eyes: as a dynamic amalgam of science, philosophy, policy, and practice, built upon antecedents in the United States and in cultures and traditions throughout the world, but responding to conditions unique in human and natural history.[17] During the Progressive Era, these constituent elements of conservation came into alignment and a new movement materialized. That movement has continually evolved ever since in response to expanded scientific knowledge, emerging ecological realities, shifting political pressures, and a constantly changing cultural context.

◂◂ ▸▸

Conservation in the Progressive Era rested, first and foremost, on utilitarian and anthropocentric premises. "The first principle of conservation is development, the use of the natural resources now existing on this continent for the benefit of the people who live here now," Gifford Pinchot wrote in his 1910 book *The Fight for Conservation*.[18] In order to provide "the greatest good to the greatest number for the longest time," natural resources were to be efficiently managed and developed in a manner informed by science. The "science" of the time was disciplinary, applied, production-oriented, pre-ecological. It sought and provided raw numbers:

tree growth rates for the forester, stocking rates for the range specialist, base flow rates for the water engineer, tonnage rates for the mining engineer. It did not seek nor provide much insight into systemic social, cultural, economic, or environmental impacts.

Policies were geared to assuring the orderly administration of resources and the prevention of waste. Such policies were to be adopted and applied "for the benefit of the many, and not merely the profit of a few."[19] The policies would be developed and carried out by professional civil servants working within government agencies responsible for particular resources. Removed from direct political influence and trained in the relevant science, government experts would discharge their administrative duties with impartial, businesslike efficiency. Pinchot oversaw the premier manifestation of Progressive Era conservation, the U. S. Forest Service. The Forest Service soon became, in the words of Pinchot biographer Char Miller, "the prime marker of the executive branch's consolidation of authority" and the standard by which other efficiency-driven federal agencies were judged.[20]

With their commitment to enlightened, honest, and restrained use of resources, the new conservationists stood in *opposition* to the rank exploiters of land and water, forests and minerals, game and grass. With their emphasis on long-term development and management of resources, they stood in *contrast* to those who placed priority on the preservation of wild nature. The preservationist impulse had grown through the 1800s, focusing on special landscape features, unique scenic sites, and dwindling game populations. The destruction of the Great Lakes pineries swelled the preservationist call through the 1870s and 1880s (and, significantly, drew attention not just to rarities like the California redwoods, but forestlands more generally). In the 1890s, the call was answered with the designation of the nation's first "forest reserves."

The contrast between proponents of wilderness and the proponents of rational resource use would intensify during Roosevelt's presidential years and beyond, epitomized by the battle between John Muir and Gifford Pinchot over the damming of the Hetch Hetchy Valley. It is an episode, and a philosophical fissure, deeply incised in the history we have told ourselves. The very drama of the episode, however, has distorted our view of the broader Progressive conservation crusade, of the events leading up to it, and of the subsequent role of wilderness protection vis-à-vis the conservation movement (and ultimately environmentalism). Only recently have historians begun to examine the Muir-Pinchot schism more carefully, and to understand how it has colored our understanding of the relationship between utilitarian conservationists and wilderness preservationists.[21]

For those whose support for reform grew out of the direct experience of rampant resource exploitation, the Progressive crusade was an appropriate response of national authority to private, corporate irresponsibility. The enhanced role of the federal government did not represent a reckless centralization of authority, Theodore Roosevelt informed Congress in December 1908. "It represents merely the acknowledgment of the patent fact that centralization has already come in business. If this irresponsible, outside business power is to be controlled in the interest of the general public, it can only be controlled in one way—by giving adequate power of control to the one sovereignty capable of exercising such power—the National Government."[22] Roosevelt had a fine gift for being simultaneously coy and convincing. Of course his policies strengthened centralized authority. Of course that centralization was evoked by decades of corporate collusion, unchecked resource destruction, and base politics.

And, of course, stronger federal authority was anathema to those still busily profiting from exploitation, those who for decades had known nothing but the doctrine of laissez-faire, those who were among the "locally powerful."[23] They tended not to reside (at least not in their former numbers) in the wasted pineries of the upper Great Lakes. They were legion in the wide-open West, where Roosevelt's national bequest of protected public lands also entailed, in Daniel Kemmis's words, a "legacy of resentment." "At the heart of that burning (and still burning) western resentment of the Forest Service lay a repeated exercise of centralized authority, one that has always made large numbers of westerners feel abused—feel, in fact, colonized."[24] Roosevelt, Pinchot, Secretary of Agriculture James Garfield, and their supporters built conservation into a movement, and they did so in part by strengthening the hand of federal authority. It may be said that they *had* to strengthen it. It must be said in the same breath that the tension between local and federal authority—and responsibility—was built into conservation from the get-go.

That tension was already long established in American history and identity. It pitted two great channels of American democratic commitment against each other. One channel issued forth from the dictum that "that government is best which governs least."[25] Flowing through colonial rebels, Jacksonian democrats, states' righters, freeholding farmers, westering homesteaders, and even Theodore Roosevelt's own hunting, ranching, and rough-riding compatriots, it was "decentralist, localist, agrarian," resistant to powerful governmental authority.[26] The second channel issued from Jefferson's words in the Declaration of Independence: that "in order to secure certain unalienable Rights . . . Governments are instituted among Men." Flowing again through the colonial rebels, and then through abolitionists, prairie populists, Mugwumps, unionists, suffragists, and Teddy Roosevelt's own fellow conservationists and scientists, it invoked governmental authority to secure political representation, civil rights, honest administration, and fair economic play.

The two channels were not separate or distinct. They had long intermingled within the American soul, on American land. During the Civil War, the tension between them became profoundly unbearable. Conservation in the Progressive Era, however, gave a new twist to the old tension. It linked the state of the body politic to the condition of the land itself. It demanded that Americans, having drawn so much of their political identity from the land, now accept their responsibility *for* the land. The conservation movement may have been primarily utilitarian in its genesis, but it insisted that there was a connection between the ultimate sources of wealth and the morality of the means by which that wealth was secured, transformed, distributed, and used. That, in time, would make all the difference in the world.

➤➤ ➤➤

Before Theodore Roosevelt assumed the presidency, "conservation" was an obscure word and concept, barely linked to the idea of stewardship. By the time Roosevelt left the presidency, it was a national watchword, policy, and ethos. But it had only begun its career. Gifford Pinchot himself noted, "Times change, and the public needs change with them."[27] As Char Miller notes, the Progressives' definition of conservation posed problems: "Who defines what the greatest good is, and on what basis? How to measure its production and equitable distribution or, more trickily, how to weigh humanity's material needs against environmental conditions over time? And would it be possible for succeeding generations to redefine the greatest good?"[28] Beyond these questions of intent lay questions of *process*. Assuming that the aims of conservation aims could and would continue to evolve, how would the *practice* of conservation be defined, pursued, and implemented?

This is where things get murky. Even historians are prone to jump directly to the present, to see environmentalism as a linear extension of Progressive Era conservation, bearing all of its heroic strengths, flaws, and discords. There is a tendency to extrapolate uncritically the bifurcation between wilderness preservation and utilitarian conservation, as if nothing much changed after Muir and Pinchot parted company. There is a tendency as well to rehash the conflict between federal authority and local interests in environmentalism as if nothing much changed after Roosevelt and Pinchot created the "midnight reserves" in 1907.

But much has changed. From the moment the Progressive agenda began to play out on the ground, it was subject to adaptation and amendment. The conservation movement was continually reshaping itself long before Rachel Carson's *Silent Spring* or Aldo Leopold's *A Sand County Almanac* appeared. To assume a static view of conservation's early decades is to miss the opportunity for a more nuanced account of its later relationship to environmentalism.

Over the next three decades, roughly 1910 to 1940, conservation's utilitarian philosophical foundations shifted as practitioners and policy makers explored a wider range of values. The science underlying conservation received its first strong influx of more integrated, ecological approaches. Conservation policies addressed an ever-broadening array of issues, including protection and management of wildlife, outdoor recreation, wilderness protection, water pollution, soil and water conservation, and urban planning. Conservation became the province not only of the federal agencies, but also of state agencies, local governments, and a growing private and nonprofit sector. And perhaps most significantly, conservation became a matter of concern not only in terms of the nation's public lands and resources, but its private lands as well.

The story of conservation in these years is not a simple one of ever-expanding federal power and control. Certainly that trend was evident in a long series of key federal actions, including passage of the Weeks Act (1911), extending the national forest system to the eastern states; creation of the National Park Service (1916); approval of the construction of Hoover Dam on the Colorado River (1928) and other federal dam projects; passage of the Flood Control Act (1928), giving the federal government primary responsibility for controlling flooding on the Mississippi and Sacramento Rivers; passage of the Migratory Bird Conservation Act (also known as the Norbeck-Andreson Act) (1929), establishing a national system of waterfowl refuges; passage of the Taylor Grazing Act (1934), restricting further disbursement of the nation's public lands; and passage of the Wheeler-Howard Act (1934), which established the Bureau of Indian Affairs and provided federal assistance for the management of tribal lands. The Great Depression and the dust bowl brought forth Franklin Roosevelt's New Deal, with its "alphabet soup" of agencies, echoing the earlier Roosevelt's response to looming economic and environmental pressures.

These developments seemed to mark conservation indelibly with the imprint of federal paternalism. Yet, there was a countervailing trend also evident in new laws and programs. The Clarke-McNary Act (1924) supported cooperative measures in federal, state, and private forestry. The Taylor Grazing Act's provisions included the establishment of grazing districts with advisory boards of local stockgrowers. The state-based Cooperative Wildlife Research Unit system (1935) and the Pittman-Robertson Act (1937) provided the states with revenues from the sales of sporting arms and ammunition for wildlife conservation purposes. All of these measures dispersed resources and devolved authority, expanding the role of landowners, local governing bodies, and state agencies and universities. Meanwhile, state and local governments increasingly asserted their own conservation responsibilities by, for example, strengthening their resource management agencies, passing pollution control measures, and establishing protected forests, parks, and wildlife areas.

But it was the challenge of soil and water conservation in the 1930s that revealed most starkly the limits of centralized governmental approaches and the need for local conservation commitment. Extensive soil erosion, agricultural development of submarginal soils, siltation of water bodies, disruption of hydrological processes, and dislocation of farmers were growing concerns long before the situation assumed crisis proportions in the 1930s. The federal government responded in the old Progressive way, creating the Soil Conservation Service (SCS) in 1935, but it had to do so in a novel manner. The SCS was not, and never would be, a land-owning conservation agency. It was the only federal agency specifically directed to work with the millions of private landowners who controlled two-thirds of the American landscape. By the very nature of its charge, it had to address the relationship between local social conditions and watersheds. If it hoped to have a salutary effect on the land, it could not work through coercive means; it had to respect the needs, knowledge, and experience of local landowners and rural communities.

The agricultural crisis of the 1930s thus prompted—at least for some— a basic reconsideration of the federal role in conservation, and hence conservation generally. As Randal Beeman and James Pritchard note in their book *A Green and Permanent Land: Ecology and Agriculture in the Twentieth Century*, the need to address root causes of land degradation in the 1930s "helps explain the shift from conservation to environmentalism." Permanent agriculture (their preferred term for the antecedents of today's sustainable agriculture) "was an idea conceived by individuals born in the Progressive Era, when conservation was generally viewed as the managing of resources for human use, and a task to be pursued mainly by extractive technocrats. . . . Despite, or perhaps because of, their solid indoctrination in conservation values, members of the permanent agriculture cadre were susceptible to nascent ecological ideas that dictated a far more complex set of values than did mainstream conservation, including interdependence and a heightened reverence for all life-forms."[29] Conservation on agricultural lands required adjustments not only in the movement's philosophical stance, but also in its implementation. The New Deal conservation programs expanded the role of the federal government in the short term, but they also revealed the ultimate limits of centralized approaches.

As much as any figure at the time, Aldo Leopold appreciated the need for conservation to adjust to these new realities. As a boy he had seen firsthand the results of unfettered markets in the deforested north woods of Michigan, the disappearing prairies of Iowa, the decimated waterfowl populations of the Mississippi River valley. As a young Progressive Era forester, he was a carrier of national authority to the newly established national forests of the American Southwest. It was his abiding concern over the degradation of watersheds, first in the Southwest and then in the Midwest, that brought him to the crux of the conservation problem: its *universality*.

> The government cannot buy "everywhere." The private landowner *must* enter the picture. It is easy to side-step the issue of getting lumbermen to practice forestry, or the farmer to crop game or conserve soil, and to pass these functions along to government. *But it won't work.* I assert this, not as a political opinion, but as a geographical fact. The basic problem is to *induce the private landowner to conserve on his own land*, and no conceivable millions or billions for public land purchase can alter that fact, nor the fact that so far he hasn't done it.[30]

The need for conservation, as Leopold once expressed it, was "co-extensive with the map of the United States," and new methods of encouraging conservation had to reflect that need.[31]

By the early 1930s, Leopold had developed firm views on what government agencies, at any level, could and could not accomplish. He had also come to distinguish between what he called "bogus individualism" and responsible citizenship.[32] His effort to calibrate the proper relationship between the public and private sectors—and private and public responsibilities—continued to the end of his life and found its final expression in "The Land Ethic":

> Government ownership, operation, subsidy, or regulation is now widely prevalent in forestry, range management, soil and watershed management, park and wilderness conservation, fisheries management, and migratory bird management, with more to come. Most of this growth in governmental conservation is proper and logical, some if it is inevitable. That I imply no disapproval of it is implicit in the fact that I have spent most of my life working for it. Nevertheless the question arises: What is the ultimate magnitude of the enterprise? Will the tax base carry its

eventual ramifications? At what point will governmental conservation, like the mastodon, become handicapped by its own dimensions? The answer, if there is any, seems to be in a land ethic, or some other force which assigns more obligation to the private landowner.[33]

In essence, Leopold's land ethic served as both a rebuke to irresponsible private, local, and individual behavior on the land (Jefferson's yeoman farmers notwithstanding) and an open admission of the limits of Progressive Era conservation methods (Pinchot's agency experts notwithstanding). We still struggle to navigate these political and ideological currents—with variable winds blowing hard from the right and left.

The winds picked up again after World War II. A renewed challenge to jurisdiction over the West's public lands in the late 1940s and early 1950s failed to wrest control away from the federal agencies and inflamed the old tension between centralized and decentralized authority. Latent dissatisfaction with the 1934 Taylor Grazing Act ("federalism in the extreme" in one congressman's words) reasserted itself.[34] Bernard De Voto, conservation's standard-bearer during this struggle, derided the "unceasing, many-sided effort to discredit all conservation bureaus of the government, to discredit conservation itself."[35]

Conservation groups, meanwhile, had rallied in response to growing threats to the nation's wildlands. The prime battleground in the late 1940s and early 1950s was Dinosaur National Monument in Colorado and Utah, where the U.S. Bureau of Reclamation had proposed to build two dams as part of a massive plan for developing the upper Colorado River basin (Echo Park, one of the planned dam sites, gave its name to the struggle). Regional support for the project was arrayed across the political spectrum and across party lines. The dams—eventually stopped by a broad coalition of wilderness advocates—symbolized more than just the growing postwar threats to wildlands; they were planned atop a deep fault line beneath conservation's political landscape. The U.S. Bureau of Reclamation was first established as the Reclamation Service, by Theodore Roosevelt's pen stroke, through the National Reclamation Act of 1902. Roosevelt was also the first to protect threatened public lands by designating national monuments under the 1906 Antiquities Act. In effect, at Dinosaur National Monument, the estranged heirs to the Progressive Era conservation tradition had split and circled around to oppose the actions of each other.[36]

Much as the universality of soil erosion had brought home the limits of centralized authority in conserving private lands, the battle at Dinosaur signaled a larger "crisis of progressive faith" (to use economist Robert Nelson's phrase) in dealing with the nation's public lands: "Created in the name of efficiency, public land agencies in practice gave little heed to efficiency. Part of the reason was that public land management proved in the event not to be scientific management, but politicized management."[37] Echo Park demonstrated that "politicized management" could involve clashes not just between local and federal interests, but between different *alliances* of local and federal interests. More was at stake, evidently, than ideological purity.

All of these events still predated *Silent Spring*, the U.S. National Environmental Protection Act of 1969, other key federal environmental laws, the first Earth Day, and environmentalism's emergence as a self-conscious movement. Environmentalism may be seen in part as a response to private and public *irresponsibility* during the economic boom years from 1945 and 1965. Roosevelt's "riot of individualistic materialism" was enjoying a long and unprecedented reprise. Leopold's land ethic seemed to have gained little currency. Although the nonprofit side of the conservation movement found temporary solidarity in wilderness advocacy, the movement as a whole was increasingly fragmented. Some conservationists were willing to explore the broader social, political, cultural, and philosophical dimensions of wilderness loss, pollution, land degradation, species extinction, and resource depletion. Others, however, were unprepared or unwilling. As Leopold had noted, "in our effort to make conservation easy," we had "made it trivial."[38] Under the strains of postwar economic expansion, social and demographic change, political realignment, philosophical disquiet, and increasingly reductionistic and specialized science, conservation was cut loose from its old Progressive moorings.

Environmentalism arose as conservation drifted. Environmentalism reconfigured the substance of, and relationships among, conservation science, philosophy, and policy. Environmental science, building on ecology's insights, was essentially integrative and systems oriented. Environmental philosophy was more accommodating of varied values and belief systems. Environmental policies contended with issues that conservation as such had not adequately addressed or anticipated: air and water pollution, nuclear and toxic waste, human population growth, energy use and production, land use and urban sprawl, endangered species, the global-scale threats of ozone depletion, climate change, degradation of the oceans. Conservation suddenly found itself in a greatly enlarged political arena, and many older conservationists were overwhelmed. Younger environmentalists rushed in to fill the expanded space. And the new ranks of environmental activists, drawing lessons from the contemporary civil rights and women's movements, turned to federal authority as a necessary tool to confront entrenched private interests and political power.

This is where we need to take a time out to define our historiographic problem.

Let us be painfully circumspect.

Let us say it this way: *When the modern environmental movement superceded the older American conservation movement and tradition, we gained a great deal, and we lost a great deal; we have yet to understand fully those losses and gains, and we are still reckoning with them.*[39]

In the transition, we gained, among other things: a global, yet more detailed view of the earth's ecosystems; appreciation of the full diversity of life and the importance of ecosystem functions; a more penetrating critique of heedless industrial and technological development; a greater appreciation of interdisciplinary science as a tool in solving problems; a greater appreciation, however, of the limits of science alone in solving problems; a broader and better informed constituency that now included urban and suburban dwellers; a more thorough understanding of the social and economic causes and consequences of environmental degradation. In short, we gained perspective on the full dimensions of humankind's environmental dilemma, as well as a broader base of support for actions to address it.

But we also lost much in the transition: the attitude of stewardship that formerly bound conservationists, hunters, farmers, ranchers, and other landowners more closely together; the focused attention on private land conservation; respect for the realities of rural life and the structural constraints facing rural economies; the connection, explicit in the 1930s and 1940s, between wilderness protection and other aspects of land conservation; the sense that the movement—call it what we will—was about more than honing legal tools to "protect the environment" (to use the lazy politician's shorthand). We lost the vision of conservation as a commitment binding people and places together across ideological and cultural divides, across landscapes, and across generations. As the institutional memory of "traditional" conservation faded, the very word itself seemed fated to slip into oblivion. It carried less and less weight with the new generation of environmentalists.

As the transition continued in the years following Earth Day 1970, the historical tension between centralized and decentralized authority in American conservation and environmental policy reasserted itself. It did so now along multiple, overlapping fault lines: federalism versus localism in managing the country's public lands; regulatory versus free market approaches in controlling pollution; the carrot of policy incentives versus the stick of enforcement in protecting endangered species; enthusiasm versus reluctance in supporting international environmental treaties and protocols. In these and other arenas there was still room for lively policy debate and, on at least some issues, creative solutions were hammered out, and real gains were made.

At the same time, however, environmentalism became a combat zone in the culture wars. The environmental politics of the 1970s begat Secretary of the Interior James Watt and the sagebrush rebellion, which begat an ever-closer alliance of Democrats and environmentalists, which begat the "Wise Use" movement, which begat the opportunism of the early presidency of Bill Clinton, which begat the "Contract with America" and Newt Gingrich's revolution, which mystified mainstream environmentalists but galvanized action by the Evangelical Environmental Network (among other culturally conservative environmentalists), which took both conservative and liberal think tanks aback, which left things in a complete muddle that neither George W. Bush, nor Al Gore, nor Ralph Nader, nor their dedicated camp followers, could clarify as the new millennium arrived. . . .

Every turn in the cycle further polarized the contestants. Partisan operatives drove political wedges in ever deeper. As the sound bites flew, it became increasingly difficult to work out a coherent story.

We still don't appreciate fully just what we lost and what we gained.

◂◂ ▸▸

Remarkably, however, conservation did not simply wither away. Environmentalism had grown up fast, overshadowing its venerable predecessor. Yet, hunkered down under the canopy of environmentalism, conservation proved to be deep rooted and shade tolerant. Written off and nearly forgotten, conservation continued, slowly and quietly, to lay on new rings of growth.

Gradually, from the late 1970s on, conservation began again to reinvent itself. Conservation biologists, building initially on new concepts in island biogeography and genetics, sought to unite multiple disciplines in the effort to understand, protect, and sustain biological diversity. Conservation of the marine environment and biota established itself as a vital new field of research and action. At least some wilderness advocates revisited their premises, retooled their science (including their anthropology), and returned to the necessary work of protecting wild places. Watershed advocates and community-based conservation organizations gave a strong positive focus to the "decentralist, localist, agrarian" strain of American democracy. Landscape ecologists and conservation-savvy planners, architects, designers, and builders lent their expertise to the effort to better coordinate human land use and resource management at various spatial scales. Practitioners of sustainable agriculture reinvigorated the tradition of "permanent agriculture" that had tapered off after World War II. The movement for environmental justice arose to address an entire suite of neglected concerns and to involve communities that neither conservation nor environmentalism had effectively engaged.[40]

A friend once observed that "we environmentalists are pretty effective at fighting against things; we are not so effective at creating solutions." Since the 1970s, ecological restoration has provided a new outlet for affirmative, hands-on action. Seeking to enhance the ecological integrity of local places, from the wild to the urban, restoration has offered many a battle-weary environmentalist something to work *for* and *at*, and not just something to *stop*. The restoration movement, as much as any development in recent decades, stood as evidence of a resurgent conservation ethic. Kenneth Brower, introducing a new edition of Leopold's *A Sand County Almanac* in 2001, predicted that "the century or two of the Preservation Era will prove to be prologue, an introductory chapter, noble but brief. Almost all the wilderness that can be saved has been saved. For the duration of our time on the planet—for whatever piece of eternity we have left here—restoration will be the great task."[41]

In all these fields, people from varied backgrounds have been seeking ways to depolarize environmental issues, reintegrate conservation, and build a new consensus for action. The common denominator is a commitment to land health on the part of individuals, neighborhoods, organizations, tribes, agencies, and businesses, and a desire to achieve tangible results, whether on private, public, or community lands. These trends suggest the possibility of an emerging "cross-landscape" constituency that can address the harmful feedback loops that encourage continued degradation of urban, suburban, exurban, rural, and wild lands alike. They reflect the emergence of a "radical center" where people (whatever their political stripe) who care about land and communities and wild things and places may meet to make common cause.[42] They point toward a new concept of economic freedom—one that realizes there can be no freedom without responsibility, and no definition of sustainability that does not embed the circle of human social and economic relationships within the greater sphere of nature. They demonstrate that the desire to build better relationships between people and land is tenacious. It will not go away.

Always, the conversation must return to the core concept of responsibility. The latest "riot of individualistic materialism" and corporate avarice cannot last forever; the peak of Enron's stock price may have served as its high-water mark (or so we can hope). In any case, a renewed commitment to conservation values must, sooner or later, find a home once again in our civic life, under a form of political leadership that does not yet exist. Where might we find it? How might we encourage it? As historian Donald Worster has suggested, "a history that is more alert to the landscape around us, looking for clues there about our past behavior and acknowledging the agency of nature in human life, is . . . a good place to start. It can help overcome one-generation thinking. It may even promote a wider area of responsibility, which is all that conservation asks."[43]

Conservation emerged in the Progressive Era, effectively broadening the "area of responsibility" in American life. It has evolved continually ever since (one dominant strain having mutated to help create what is now a global environmental movement). Changes in science and in ethics, in society and in the world, continue to prompt us to reconsider our responsibilities, not just in terms of long-term economic self-interest, but in terms of our obligations to our neighbors, our communities, future generations, and non-human nature. In the long run, our own self-interest and well-being are bound up with these broader responsibilities in intricate and inescapable ways.

The Progressives of the early 1900s could not foresee the utter transformation of the world that the ensuing century would bring. Neither, for that matter, could the stalwarts and plutocrats and reactionaries they opposed. In three generations we have built a world that their generation would not recognize. The solutions that the Progressives devised to meet the problems of their time will not suffice for us to meet ours. However, the basis upon which they acted is of the essence. They saw the need, as we must again, for public responsibilities to keep pace with private privilege. To that end they sought to make democracy work, as we must again, "to secure the social and political betterment of the people as a whole."

3

Conservation Biology and Sustainable Societies

We cannot extend our concern for wild nature
unless we are also concerned for the welfare of
people, because the two cannot be separated.
—RAYMOND F. DASMANN (1987)

ON THE first Earth Day a group of students in California decided to make a statement about the pervasive environmental effects of the automobile. They buried one. In so doing, they symbolically interred all the pollution-burdened skies, lost wildernesses, bulldozed neighborhoods, gridlocked cities, and *ad infinitum* urban sprawl that the automobile represented. Earth Day 1970 was nothing if not fresh.[1]

Afterward, it is said, on the other side of town, the leaders of a money-strapped community assistance organization objected to the display. They protested, quite naturally, that they could have used the car to transport the elderly and deliver food to the needy.

It was so easy to be environmentally aware in 1970. One sensed threats keenly, as would a wild creature. The cause was clear, the symptoms obvious, the solutions self-evident. One felt the righteousness of the crusade in one's bones. The simple answer was simplicity itself. In nature one could find order, peace of mind, and the foundations for a philosophy that would save the world, if not one's soul. Love of money was the root of all evil, and all corruptions would wither once an understanding of ecology spread and a change in values occurred. The problems of human society? Return to nature, and all would be well.

And it was so easy *not* to be environmentally aware in 1970. The threats to durable human societies were strictly political and economic in nature, and once political repression and impediments to economic growth were done away with, all would be well. Insufficient and inequitably apportioned wealth was the root of all evil, and all corruptions would diminish once the economic pie was made larger and/or (depending on one's political philosophy) distributed differently. The *real* problems of the *real* world would be solved through economic expansion and restructuring. These new "environmentalists" were irrelevant at best, dangerous at worst—a strange collection of impractical utopians, discontented Luddites, misguided misanthropes, and probably atheistic anarchists, supplemented by the odd scientist or two. Ecology? What was that? Nature? Nature is resilient. It's backdrop.

The polarity that marked environmental attitudes in 1970 has not disappeared. We remain susceptible to stereotype and dogma, simple answers and narrow definitions. It's easy! Go for the rough rhetoric and bloody politics, the sharp bumper sticker and hot news footage. It's so much less of a drain on our psychic energies than lifelong devotion to what Edward Abbey called "Reason with a capital *R*—Sweet Reason, the newest and rarest thing in human life, the most delicate child of human history. . . . Intelligence informed by sympathy, knowledge in the arms of love."[2]

But since 1970 the sheer weight of environmental pressures, if nothing else, has deepened the discussion. In some arenas—protection of North America's remaining old growth forests in the Pacific Northwest, oil drilling in the Arctic National Wildlife Refuge (to cite two obvious examples)—the polarity remains potent, and for good reason. On these far borders, the final scenes of a very old drama unfold. In these largest remaining intact corners of wild America, our culture's unresolved tensions, conflicting values, and divided way of life play out.

More broadly, the conflicting views are now heard on a global scale in a way that they were not in 1970. Developed nations have grown increasingly aware of the hidden costs—social, economic, environmental—of the trail they have blazed over the last few tumultuous centuries of industrialization. Developing nations have naturally protested that environmental concern is a luxury of the already prosperous, that more immediate concerns preclude such investments of time, money, and human ability. The wealthy nations, having driven the sleek automobile, pause (occasionally) to consider its impacts. The poorer nations could use the car to transport the elderly and deliver food to the needy.

But Sweet Reason, rare, demanding, and delicate though it is, is also a caustic agent. Eventually it can erode even the most granitic stereotype. An appreciation of history, complexity, diversity, and humanity must eventually penetrate the cracks in dogma's solid edifice. It dissolves hard attitudes—though, it seems, only after those attitudes have themselves scarred ecosystems and societies.

Of course, the stereotypes and dogmas were never so simple to begin with; there were just too few souls intrepid enough to explore the underlying premises. One of those, George Perkins Marsh, warned in 1864 that "the earth is fast becoming an unfit home for its noblest inhabitant, and another era of equal human crime and human improvidence . . . of like duration . . . would reduce it to such a condition of impoverished productiveness, of shattered surface, of climatic excess, as to threaten the depravation, barbarism, and perhaps even extinction of the species."[3] Having devoted himself to careful study and documentation of the processes by which "man had changed millions of square miles, in the fairest and most fertile regions of the Old World, into the barrenest deserts," Marsh was among the first to concern himself with what we now awkwardly call "sustainability."

More poetically, Marsh challenged his contemporaries to "renovate a nature drained, by [human] improvidence, of [the] fountains which *a wise economy* would have made plenteous and perennial sources of beauty, health, and wealth."[4] Few in Marsh's time accepted the challenge. The era of "human improvidence" continued. One result, a century later, was an Earth Day spectacle of buried automobiles, mixed signals, and polarized attitudes. In 1970 the larger questions, questions as pervasive and encircling and ignored as the air itself, went largely unanswered: How did we manage to work ourselves into this bind? What would a "wise economy" look like? How might we achieve it?

◄◄ ►►

Throughout his career Aldo Leopold thought carefully about ultimate sources of conservation disputes. He gave the theme especially poignant expression in one obscure and fragmentary manuscript: three paragraphs scrawled on the back of a piece of hotel stationery. The year was 1935. The hotel was in Berlin, where Leopold was staying during an extended tour of Germany and neighboring lands. He had undertaken the tour to examine the history and status of forestry and wildlife conservation in central Europe. One can imagine the scene: cold, confining, uneasy; Leopold, his conservation philosophy forged in the freewheeling and spacious American context, sitting quietly at a desk, increasingly cognizant of the political forces then upheaving Germany, trying to come to terms with the seeming irrelevance of conservation under such circumstances. At the top of the sheet of paper he scrawls a title: "Wilderness." He begins his thought by reaching back in time to broaden the context:

> The two great cultural advances of the past century were the Darwinian theory [of evolution] and the development of geology. The one explained how, and the other where, we live. Compared with such ideas, the whole gamut of mechanical and chemical invention pales into a mere matter of current ways and means.

He then focuses on the present, and on his own most absorbing interest:

> Just as important as the origin of plant, animals, and soil is the question of how they operate as a community. Darwin lacked time to unravel any more than the beginnings of an answer. That task has fallen to the new science of ecology, which is daily uncovering a web of interdependencies so intricate as to amaze—were he here—even Darwin himself, who, of all men, [would] have the least cause to tremble before the veil.

And then Leopold casts his thoughts forward:

> One of the anomalies of modern ecology is that it is the creation of two groups, each of which seems barely aware of the existence of each other. The one studies the human community, almost as if it were a separate entity, and calls its findings sociology, economics, and history. The other studies the plant and animal community [and] comfortably relegates the hodgepodge of politics to "the liberal arts." *The inevitable fusion of these two lines of thought will perhaps constitute the outstanding advance of the present century.*"[5]

Leopold left his thought unrefined and never completed the essay it was intended to introduce.[6] The statement, as it stood, reflected Leopold's typical unwillingness to treat the human community and the natural community—and analogously, the liberal arts and natural sciences—as "separate entities." It reflects, too, his dawning sense that the split was destined to be but of short duration, not necessarily (to use his own later phrasing) because it was bad for wildlife, but because it was bad for people.[7]

Has Leopold's prediction come true? Have the "two lines of thought" fused? The evidence on Earth Day 1970 was certainly mixed. That season, Richard Nixon declared a clean environment "the birthright of every American," while the *New Republic* disparaged environmentalists as "the biggest assortment of ill-matched allies since the Crusades."[8] The 1970s, 1980s, and 1990s would each be proclaimed "the decade of the environment" at one point or another. (As if all previous decades had nothing to do with "the environment." As if at some point in the future we will enter a decade *not* "of the environment.")

Instead of searching for direct evidence of fusion, we might look for circumstantial evidence of less polarized attitudes, of a stronger foundation of shared assumptions . . . maybe even of those rare flowerings of "intelligence informed by sympathy, knowledge in the arms of love." Here there is some cause for optimism. Environmental values are no longer marginal, as they were in 1970. Despite partisan excess and periodic waves of political backlash, environmental policies in general are solidly supported. Our ideas about what constitutes "environmental concern" have grown beyond (without outgrowing) considerations of clean air, clean water, wilderness, and wildlife. At the same time, our ideas about social justice, economic health, and community well-being no longer exist in an absolute environmental vacuum.

The apparent shift in the old polarity raises many further questions: Are we truly reaching the "fusion point"? Are we moving toward that point quickly enough? How deep do the convictions go? Have we merely succumbed to ineffective, but feel-good, compromise? In our understanding of the relationship between human and environmental well-being, have we forged links between causes and effects strong enough to withstand unanticipated social and economic pressures? If consensus exists, will it be strong enough, ingrained enough, to endure harsher times, and the changing priorities and attitudes that such times bring?

These questions lead back to the "two lines of thought" that Leopold saw converging: the study of the human community and the study of plant and animal communities. Since Earth Day 1970 both lines have changed in response to more widespread and more immediate environmental concerns. Participants in the first Earth Day observance would recognize most of our current principles, but might not understand today's language. As we have redefined the issues (and as the issues have redefined us), new terms have emerged to frame our discussion.

This is nothing new. Words, like species, inhabit particular niches and evolve with time. Their linguistic and rhetorical ranges shrink and grow in response to changing conditions. Throughout history, conservation and the environmental movement have required new words, and shed inflexible words like snake skins. The more useful and adaptable words (for example, "wildlife," "ecology," even "environment" itself) remain.

Two of the more recent coinages, or at least new uses of older words, bear examination. In 1970 it was assumed that the established scientific disciplines provided firm footing for conservation. Since then, the field of *conservation biology* has helped to reconfigure the scientific foundations of conservation. The emergence of conservation biology in the mid-1980s signified the belief of many that conservation's scientific energies had to be redirected, particularly with regard to the core attribute of Earth's "plant and animal community": its diversity. And whereas in 1970 the basic durability of human communities, in all their permutations, was also assumed, many soon began to speak of the need for *sustainable* societies. By the mid-1980s "sustainability" had worked its way into the highest government circles as both a policy objective and an environmental goal. Its use signified the belief of many that the foundations of healthy human communities also had to be reassessed.

Conservation biology and *sustainability* may be thought of as "indicator terms." But what do they indicate? What do they tell us about the shifting relationship between Leopold's "two lines of thought" over the last century, and especially since the first Earth Day? Do they offer insights into the changing physics of our planetary dilemma—the degree of fusion or polarity on matters environmental?

⤛ ⤜

In 1986, concerned conservationists banded together to form the Society for Conservation Biology. The new organization was one expression of growing concern over the accelerated loss of genetic, species, and ecosystem diversity around the world. "The society," noted its first president, Michael Soulé, "is a response by professionals, mainly biological and social scientists, managers and administrators, to the biological diversity crisis that will reach a crescendo in the first half of the twenty-first century. We assume implicitly that we are in time, and that by joining together with each other and with other well intentioned persons and groups, the worst biological disaster in 65 million years can be averted."[9]

These concerns, of course, predated the rise in popular understanding of ecology and human environmental impacts that Earth Day 1970 embodied. The scientific foundations of conservation had been built over the previous century in a wide variety of relevant disciplines: geology, geography, hydrology, limnology, soil science, botany, marine biology, zoology, ornithology, entomology, ichthyology, forestry, plant ecology, wildlife ecology, genetics, agronomy, and so on through the catalogue of specialties. The application of biological research to conservation work, in short, already had a long and rich history.

There was, however, no one interdisciplinary organization of biologists devoted to the broad range of applied conservation knowledge. None of these fields alone provided the information, techniques, or perspective sufficient to counter the quickening trends of environmental degradation and biological impoverishment. In the 1970s the expanded environmental movement attempted to address those trends through a series of conferences and agreements at the global scale. The United Nations Conference on the Human Environment in Stockholm in 1972 brought the full array of environmental issues, for the first time, before the international community. The 1972 conference built upon the 1968 Conference on the Use and Conservation of the Biosphere, sponsored by the United Nations Educational, Scientific, and Cultural Organization (UNESCO). One result of the earlier conference was the Man and the Biosphere (MAB) program, which included the designation of internationally significant biosphere reserves, an important step in defining the issues that conservation biology would soon focus on.

Another important milestone came in 1973, with the adoption of the Convention on International Trade in Endangered Species of Wild Fauna and Flora (CITES), which provided scientific and administrative procedures for the protection of commercially exploited endangered species worldwide.

Meanwhile, in the United States, the National Environmental Policy Act (1969)—in particular its provision requiring federal agencies to prepare environmental impact assessments before undertaking proposed actions—gave biologists a stronger role in the process of environmental analysis. This in turn would demonstrate a fundamental reality: to solve conservation problems, disciplinary expertise had to be combined with interdisciplinary coordination. Passage of the 1973 Endangered Species Act reflected growing public concern over the loss of native plant and animal species. It provided new legal tools for protecting and restoring vulnerable species and, importantly, their habitats. These and other laws of the period gave conservationists hope that threatened flora and fauna would gain fuller consideration in the face of human economic pressures.

Translating that hope into effective management would not be so simple. Through the 1970s and 1980s, the old truth, confirmed throughout history, had to be proven once again: that however necessary legal measures were, they alone could not *achieve* conservation. People achieve conservation. Ultimately, attaining conservation goals depended on understanding and changing entrenched patterns of resource use and abuse that degraded ecosystems and threatened plant and animal populations.

Something seemed to be lacking, too, in the ability of the various conservation-related sciences, acting in isolation, to respond to these challenges, and especially the speed and scale at which they were occurring. Whole systems seemed to be increasingly at risk. In the temperate zones, intensified land use accelerated long-term trends in the development, fragmentation, isolation, and outright destruction of forests, savannahs, grasslands, wetlands, and deserts, as well as the worked landscape of agricultural lands—croplands, pasturelands, woodlots, rangelands. Aquatic ecosystems and the fisheries they supported were increasingly taxed by declining water quality and quantity, heavy harvesting, species introductions and invasions, and shortsighted fisheries management strategies. Desertification threatened already sensitive arid lands around the world. In the humid tropics, the conflagration of massive deforestation was stimulating greater scientific interest in the prime attribute of rainforests: the sheer diversity of life forms they supported.

Prior to the 1970s, biological diversity was a relatively neglected concept in conservation, not so much because its importance was doubted, but because it was taken for granted. For centuries, taxonomists had gone about the quiet, meticulous work of describing and cataloguing life's diversity. Biogeographers had charted the patterns of distribution of that diversity in time and space. For decades, theoretical ecologists had debated the question of biological diversity and its complex relationship to ecosystem stability. Meanwhile, conservationists in the field were focused on practical efforts to protect and manage particular populations, species, and wild places. Biological diversity, in short, was the medium in which conservation took place—so pervasive, definitive, and self-evident that even conservationists seemed unable to regard it with objectivity or urgency. It was assumed. It was as obvious as life itself.

Extinction, diversity's partner in the evolutionary process, was likewise a relatively neglected area of study from a conservation standpoint. Paleontologists, of course, studied ancient extinctions and so provided the foundation of knowledge on which appreciation of diversity was built. The basic biology, however, of contemporary extinctions went largely unstudied. Perhaps this reflected an understandable reluctance among conservationists to examine objectively a process they were sworn to forestall.

The prospect, however, of frequent, imminent, and prominent extinctions and extirpations—in North America, the California condor and grizzly bear, the whooping crane and bald eagle, the snail darter and Owens pupfish, the Furbish lousewort and grey wolf and blue whale—forced biologists to focus on extinction *as a process*, and to do so *at the global scale*. This in turn led field biologists back to the smaller, quieter, less gaudy members of the biological community, the vast majority of which, it was acknowledged, science had yet even to dignify with proper Linnean nomenclature. Even the extent of this great unnamed majority was a matter of speculation—unknown, as biologist E. O. Wilson would note, "even to the nearest order of magnitude."[10] Wilson would be a leader in drawing conservationists' attention to the full spectrum of life forms. Through his landmark studies of colonization and extinction in island ecosystems, Wilson would also help to revolutionize the way scientists studied and understood human impacts on diversity.

Even as conservationists began to pay closer attention to less conspicuous members of the biological community, they stepped up efforts to protect habitat at larger landscape, watershed, ecosystem, and regional scales. In the United States this was especially evident through the 1970s in regard to the nation's public lands: in efforts to designate wilderness areas in accordance with the Wilderness Act of 1964 and to stem the loss of diversity on national forests, rangelands, wildlife refuges, and parklands.[11] At the global level, the preeminent locus of ecosystem-level conservation action was the equatorial belt of rainforests, where the loss of diversity was assuming crisis dimensions. Conservationists and scientists had long expressed concern about tropical forests, but these voices had gone largely unheeded. Field biologists, ecologists, and taxonomists, alarmed by the rapid conversion of the species-rich rainforests, began to sound louder alarms in the 1970s. By the end of the decade, the issue of rainforest destruction was highlighted through a surge of articles, books, studies, and reports.[12]

As the magnitude of the threats to biological diversity became more apparent and better understood, policy makers and scientists not traditionally focused on conservation came alive to the issue. In 1981, the U.S. Department of State sponsored an International Strategy Conference on Biological Diversity. Meanwhile, accelerated losses of domestic livestock breeds and crop plant germ plasm focused attention on the value of genetic diversity, heretofore a relatively neglected area of conservation research. In 1980 and 1981, the United Nations Food and Agriculture Organization and the U.N. Environmental Programme hosted four conferences in Rome on the conservation of genetic resources of fish, domestic animals, forests, and crops. In 1982, several conservation groups, U.S. agencies, and UNESCO sponsored a conference in Washington on the "Application of Genetics to the Conservation of Plants and Animals." As a result of these efforts, the conservation of germ plasm and analysis of the genetic basis of "viable" populations gained a more prominent place on the research agenda. Many of those who began to identify themselves as "conservation biologists" in fact had their scientific roots in biology at the genetic rather than the organism, population, or ecosystem level.[13]

The term "conservation biology" itself was not new. It had been used previously, although in an inchoate sense.[14] In 1978, the first International Conference on Conservation Biology was convened at the University of California, San Diego.[15] After that, the term began to denote a more direct infusion of research in genetics, evolutionary biology, theoretical ecology, and biogeography into conservation programs. New insights from the earth sciences were also enriching the intellectual atmosphere surrounding conservation issues. Geophysicists were increasingly interested in the role that rainforest vegetation played in regional and global climatic patterns and water and carbon cycles. The revolutionary synthesis of plate tectonics in geology and the provocative elucidation of the Gaia hypothesis drew the life sciences and geophysical sciences closer together. In the early 1980s, Luis and Walter Alvarez stimulated scientific discussion of mass extinction with their novel theory that a devastating asteroid impact caused the extinction event at the Cretaceous-Tertiary boundary. The theory (and, importantly, related debates surrounding "nuclear winter" scenarios in 1984–1985) put biological diversity into a revised evolutionary and ecological context and gave it enhanced visibility at both the professional and popular level.

In 1986, a second international conference on conservation biology was held at Ann Arbor, Michigan. By this time, interest had grown enough to encourage establishment of a new professional organization. Growing numbers of scientists and conservationists, especially younger professionals trained with post–Earth Day sensibilities, found in conservation biology a refreshing perspective on problems confronting their varied fields and professions. It provided opportunities to address conservation issues as they must inevitably be addressed: through the integration of conservation theory, policy, and practice, underpinned by solid interdisciplinary research and application, involving all levels of biological organization.

The shifting intellectual forces reached critical mass in September 1986, when the U.S. National Academy of Sciences and the Smithsonian Institution sponsored a four-day "National Forum on BioDiversity." The forum (which included thousands of satellite-linked participants) brought

together not only prominent biologists, but also anthropologists, economists, philosophers, policy makers, artists, theologians. The National
Academy published the proceedings in the book *Biodiversity* (1988). The
abbreviated term "biodiversity" was suggested by Walt Rosen of the
National Academy, who assisted in planning the forum.[16] The volume
quickly became a standard reference. Its lead editor, E. O. Wilson, stated
the basic goal of the forum in the opening paragraph: "Biological diversity
must be treated more seriously as a global resource, to be indexed, used,
and above all, preserved. . . . We must hurry to acquire the knowledge on
which a wise policy of conservation and development can be based for centuries to come."[17]

This, to a large degree, would become the mission of those who
adopted the label "conservation biologist" and who in 1987 founded the
Society for Conservation Biology and its flagship journal *Conservation
Biology*. The new phrase, field, and organization were not without their
critics, especially in forestry, wildlife management, and other "traditional"
conservation disciplines.[18] And the criticism was not without merit. The
newcomers tended to overlook precedents and connections within the
older disciplines. Traditionalists, by the same token, tended to dismiss the
dissidents in their own ranks, to resist interdisciplinary approaches, and to
treat emerging concepts as mere buzzwords.

But the terms "conservation biology" and "biodiversity" had staying
power. They captured new emphases in the relevant science and its application: the basic appreciation of diversity; the crisis-orientation; the
importance of ecosystem processes, geographical scales, and biological
hierarchies in conservation; the need to expand concern beyond a few
large, beautiful, watchable, huntable, edible, or otherwise economically
important species; the need to place conservation actions within a longer-
term evolutionary and ecological framework; growing knowledge of the
impact of rapid human population growth, resource consumption, climate
change, invasive species, and other global phenomena on floras and faunas;
accordingly, the effort to bring a more balanced international perspective
to conservation and to anticipate problems in exporting the traditional
American or temperate zone models; and the need to counter the "harden-
ing of the categories" to which modern disciplines—and life!—are prone.

By the early 1990s, conservation was rapidly reconfiguring itself. The emergence of conservation biology and the rise of biodiversity as a unifying concept signaled that conservation's scientific foundations were shifting, out of necessity and through new understanding. In this, conservation biology emerged not so much as a new science as a more comprehensive, better-integrated response to problems that were themselves more extensive, more urgent, and more complicated than most had realized in 1970. In doing so, it built upon a tradition of applied ecological knowledge in conservation that had long been present but that had been stifled by narrower approaches. Universities, agencies, businesses, professional groups, and conservation organizations began to adapt, in varying degrees, to the reorientation. Those who (recalling Leopold) studied the plant and animal community, and "comfortably [relegated] the hodgepodge of politics to 'the liberal arts,'" had moved closer to the fusion point.

⟶⟵ ⟶⟶

In *Biodiversity* E. O. Wilson noted "the close linkage between the conservation of biodiversity and economic development."[19] Recognizing that linkage was only the first step toward understanding the complex and ever-changing feedback loops between human economic development and environmental change. Attention to these dynamics grew quickly in the 1970s and 1980s as ambitious international development policies and projects, many of them profoundly threatening to biological and cultural diversity, failed to fulfill their promise. The industrialized nations too began to recognize the accumulated social and economic costs of environmental neglect and to reassess the meaning of what George Perkins Marsh had called, so perfectly, so long ago, "a wise economy."

In 1970, the possible paths to such an economy, and a society around it, were hard to see. Biologists and conservationists who appreciated the evolutionary foundations and ecological context of human society were generally unprepared, by training and often by temperament, to tackle perplexing questions of socioeconomic reform and readjustment. They had their hands full just trying to stem losses. Those who focused on the development side of the equation had their training in economics, education, history, international relations, sociology, public health, political science— disciplines that had traditionally viewed human society "almost as if it were a separate entity." They too had their hands full, addressing intractable problems of poverty, disease, dislocation, and political corruption. They were often unschooled in the intricacies of the natural and environmental sciences. Of course, the social sciences were not alone in this regard. They simply reflected dominant social attitudes and the ever-greater specialization of the professions and disciplines.

The prospects, then, circa 1970, were not encouraging. That these two broad human "taxa" could learn important lessons from one another seemed a faint hope. That they would *have to* learn from one another would, in the following decades, become evident to a growing number of citizens, scientists, and policy makers.

As noted above, conservation biologists played a valuable role in changing the terms and atmosphere of the conversation. By broadening the traditional focus on protected areas, habitat preservation, and single species management, they had begun to put biological diversity into a fuller cultural and geographical context. Ray Dasmann, a respected elder in conservation biology, wrote in 1987 that "If efforts to conserve biological diversity are to succeed, nature conservation must become part of the total land use pattern. . . . Sustainable use and management must have a role." Dasmann himself noted that "a decade or two ago these words would not have been received with much enthusiasm."[20] In the intervening years, however, the connections between social and economic pressures and environmental decline, particularly in the developing world, became plain. There was little room, and less time, for piecemeal approaches.

During these years, the term "sustainable" emerged to describe the new orientation. Like "conservation biology," it faced serious obstacles to acceptance: the red pencil of editors, the coolness of entrenched academics, the caution of reluctant bureaucrats, the ardor of its own adherents. Many ran with it, not pausing to look back. Others objected to its lack of definition, as if this were some horrible disease, and not a sign of ideas seeking expression. Still others were insulted. Among development theorists, analysts, and administrators, "sustainability" was a given. Just as conservationists had taken biological diversity for granted, so had those promoting development rarely stopped to ponder the ecological preconditions of social cohesion and continuity; in a sense, "sustainability" was the medium in which *their* work took place. Now, however, basic environmental factors had to be given greater weight.

In many ways, Thomas Malthus began the modern discussion of the theme in 1798 with his *Essays on the Principle of Population*, applying to human society a primitive version of the concept later ecologists would call "carrying capacity." Malthus's scenario was not optimistic. Extrapolating the trends as he saw them, he discerned an inevitable tendency toward overpopulation and resource scarcity. Marsh, assessing in 1864 the influence of prevailing patterns of resource use on "the social life and social progress of man," was a bit more sanguine. Although he held only "faint hope that we shall yet make full atonement for our spendthrift waste of the bounties of nature," he did look forward to "an epoch when our descendants shall have marched as far beyond us in physical conquest as we have marched beyond the trophies erected by our grandfathers."[21] The problems arising from prior "physical conquests" of nature would presumably be overcome by the triumph of reason.

With the rise of the Progressive Era conservation movement, the idea of sustainability appears under the rubric of "sustained yield" of timber, water supplies, range forage, fisheries, and, somewhat later, wild game populations. Given the lack of restraint that had characterized resource use through the 1800s, the notion that resources could and should be managed rationally for perpetual economic benefits was revolutionary. But the underlying reductionist and utilitarian assumptions—that these were discrete "resources" that *existed* solely for the perpetual economic benefit of human beings—would be challenged in turn by a yet broader view of conservation that combined science, ethics, aesthetics, and long-term economics in its rationale.

In the 1930s a vanguard of scientists and conservationists began to explore the social, economic, and cultural as well as biological ramifications of the emerging science of ecology. To the discussion they brought the realization that what we now term "sustainability" was in fact predicated not only on the intricate latticework of human relationships, but on basic ecological facts of life as well. That, in essence, is what Aldo Leopold tried to capture in his fragmentary notes in his hotel room in Berlin in 1935.

In a lecture that same year, Leopold noted that "philosophers have long since claimed that society is an organism, but with few exceptions they have failed to understand that the organism includes the land which is its medium. The properties of human populations, which are the joint domain of sociologist, economist, and statesman, are all conditioned by land."[22] (His statement likely reflected the dark reality of the midwestern dust storms that spring.) By the end of the 1930s, Leopold had turned the thought inside out: ecology, the "fusion point of sciences and all the land uses," provided a view of land as the whole that included human society. The study of land and its life could, he held, help human beings to live more wisely within it. He charged his own scientific colleagues with the task: "We might get better advice from economists and philosophers if we gave them a truer picture of the biotic mechanism."[23]

World War II put the task on hold. The struggle for dominance and survival in the human community drained attention away from broader considerations of the relationship between the human and biotic communities. But in ways not immediately apparent, the war also redefined the context of conservation and environmental debate. Among the factors contributing to this change was the employment of atomic weaponry—the most concerted threat to "sustainability" yet devised.

In the immediate postwar years, a series of ecologically informed, international-scale assessments of the global condition appeared that were, in Robert Paehlke's words, "precursors of a coming change in public consciousness."[24] Two of these, Fairfield Osborn's *Our Plundered Planet* and William Vogt's *Road to Survival* (both published in 1948), were especially important in articulating the message of conservation for a broad audience. Osborn, in what amounted to an updating of Marsh, wrote, "Man must recognize the necessity of cooperating with nature. He must temper his demands and use and conserve the natural living resources of this earth *in a manner that alone can provide for the continuation of his civilization.* The final answer is to be found only through comprehension of the enduring processes of nature. The time for defiance is at an end."[25] "Above all," Vogt wrote, "we must learn to know—to feel to the core of our beings—*our dependence upon the earth and the riches with which it sustains us.*"[26]

This same intellectual climate yielded Leopold's concurrent expression of the land ethic. Such expressions, little heeded in the postwar rush to normalcy and prosperity, nonetheless would have a tenacious hold on readers who, by one route or another, came to them. Those readers, in turn, would over the next two decades lead the nation to Earth Day 1970 and the world to the international Conference on the Human Environment in Stockholm in 1972.

The ways in which the various strands of "sustainability" came to be woven together in the ten years before and after Earth Day are complex. The emergence of concern about biological diversity, summarized above, was an important part of the process. With *Silent Spring* (1962), Rachel Carson brought basic concepts of ecology to an audience of unprecedented size. Paul Ehrlich's best-selling *The Population Bomb* (1968) picked up the Malthusian theme, reigniting that aspect of the discussion. Garrett Hardin's classic essay "The Tragedy of the Commons" (1968) showed the power of carrying capacity as a conceptual tool in framing discussions about the environmental impact of human population pressure and economic behavior. Barry Commoner's writings in the 1960s and 1970s stressed the role of technological choice and socioeconomic systems in determining the actual impact of population growth on environmental systems. The energy crises of the 1970s brought home the essential role of energy production, transport, and consumption in determining not just environmental quality, but the very character of modern society. Amory Lovins's *Soft Energy Paths* (1977) led the way to alternative analyses of this fundamental issue. Kenneth Boulding, E. F. Schumacher, and Herman Daly, among others, helped to move economics toward not just a more rational approach to environmental resources and conditions, but toward a new economics that drew upon and applied basic ecological principles to human economic systems.[27]

This basic list of key publications and figures serves, at best, as an index to the general upwelling of environmental thought and analysis in varied fields. One area of reform proved to be especially noteworthy in the evolution of the idea of sustainability: agriculture. As connections among the many factors that define "sustainability"—population, technological change, pollution control, energy, economics, biodiversity—became better defined, American agriculture proved to be an especially important arena for their integration.

Agriculture, in the pattern that characterized other fields of resource use, management, and conservation in the industrial world after World War II, became more specialized, intensive, and commodity driven. Traditional techniques of soil conservation and management were, for a time, neglected or even abandoned. However, having secured a foothold in modern agricultural policy and science earlier in the century, conservationists held on through the postwar decades. In addition, the strong tradition of more holistic approaches to farming, though overshadowed, never disappeared entirely. With the rise of ecology these approaches began to gain the attention and imprimatur of science.[28]

The manifold social and environmental impacts of industrial agriculture—groundwater contamination, surface water degradation, accelerated soil erosion, soil compaction, nutrient depletion, salinization of irrigated lands, pesticide resistance, diminished soil floral and faunal diversity, decreasing wildlife populations, loss of crop germ plasm and livestock breed diversity, farmer health problems, declining rural communities, economic insecurity—became increasingly evident in the late 1970s and 1980s, reinforcing one another in a cycle that fragmentary approaches could not effectively address.

Mainstream agricultural science, education, and policy, locked into strong traditions of their own, responded slowly to the situation. The result was a grassroots "sustainable agriculture" movement (though it had, and has, many other names) that brought the term *sustainable* into wide usage among a constituency that gave it greater definition on the ground. Economic pressures and droughts in the mid- to late 1980s forced thousands of midwestern farmers off the land but gave the movement for sustainability even greater impetus. Many farmers took a hard look at the economics of modern, large-scale farming, especially the high cost of purchased inputs. More and more of them began to experiment with alternative practices for economic reasons, but in the bargain realized other benefits as well.

By no stretch of the imagination did sustainable agriculture win the day, and the formula for achieving it may never be fully determined (and indeed will vary by site and circumstance). But the very process of research, demonstration, and application, led effectively by farmers themselves, gave strength and durability to the movement. Along the way, the term "sustainable" came to imply a broadened approach that sought to address simultaneously the social, economic, agronomic, environmental, and intergenerational costs of conventional agriculture.

A parallel shift was occurring at the international level. International development programs, which by their nature involve a large component of *rural* and *agricultural* development, had for decades been dominated by efforts to export the American model of high-input production agriculture. The technologies that collectively comprised the Green Revolution succeeded in raising raw yields of crops in many regions of the world but entailed high social, economic, and environmental costs. As gains in yield showed signs of plateauing, additional arable lands grew scarce, and the quality of the soil and water resource base suffered the effects of widespread neglect and abuse. The environmental and cultural impacts of large-scale, energy-intensive methods called into question many basic assumptions of the prevailing agricultural development model.[29]

At the same time, international development agencies and lending institutions were coming under greater scrutiny for supporting environmentally destructive development projects, backing economically perverse policies, and leading developing countries deeper and deeper into the ruts of debt. The most dramatic and well-publicized example of the traditional approach—the subsidized conversion of the rainforests of the Amazon basin—represented the extreme in a way of thinking about human communities and their development that, by the late 1980s, was undeniably flawed. In this environmental crucible, concerns over biodiversity loss, poverty, decline of indigenous cultures, and inappropriate approaches to development melded together in sadly spectacular fashion. However difficult it was to define sustainability, it was not hard to recognize its opposite.

Importantly, these changes occurred as other global scale environmental matters—depletion of the earth's ozone layer, early warnings of global climate change, the Law of the Sea negotiations—came to the fore. In 1987 the United Nations' World Commission on Environment and Development released its widely publicized report, *Our Common Future* (or, as it came to be known, the "Brundtland Report"). The report called for the redirection of international development policies to foster sustainable economic development and resource management. It also provided a standard (and much criticized) definition of sustainable development, as "development that meets the needs of the present without compromising the ability of future generations to meet their own needs."[30]

The Brundtland Report was only the most prominent summary statement on international development and environmental policy that came out in the late 1970s and 1980s. Advocates of sustainability had been busily refining their alternative analyses. Building in particular on the insights (and flaws) of the landmark Club of Rome report *The Limits to Growth* (1972), this work was reflected in a thicket of new publications on sustainability and international policy. A far from complete list from this period includes *Alternatives for Growth: A Search for Sustainable Futures* (1977), *The Dispossessed of the Earth: Land Reform and Sustainable Development* (1979), *World Conservation Strategy: Living Resource Conservation for Sustainable Development* (1980), *Building a Sustainable Society* (1981), *Sustainable Food Systems* (1983), *Agricultural Sustainability in a Changing World Order* (1984), *Sustainable Development in an Industrial Economy* (1985), *Sustainable Resource Development in the Third World* (1987), *Sustainable Development: Exploring the Contradictions* (1988), *Sustainable Environmental Management: Principles and Practices* (1988), and *Fragile Lands in Latin America: Struggles for Sustainable Development* (1989).[31]

Some saw this outpouring as a mere bandwagon phenomenon; others held that the bandwagon had been long overdue. Some suggested that the concept of sustainability finally ushered ecosystem values into the inner sanctums of economics. Others responded that the mere invocation of "sustainability" did not portend any meaningful concern for the broader community of living things except as it served and concerned human welfare—thus perpetuating the root cause of nonsustainability.[32]

By the early 1990s, acceptance of sustainability as a guiding concept was evident in a wide range of activities undertaken by national, international, scientific, and nongovernmental organizations. In 1991, for example, the Ecological Society of America issued its "Sustainable Biosphere Initiative," highlighting "the necessary role of ecological science in the wise management of the Earth's resources and the maintenance of Earth's life support systems."[33]

In 1992, the Royal Society of London and the U.S. National Academy of Sciences issued an unprecedented joint statement, "Population Growth, Resource Consumption, and a Sustainable World."[34] The World Conservation Union, United Nations Development Programme, and World Wide Fund for Nature identified sustainability principles, actions, and indicators in "Caring for the Earth: A Strategy for Sustainable Living."[35] The varying definitions and interpretations of "sustainable development" were at the heart of the June 1992 United Nations Conference on Environment and Development in Rio de Janeiro (the "Earth Summit"). In many ways the Rio summit represented the culmination of a generation's effort to put environmental issues on the global political agenda.[36]

Coming along as it did in the wake of the Cold War, the Rio summit generated high hopes. As one participant put it, "the world felt it was finally getting its act together. . . . Anything seemed possible."[37] The decade that followed would temper those hopes. In the feverish 1990s, sustainability continued to gain acceptance as a general goal—and to fall short of serious commitment. For every creative action to better harmonize ecology and economics, there was an opposite reaction in defense of conventional economics and political self-interest. As "the world's only remaining superpower," the United States had a unique leadership role to play. It had lapsed in that role even before September 11, 2001. At the August 2002 "Rio-Plus-10" summit in South Africa, the United States found itself isolated by its growing unilateralism. The great irony from a historical perspective was that the nation that for a century had led the global conservation movement was now being left behind. And the great tragedy was that it had missed a unique opportunity to explore, and explain, the connections between international security and sustainability.

Whatever else the term "sustainability" has come to signify since 1970, it marks a basic shift in rhetoric and *potentially* in practice. Taken in sum, the calls for sustainability offer a far more sophisticated critique of blind economics than had been available on the first Earth Day. The emergence of sustainability as a unifying concept, however flawed, reflected the need for more judicious approaches to complex social and environmental problems. It forced those who worked in these arenas to confront fundamental questions about their means and ends, and to take into account—quite literally—the ecological basis of secure human communities. And for some, at least, it opened the way to a wider ethical perspective that would allow ecosystems to be "sustained" not only for the human benefits they yield, but for their own inherent value.

As with conservation biology, this reorientation compelled universities, aid agencies, professional groups, businesses, and nongovernmental organizations to respond. Those who had formerly studied the human community "almost as if it were a separate entity" could no longer afford to do so. They, too, had moved closer to the fusion point.

←← →→

There will always be those who insist on framing any and all environmental issues in terms of "jobs versus the environment," "people versus trees," "progress versus stagnation." But people have become increasingly aware of the fallacies, simplistic assumptions, and myopic perspectives that underlie such sentiments and are searching for practical alternatives that do not involve choosing the short-term evil of social and economic hardship or the long-term evil of environmental decline.

Since Earth Day 1970, conservation biology has emerged as an integrative area of scientific endeavor. It has sought to fathom the full diversity of life on Earth, to understand the impact of human activities on that diversity, and to devise means to maintain and restore it. To do so, it has had to pay increased attention to the human side of the dilemma: the historical patterns, social conditions, educational approaches, economic forces, cultural traditions, and development goals that so largely determine the fate of biological diversity around the world and in our backyards.

Over this same period, sustainability has emerged as an umbrella term that has sought to reframe social and economic development in a manner that respects the essential importance of ecosystem health and the diversity of life—the ultimate sources and bases of healthy human societies. Although often defined in primarily economic terms, sustainability does imply that constant attention must be given to long-term environmental quality. It may yet come to imply that the biotic community, with which human society has coevolved and must finally coexist, has intrinsic value as well.

The advent of conservation biology and the wide acceptance of the goal of sustainable societies indicate that Leopold's "two lines of thought" have, if not fused, at least converged. Both concepts survey vast realms of knowledge and activity. We find now that these spheres, the biotic and the human, can no longer be considered separately. If on Earth Day 1970 those concerned with the health of the environment and those concerned with the health of human society generally spoke past one another, this is no longer the case. Their words were stones, cast into the same pool. The circles have rippled across the water, growing ever outward over time, meeting and overlapping. They may yet merge within the common circle of concern.

Leopold's Legacy |

PART TWO

4

Leopold's Fine Line

*There is nothing more practical in the end
than the preservation of beauty, than the
preservation of anything that appeals to the
higher emotions of mankind.*
—THEODORE ROOSEVELT (1903)

*Conservation, without a keen realization of
its vital conflicts, fails to rate as authentic
human drama; it falls to the level of a mere
Utopian dream.*
—ALDO LEOPOLD (1937)

SCHOLARS HAVE long focused on the split between utilitarian conservationists and preservationists in interpreting the human–nature relationship. This has shaped our standard view of American conservation and environmental history: as an ongoing struggle between those who see the natural world as a collection of resources that ought to be controlled, managed, and used (albeit "wisely"), and those who see nature as a beautiful unity, possessed of inherent value, that ought to be preserved. The prototypical joiners of the battle, Gifford Pinchot and John Muir, are seen continuing through their ideological successors to vie for the hearts and minds of the committed.

That the paradigm is useful is affirmed by its durability as a historical device. It has illuminated the unfolding of conservation as a human endeavor and a force on the landscape. It has helped us to gauge society's response to rates of environmental change unprecedented in the human experience—and to develop, we hope, appropriate responses. Yet the line between utility and preservation is not always so easily traced. Depending on definitions and circumstances, waste may contain wonder, preservation may lead to destruction, and one generation's "wise use" may become the height of folly to those who follow. Analogously, there are problems in applying a strict utilitarian/preservation dichotomy to conservation history.

Conservation is a big thing, and the device is better suited for certain tasks than for others. The utility-versus-preservation approach has different shades of meaning when applied to minerals, oceans, the atmosphere, groundwater, surface waters, wetlands, soils, vegetation, forests, rangelands, agriculture, parks, wilderness, recreation, game, fish, wildlife, biodiversity, cultural resources, the built environment. The need for better-integrated approaches to these "parts" of conservation grows only more apparent with time; yet each "part" has its own needs and dynamics. The formula for conservation, like the formula for human wisdom itself, is complicated.

The use/preservation paradigm has been most useful in understanding especially sensitive—and, to be sure, important—issues: the status of the early national forests, the damming of the Hetch Hetchy valley, the demise of old-growth forests, the fate of roadless areas, the exploitation of Alaska's oil fields, the protection of endangered species. Yet, conservation has always involved quieter, more pervasive skirmishes, away from the major battlegrounds. Those conflicts continue—on acres of tired farmland, over poisoned plumes of groundwater, on the outskirts of cities whose fringes sprawl as their guts decay, in ecosystems whose degradation is too slow and incremental to draw cameras or concern. These may demand attention as much as the spectacular, scenic, and charismatic, but the traditional "sides" in environmental disputes speak less directly to the issues here.

The division tends to oversimplify. "Use" can connote a wide range of relationships, from outright slavery and rank exploitation to communion and symbiosis. All living creatures "use" their environments. Some would convert this biological truth into economic dogma, and so sanction the intensive exploitation of all natural objects and processes. But preservation does not preclude utility. To the contrary, if we breathe, it is because the oxygen-producing capacity of our photosynthetic planet-mates persists; if we drink, it is because the world's hydrologic cycle continues to function;

if we eat, it is because we draw upon nature's original provisions of chlorophyll, germ plasm, and fertility. And if we dream, it is because there still exist spaces expansive enough to contain the human imagination.

The use/preservation tension strongly reflects the American experience. The European conquest of this continent was so fast, so complete, and remains so important a part of American myth and symbolism that the environmental lessons drawn from it can be applied only with caution to other landscapes and cultures. Conservation knows no boundaries, and the American experience, crucial though it has been to the development of an environmental ethic, was not and cannot be its sole source.

The use/preservation paradigm too easily glosses over some basic historical connections: that, for example, but for the Progressive utilitarian conservation movement of the early 1900s, we would still be arguing over stumps and gullies; that the movement for wilderness protection emerged largely from within the utilitarian confines of the U.S. Forest Service; that programs for protecting and restoring rare and endangered species had their "test runs" on game species; that before ecology got "deep" it had to get *born*.

A further flaw in the paradigm is that it all but automatically opposes active development or use of "resources" with passive preservation. It establishes a polarity instead of a spectrum. It provides scant space for alternative human activity or evolving attitudes or adaptive policies. Yet history demonstrates that neither free-for-all markets nor compulsory governmental restrictions are conservation panaceas. Rather, conservationists have tended to work pragmatically to create new opportunities for people to fit more healthfully within their landscapes. The point: neither "hands on" nor "hands off" approaches have sufficed to address all conservation dilemmas, in all places, for all time.

Finally, and more abstractly, strict adherence to the worldview implied by the utility-versus-preservation split may only reinforce the alienation that afflicts the human/nature relationship in the modern age. This core concern has recently motivated scholars and conservationists alike to reexamine the basic premises upon which environmental philosophies and policies rest.[1]

Such flaws do not diminish the real value of the utility-versus-preservation paradigm in understanding environmental history. I state them here mainly to bound a conversation. Aldo Leopold does not easily fit the standard pattern in this venerable debate. Leopold is often portrayed as having moved through his career from a youthful, Pinchot-like utilitarianism to a mature, Muir-like preservationist philosophy. The record is far more complex. Leopold clearly perceived this tension in his own work and thought, and in the conservation movement. Using that tension, he challenged himself, his colleagues, and his fellow citizens to confront ultimate conservation questions. What follows, then, is a conversation about utility and preservation with Aldo Leopold, in three areas that absorbed him throughout his career: wildlife management, wilderness preservation, and conservation philosophy.

✦ ✦

The place to begin the conversation is at the end, when Leopold was in the fullness of his creative powers, when his aspiration for conservation was equal to his abiding concern, when he was confident in both his emotion and his intellect. He is standing before a room of post–World War II students, pausing midway in his wildlife ecology course to discuss, briefly, his aims and motives: "If the individual has a warm personal understanding of land, he will perceive of his own accord that it is something more than a breadbasket. He will see land as a community of which he is only a member, albeit now a dominant one. He will see the beauty, as well as the utility, of the whole, and know the two cannot be separated. We love (and make intelligent use of) what we have learned to understand." He rejected the notion that "the human relation to land is only economic. It is, or should be, esthetic as well."[2]

It was the statement of a teacher who had learned the value of reason and enthusiasm in communicating lessons that mere propaganda could not. It was also the declaration of a human being who had wrestled with the tensions in his own vision through a lifetime of constant inquiry. Leopold's reference to "the beauty, as well as the utility, of the whole" and his emphasis on their essential coherence were not anomalous. It was in fact just the latest expression of a theme that had grown in Leopold's thinking and writing over his forty-year career, evolving alongside his emerging ecological worldview and culminating in the framing of his land ethic.

In the realm of wildlife conservation, one cannot divorce Leopold the protector of wildlife from Leopold the hunter, although that tension has often been bitter and deeply problematic. As a naturalist and sportsman, Leopold from his earliest outings practiced his pastimes with enthusiasm, self-discipline, and self-criticism. Born in 1887, he came to maturity during the heyday of Teddy Roosevelt as president, conservation leader, and outdoor cult figure, and Leopold absorbed the flavor of the era. In some ways, he resembled Roosevelt more than either of the rivals for Roosevelt's conservation heart, soul, and ear—Muir and Pinchot. Roosevelt lived the extremes of their positions, bringing the same brio to the creation of national parks, forests, and refuges that he brought to the buffalo plains of North Dakota and the savannas of Africa. If ever the split between Muir and Pinchot was manifest, it was in the person and presidency of Roosevelt.

Leopold's training at the Yale Forest School placed him in conservation's avant-garde.[3] Forestry in the first decade of the twentieth century was quickly gaining all the statistical, technical, and bureaucratic accoutrements of an established profession. Yet the fire that fueled many young foresters was not board-feet figures, or potential sales, or tensile strengths, but *forests*, especially *western* forests. So with Leopold. In 1909 he arrived on the Apache National Forest in the Arizona Territory prepared to apply forestry, but just as eager to explore wild country.

Leopold's abiding boyhood interest in birds, game, and hunting necessarily slackened during his first busy years in the U.S. Forest Service, but it never completely faded. It took its place within Leopold's expansive definition of forestry. An important early expression of this came in a letter to his fellow foresters on New Mexico's Carson National Forest in 1913. Sidelined by a protracted illness, he took the opportunity to consider the Forest Service's mandate: "We are entrusted with the protection and development, through wise use and constructive study, of the Timber, water, forage, farm, recreative, game, fish, and esthetic resources of the areas under our jurisdiction. I will call these resources, for short, 'The Forest.' . . . And it . . . follows that the sole measure of our success is the *effect* which [our efforts] have on the Forest."[4] Already Leopold was thinking of the forest as something more than trees, and of trees as something more than just timber. As a newly minted forester Leopold made his share of youthful mistakes, but he would not make the more serious blunder of placing a narrow concept of the forest's economic value above the forest's functional integrity.

After his recuperation, Leopold began to devote more of his energies to the cause of game protection. In general, conservationists were not yet much concerned about nongame species (except in a few special cases), nor were they thinking in terms of positive restoration measures. Yet Leopold as leader of the game protection movement in the Southwest plainly understood both the ethical and political import of a balanced approach to wildlife conservation. Speaking to Albuquerque's Rotary Club in 1917, he stated:

> We conceive of these wild things as an integral part of our national environment, and are striving to promote, restore, and develop them not as so many pounds of meat, nor as so many things to shoot at, but as a tremendous social asset, as a source of democratic and healthful recreation to the millions of today and the tens of millions of tomorrow. . . . It is our task to educate the moral nature of each and every one of New Mexico's half million citizens to look upon our beneficial birds and animals, not as so much gun fodder to satisfy his instinctive love of killing, but as irreplaceable works of art, done in life by the Great Artist. They are to be seen and used and enjoyed, to be sure, but never destroyed or wasted.[5]

Of course, not all species qualified as "irreplaceable works of art" in Leopold's estimation (or in the sights of most sportsmen of the day). His ethical and aesthetic boundaries excluded "varmints"—those species not deemed "beneficial." Already, however, Leopold was beginning to lay the foundations for a more positive approach to game management. Over the next decade he would articulate the need to preserve and improve habitat conditions so that game populations could better sustain themselves. This stood is contrast to the techniques that conservationists had heretofore used: game farming, tighter hunting restrictions, predator control, the establishment of refuges.

This approach allowed Leopold to rise above—or at least sidestep—the rancorous debates, often across the utility/preservation line, that rocked "wild life" conservation efforts in the 1920s and early 1930s. That line cut somewhat differently than it had earlier in the century, when debate revolved around public parklands, forests, rangelands, and waters. The use and/or preservation of those features involved large institutions, federal agencies, and corporate interests. Much of the action occurred in the halls of government. With regard to game, the institutions were often more local, the habits and attitudes more personal. Through the 1920s, Leopold became familiar with all the key players and issues in the game conservation arena. He spoke out when necessary, but devoted most of his energies, especially after leaving the Forest Service in 1928, to the background work necessary to establish game management as a viable field.

Although busy building these foundations, Leopold was too prominent a figure in the conservation community to avoid the divisions within it. He was in a precarious position. Under the employ, at first, of the arms and ammunitions industry, he was an object of suspicion among hunting's vocal opponents, in particular the bird-watching contingent (despite Leopold's credentials as an ornithologist). Many hunters were skeptical of, if not openly hostile to, Leopold's game management theories, especially as they affected—or so they feared—the traditional American freedom to hunt on private lands. Game farmers did not share Leopold's view that game populations could and should be restored primarily by preserving and creating habitat. Few zoologists concerned themselves with the applied arts of conservation; those who did often saw Leopold as an agent of the hunting fraternity. Among all these factions, there was only scattered appreciation of Leopold's vision of a new profession skilled in the study, preservation, and careful manipulation of environmental conditions so as to bolster the survival of game species in the wild, under conditions as close to natural as possible.

Delicate though his position was, Leopold benefited from his direct confrontation with antagonistic attitudes. In the late 1920s Leopold was asked to chair an expert American Game Policy Committee, the purpose of which was to forge a new national policy to guide game conservation. The assignment gave Leopold an opportunity to examine the contemporary state of conservation and his own aims as a promoter of an alternative vision. In an unfinished manuscript, he assessed the relationship between the "wild lifers" and the "gunpowder faction":

The devotees of each [faction] like to consider it the antithesis of the other. The nature student is at small pains to conceal [the belief] that he

is superior to mere atavistic blood-letting, while the sportsman sees a
lack of Rooseveltian robustness in hunting with field glass or camera.
This mutual intolerance would be amusing if it were merely personal.
The fact is, however, that each side is nationally organized, and that a
state of deadlock between the opposing factions has more than once prevented action on measures obviously advantageous to both, not to mention the development of ideas which might lessen the apparent conflict
of interest.[6]

As Leopold saw it, those who appreciated the utility of wild creatures as game animals, and those who appreciated their beauty and
worked to protect them, were both missing the point. Whether useful, or
beautiful, or both, no creature could survive and perpetuate its kind if its
basic biological and ecological needs were not met. By this time Leopold
had moved to Wisconsin, and the impact of intensified agriculture on
wild game populations in the Midwest in the 1920s made this a point of
utmost concern.

Leopold was a superb diplomat. When the committee's game policy
statement came out it called explicitly for greater cooperation among the
interested factions, as well as greater attention to habitat needs (including
those of nongame species). This did not guarantee the policy's success,
however. Leopold took the initiative in selling it through speeches, articles,
and editorials, in cornfields and classrooms and offices. He met continued
resistance from all sides. In a reply to one protectionist broadside against
the policy and Leopold's work, Leopold laid his feelings on the line:

> Does anyone still believe that restrictive game laws alone will halt the
> wave of destruction which sweeps majestically across the continent,
> regardless of closed seasons, paper refuges, bird-books-for-school-
> children, game farms, Izaak Walton Leagues, Audubon Societies, or the
> other feeble palliatives which we protectionists and sportsmen, jointly or
> separately, have so far erected as barriers in its path? . . . I have tried to
> build a mechanism whereby the sportsmen and the Ammunition Indus-
> try could contribute financially to the solution of this problem, without
> dictating the answer themselves. . . . Another mechanism which I have
> tried to build is the committee of sportsmen and protectionists charged

with setting forth a new wild life policy. . . . These things I have done, and I make no apology for them.[7]

Leopold's reply demonstrated that, for him, on this front at least, pragmatism took precedence over purism. Never one to be content with platitudes, Leopold may have begun his conservation career with romantic visions, but practical considerations had long since tempered them. To achieve conservation, attitude change was essential, but not sufficient; success required solid science, political will, effective technique, and much education. "It takes all kinds of motives to make a world," he wrote during the same period. "If all of us were capable of beholding the burning bush, there would be none left to grow bushes to burn. Doers and dreamers are the reciprocal parts of the body politic: each gives meaning and significance to the other. So also in conservation. Just now, conservation is short of doers. We need plants and birds and trees restored to ten thousand farms, not merely to a few paltry reservations."[8]

In 1933, Leopold's textbook *Game Management* was published after several years of concentrated work. He defined the new field unambiguously in his opening line: "Game management is the art of making land produce sustained annual crops of wild game for recreational use"—a utilitarian statement sure to raise the hackles of many wildlife protectors.[9] To sense Leopold's vision, and to realize how far he was moving beyond the utilitarianism that had marked his own training, one had to read beyond the opening line. At the end of his first chapter, Leopold answered those who for aesthetic reasons were reluctant to hunt, or even observe, wild animals tainted, however faintly, by intentional management:

> There are still those who shy at this prospect of a man-made game crop as at something artificial and therefore repugnant. This attitude shows good taste but poor insight. Every head of wild life still alive in this country is already artificialized, in that its existence is conditioned by economic forces. Game management merely proposes that their impact shall not remain wholly fortuitous. The hope of the future lies not in curbing the influence of human occupancy—it is already too late for that—but in creating a better understanding of the extent of that influence and a new ethic for its governance.[10]

Even as Leopold was writing these words, his understanding of ecologically informed management practices was deepening. This showed in the later portions of *Game Management*, especially the chapters on "Economics and Esthetics" and "Game as a Profession." In the former, Leopold devoted several pages to "Management of Other Wild Life," a clear indication that he saw management for direct consumptive use of game animals as only a necessary first step toward conservation of a wider array of species.[11] Leopold again displayed his impatience with factionalism and grandstanding. He described the advances that even the most basic research into wildlife habitat needs could promote, to the benefit of all factions (not to mention the oft-forgotten animals):

> The crying need at this stage of the conservation movement is *specific definitions* of the environment needed by each species. . . . There is . . . a fundamental unity of purpose and method between bird-lovers and sportsmen. Their common task of teaching the public how to modify economic activities for conservation purposes is of infinitely greater importance, and difficulty, than their current differences of opinion over details of legislative and administrative policy. Unless and until the common task is accomplished, the detailed manipulation of laws is in the long run irrelevant.[12]

In the final pages of *Game Management*, under the heading "Social Significance of Game Management," Leopold expressed his hopes for the profession he and his contemporaries were birthing. In the process, he alluded explicitly to the utilitarian, preservationist, and aesthetic attitudes toward land that he sought to meld. The passage is worth quoting in its entirety, for in it one reads Leopold defining himself:

> The game manager manipulates animals and vegetation to produce a game crop. This, however, is only a superficial indication of his social significance. What he really labors for is to bring about a new attitude toward land.
>
> The economic determinist regards the land as a food-factory. Though he sings "America" with patriotic gusto, he concedes any factory the right to be as ugly as need be, provided only it be efficient.

There is another faction which regards economic productivity as an unpleasant necessity, to be kept, like the kitchen, out of sight. Any encroachment on the "parlor" of scenic beauty is quickly resented, sometimes in the name of conservation.

There is a third, and still smaller, minority with which game management, by its very essence, is inevitably aligned. It denies that kitchens or factories need be ugly, or farms lifeless, in order to be efficient.

That ugliness which the first faction welcomes as the inevitable concomitant of progress, and which the second regretfully accepts as a necessary compromise, the third rejects as the clumsy result of poor technique, bunglingly applied by a human community which is morally and intellectually unequal to the consequences of its own success.

These are simply three differing conceptions of man's proper relation to the fruitfulness of the earth: three different ideas of productivity. Any practical citizen can understand the first conception, and any esthete the second, but the third demands a combination of economic, esthetic, and biological competence which is somehow still scarce.

It would, of course, be absurd to say that the first two attitudes are devoid of truth. It seems to be an historical fact, however, that such few "adjustments" as they have accomplished have not kept pace with the accelerating disharmony between material progress and natural beauty. Even the noble indignation of the second school has been largely barren of any positive progress toward a worthier land use.

Quite evidently we are confronted with a conflict of priorities—a philosophical problem of "what it is all about." Our moral leaders are not yet concerned with this issue. . . . Examples of harmonious land-use are the need of the hour.[13]

Even in his most technical discussions of game management, Leopold rarely failed to highlight the aesthetic dimension of the work; conversely, even in his most preservation-oriented writings on wilderness, landscape features, and rare species, he never dismissed or ignored the utilitarian argument, but faced it directly. The two "conceptions" of conservation were not incompatible; in most cases, Leopold held, they could be harmonized to the mutual benefit of people and nature.

By the late 1930s, Leopold was convinced that they *had to be* better harmonized. The influences on him at the time were manifold: his university appointment in 1933; his purchase in 1935 of a worn-out farm along the Wisconsin River; his travels in Germany and Mexico in 1935–1937; the dust bowl and the economic upheaval of the Great Depression; the intellectual syntheses in biology. As *Game Management* was being studied in classrooms, Leopold was beginning to explore the essential question that ecology now raised: where does the utilitarian value of nature end and the health of natural systems (people included) begin? To conservation's intellectual leaders, the old message of George Perkins Marsh was resounding with new clarity and immediacy: ultimate utility lay in the functional health of the environment. Ecology and evolutionary biology had emerged as intersecting axes on which to gauge that state of health.

Leopold's published and unpublished work from the time is rich in consideration of this new world of understanding, with his topics overlapping and his interests fusing. Wildlife management was no longer an obscure, foundling field; it was now a crucial area of inquiry. Hardly had it gained its legs when it was being asked to run. Leopold summarized the changes, and his own comprehension of ecology's full meaning, in his 1939 paper "A Biotic View of Land":

> The emergence of ecology has placed the economic biologist in a peculiar dilemma: with one hand he points out the accumulated findings of his search for utility, or lack of utility, in this or that species; with the other he lifts the veil from a biota so complex, so conditioned by interwoven cooperating and competitions, that no man can say where utility begins or ends. No species can be "rated" without the tongue in the cheek; the old categories of "useful" and "harmful" have validity only as conditioned by time, place, and circumstance.[14]

With that, all bets were off in terms of utilitarian value and indiscriminate environmental manipulation. The game of conservation was gaining new rules, and the "line" had to be redefined.

Leopold's wildlife work in his final decade focused on field research and the refinement of management techniques, though not at the expense of this broader vision. To the contrary, Leopold held that wildlife ecologists had a responsibility to oppose the excesses in what he had begun to refer to as "power science." He saw the need, and potential, for this new field to respond to the increasing intensity of land-use technologies. Even while working in that high temple of utilitarian research and development—the land grant college of agriculture—he did not hesitate to state his case.

In a 1946 review, "The Outlook for Farm Wildlife," Leopold depicted rural development as a competition between two divergent attitudes toward farm life: "1. *The farm is a food-factory*, and the criterion of its success is salable products. 2. *The farm is a place to live*. The criterion of success is a harmonious balance between plants, animals, and people; between the domestic and the wild; between utility and beauty." The divergent attitudes tended to produce vastly different farm landscapes: one a monoculture with no room for wildlife (and a diminishing role even for people), the other a place for farmers to live and make a living, with "as rich a flora and fauna as possible." Leopold offered his diagnosis:

> It was inevitable and no doubt desirable that the tremendous momentum of industrialization should have spread to farm life. It is clear to me, however, that it has overshot the mark, in the sense that it is generating new insecurities, economic and ecological, in place of those it was meant to abolish. In its extreme form, it is humanly desolate and economically unstable. These extremes may die of their own too-much, not because they are bad for wildlife, but because they are bad for farmers.[15]

Economic pressures and technological advances had changed the very definition of utility in conservation. The unnecessary disappearance of natural and cultural amenities from the farm landscape was not just an unfortunate collateral effect; it was a predictable response and a warning sign.

Through the late 1930s and 1940s, Leopold had buttressed his conservation science and ethics with aesthetic appreciation, built on a combination of natural history, cultural history, and ecology.[16] This mixture would, like estuarine waters, prove uncommonly rich and productive. Leopold composed most of the *Sand County Almanac* essays at this time. His teaching began to highlight perception—as opposed to manipulation—as the first priority. Ironically, ecology had wrought a revolution in the old conservation debate: keen perception had *survival value*; aesthetic sensitivity, as enhanced by the new science, was *useful*; development that left land ugly, oversimplified, and dysfunctional was fundamentally flawed from an economic standpoint.

Leopold made the point more wryly. In *Sand County* he described an educated acquaintance who was "banded by Phi Beta Kappa" but who had "never seen or heard the geese that twice a year proclaim the revolving seasons to her well-insulated roof." He mused: "Is education possibly a process of trading awareness for things of lesser worth? The goose who trades his is soon a pile of feathers."[17]

⊰⊱ ⊱⊰

With his 1921 article "The Wilderness and Its Place in Forest Recreation Policy," Leopold opened a new round in the debate over the fate of wilderness within the nation's public lands. "Very evidently," he asserted, "we have here the old conflict between preservation and use, long since an issue with respect to timber, water power, and other purely economic resources, but just now coming to be an issue with respect to recreation. It is the fundamental function of foresters to reconcile these conflicts, and to give constructive direction to these issues as they arise."[18]

Appearing in the *Journal of Forestry*, Leopold's discussion of "wilderness conservation" (his phrase) and his specific call to establish permanent wilderness areas on the national forests were sure to provoke consternation among many of his professional peers. Sensitive to bureaucratic politics and traditions, he made his case by invoking holy writ: "The argument for such wilderness areas is premised wholly on highest recreation use."[19] As an example, Leopold recommended protecting the headwaters of the Gila River in the Gila National Forest in western New Mexico. In so doing, he provided a fine oxymoron for foresters (and future environmental historians) to ponder: "Highest use," he insisted, "demands its preservation."[20]

Wilderness protection was different from game and wildlife protection. The grain of attitudes ran at a different angle. The economic arguments for protection were less obvious. A sense of history was more essential. The core constituency was harder to define. And after all, the country already had a National Park Service devoted to preserving wild wonders; wasn't that enough?

It was not enough for Leopold and his like-minded colleagues in the Forest Service. The national parks were closed to hunting and in any case were being riddled with roads and tourist accommodations. And scenery was not enough. Leopold wanted a *functional* wilderness, "big enough to absorb a two weeks' pack trip," yet accessible to those not wealthy enough to travel to the far ends of the earth.[21] His 1921 call for wilderness protection was both progressive and utilitarian in this sense. It launched him on a career of wilderness advocacy that would again demonstrate that the line dividing utility and preservation was not simple, and not immutable.

That Leopold's initial interest in wilderness was more than aesthetic—that it involved more than scenic values—became plain when the idea of wilderness designation first arose in a discussion with his colleague Arthur Carhart in 1919.[22] Carhart, a landscape architect, hoped to preserve the scenic quality of Trapper's Lake in Colorado's White River National Forest through protection of its immediate shoreline. Leopold had something more in mind. In "The Wilderness and Its Place in Forest Recreation Policy" he stressed the recreational value of wilderness areas, with hardly a word given to scenic, biological, or ecological values, and only a hint of social, cultural, economic, historical, and spiritual values. And yet, aesthetic quality underlay the type of recreation he was seeking to protect. The sort of travel, hunting, and fishing that Leopold himself most enjoyed required a large, wild, and reasonably accessible environment.

By 1924, when the Gila Wilderness Area was designated, Leopold was expressing other reasons to protect wild places. There was always a practical tack to his arguments. Preservation, evidently, had other important "uses": "What I am trying to picture is the tragic absurdity of trying to whip the March of Empire into a gallop. . . . In this headlong stampede for speed and ciphers we are crushing the last remnants of something that ought to be preserved for the spiritual and physical welfare of future Americans, even at the cost of acquiring a few less millions of wealth or population in the long run. Something that has helped build the race for such innumerable centuries that we may logically suppose it will help preserve it in the centuries to come."[23] Leopold was asking the Forest Service to commit itself, in a real way, to forest values other than those most readily translatable into the "ciphers" of economics. He was declaring the ultimate usefulness of wilderness preservation. The line between utility and preservation had become very thin indeed.

After moving to Wisconsin in 1924, Leopold produced a series of articles rounding out the argument behind "the wilderness idea." Directed to diverse audiences, these articles laid out common themes: wilderness as a complement to civilization; the central role of wilderness in American history; the limits of standard economic reasoning; the need for a balanced vision of land use. Fighting a rearguard battle, Leopold did not deny the conventional economic value of the lands in question, but used this as a starting point. Realism, again, was his hallmark:

> The Forest Service will naturally select for wilderness playgrounds the roughest areas and those poorest from the economic standpoint. But it will be physically impossible to find any area which does not embrace some economic values. Sooner or later some private interest will wish to develop these values, at which time those who are thinking in terms of . . . national development in the broad sense and those who are thinking of local development in the narrow sense will come to grips. And forthwith the private interests will invoke the aid of the steam roller. They always do. And unless the wilderness idea represents the mandate of an organized, fighting, and voting body of far-seeing Americans, the steam roller will win.[24]

To build such a mandate, Leopold resorted less to Muir-like evocations of wild beauty and sublime majesty than to appreciation of the contrast value of wilderness. This called for a sense of history and cultural wholeness that defied the prevailing mood in the United States during the Roaring Twenties: "The measure of civilization is in its contrasts. A modern city is a national asset, not because the citizen has planted his iron heel on the breast of nature, but because of the different kinds of man his control over nature has enabled him to be. . . . If, once in a while, he has the opportunity to flee the city, throw a diamond hitch upon a packmule, and disappear into the wilderness of the Covered Wagon Days, he is just that more civilized than he would be without the opportunity. It makes him one more kind of man—a pioneer."[25]

At a time when wilderness preservation was little more than a fragile hope, Leopold recognized the pragmatic need to gather potential supporters through an expanded vision of the national saga, and the national landscape. Building on the ideas of Muir and Pinchot, Roosevelt and Frederick Jackson Turner, drawing on such writers and poets as Walt Whitman, Stephen Vincent Benet, and Sinclair Lewis (and maybe even F. Scott Fitzgerald), and sharing the views of such contemporaries as Benton MacKaye and Lewis Mumford, Leopold argued for wilderness preservation, not as a denial of the American myth of progress, but as a radical new fulfillment of it.

Yet, the economic dogma had to be faced. "Economic development," then as now, was roughly synonymous with "road building." To Leopold, it was a matter of scale and balance: roads were not inherently good or bad; their utility, or lack thereof, was a function of time, place, and density. Viewed on a national scale, and in historical context, the rise of the automobile culture demanded a parallel commitment to wilderness preservation:

> The wilderness idea is assumed to be an anti-road idea. The assumption is incorrect. . . . Roads and wilderness are merely a case of the pig in the parlor. We now recognize that the pig is all right—for bacon, which we all eat. But there was no doubt a time, soon after the discovery that many pigs meant much bacon, when our ancestors assumed that because the pig was so useful an institution he should be welcomed at all times and places. And I suppose that the first "enthusiast" who raised the question of limiting his distribution was construed to be uneconomic, visionary, and anti-pig.[26]

In a 1925 article, "Wilderness as a Form of Land Use," Leopold made the point more formally:

> Our system of land use is full of phenomena which are sound as tendencies but become unsound as ultimates. . . . The question, in brief, is whether the benefits of wilderness-conquest will extend to ultimate wilderness-elimination. . . . To preserve any land in a wild condition is, of course, a reversal of economic tendency, but that fact alone should not condemn the proposal. A study of the history of land utilization shows that good use is largely a matter of good balance—of wise adjustment between opposing tendencies.[27]

Leopold did not expand here on what he thought the benefits of "wilderness-conquest" had been, and it is difficult to know how deeply he might have been holding his tongue in his cheek while making his argument. But if one of the benefits of wilderness conquest had been a heightened appreciation of the *remaining* wilderness, then use and preservation were inevitably and closely coupled. That coupling had to be considered in any future use that aspired to the adjective "wise."

Leopold put his reasoning into a particularly American context. Scorning the superficial definitions of utility and Americanism that marked the "Babbittian" decade of the 1920s, he presented wilderness not as a source just of use *or* beauty, but as *the* source of a still incomplete, evolving republic: "Is it not a bit beside the point for us to be so solicitous about preserving [American] institutions without giving so much as a thought to preserving the environment which produced them and which may now be one of our effective means of keeping them alive?"[28] Later, the American experience of wilderness would be overshadowed in Leopold's wilderness philosophy by globally applicable concerns for ecological health and diversity. Through the 1920s, however, this was a principal and effective part of his argument. The wilderness, at least as Euro-Americans had defined and experienced it, was forever gone—that too was a lesson of history—but its cultural resonance remained potent. By forcing those who patriotically invoked wilderness symbolism to confront the stark reality of dwindling wild spaces, Leopold explicitly and implicitly invited action. To those who questioned whether there was any place for wilderness in an America whose business was business, Leopold asked, "Shall we now exterminate this thing that made us American?"[29]

After producing this mid-1920s pulse of wilderness advocacy papers, Leopold turned his attention to laying the groundwork for wildlife management. When he resumed an active role in the wilderness protection movement in the mid-1930s, he did so with all the additional insight that his intellectual evolution could bring to the cause. The significance of wildlands now included their scientific and ecological value. With this came an intensified sense of the benefits to be gained by preserving wilderness.

Leopold made the point in his contribution to the inaugural issue (1935) of *Living Wilderness*, the journal of the new Wilderness Society: "I suspect . . . that the scientific values [of wilderness] are still scantily appreciated, even by members of the Society. . . . The long and short of the matter is that all land-use technologies—agriculture, forestry, watersheds, erosion, game, and range management—are encountering unexpected and baffling obstacles which show clearly that despite superficial advances in technique, *we do not yet understand and cannot yet control* the long-time interrelations of animals, plants, and mother earth."[30] The logical corollary? We needed the dynamic of wilderness as a contrast to the dynamic of civilization. Leopold had said as much in the 1920s, but his emphasis then was on the benefits to individuals and to society. Now he stressed the benefits to the combined natural and cultural community.

Humbled by his growing appreciation of the complexity of population ecology (the "yet" would evaporate from the statement above), focused by field experiences in Germany's forests and Mexico's Sierra Madre, and tempered by the harsh lessons of the dust bowl years, Leopold would henceforth employ this argument for wilderness above all others. Wildlands took their place at one end of the full spectrum of his conservation philosophy, inseparable from his other conservation interests. As Leopold worked to translate his "biotic view of land" into on-the-ground conservation strategies, wilderness became the vital control against which to check the human experiment in land use: "Just as doctors must study healthy people to understand disease, so must the land sciences study the wilderness to understand disorders of the land-mechanism."[31]

Leopold employed the "land health" analogy regularly in the late 1930s and early 1940s as he worked to instill ecological understanding among his students and colleagues. The preservationist sounded very practical at this point: "All wilderness areas, no matter how small or imperfect, have a large value to land-science. The important thing is to realize that recreation is not their only or even their principal utility. In fact, the boundary between recreation and science, like the boundaries between park and forest, animal and plant, tame and wild, exists only in the imperfections of the human mind."[32] Leopold was expanding traditional notions of utilitarianism in a manner that would not come to be appreciated for another half century. Foresters, farmers, ranchers, fishers, conservationists, scientists now wonder: what knowledge might we reap if we had access to a large functioning bison range, a county or two of midwestern tallgrass prairie, a fully self-sustaining salmon or cod fishery, a cylinder of preindustrial atmosphere? (One suspects that even the most sober of utilitarians would stand back in wonder as well.)

Although Leopold regularly explained the practical benefits to be gained through preservation, his aesthetic response remained acute. One has only to read his *Sand County Almanac* accounts of Arizona and New Mexico, of Manitoba and the Colorado River delta, of the less monumental but still entrancing wilds of Wisconsin. These essays were composed in the early 1940s, when his mature wilderness philosophy gave context to his memories. At the same time, he remained an ever-vigilant defender, in print and in person, for threatened wildlands from the Arctic to the Mexican borderlands to Wisconsin's rivers and remnant prairies. His art, his advocacy, his science, and his ethics, were of a piece.

Reconciliation of the utilitarian and preservationist traditions on the issue of wilderness protection has, of course, remained elusive. In Leopold's view, such reconciliation could be achieved only if enough "far-seeing Americans" came to understand the larger ecological, historical, and cultural context of wildness, and allowed that understanding to inform their worldviews and commitments. This is the point to which Leopold's evolving wilderness philosophy—and his land ethic—finally led. In his final essay on wilderness, he wrote:

> Wilderness is the raw material out of which man has hammered the artifact called civilization. . . .
>
> To the laborer in the sweat of his labor, the raw stuff on his anvil is an adversary to be conquered. So was wilderness an adversary to the pioneer.
>
> But to the laborer in repose, able for the moment to cast a philosophical eye on his world, that same raw stuff is something to be loved and cherished, because it gives definition and meaning to his life.[33]

Wild places have given "definition and meaning" even to the lives of those most removed from, unaware of, and even hostile toward, their existence. This "use" goes to the very essence of our identities, dives to the depths of our evolutionary origins, asks profound questions of human intentions, calls us to creation's brink. Though not always pleasant or comfortable, the human experience of the wild has *made us* human. This holds for each of us as individuals, and all of us as members of the species. Lose the wild, and we lose the human. That would be wasteful, and inefficient, and impractical. And very ugly.

-<+- -+>-

The same independent thinking that fueled Leopold's breakthroughs in wildlife conservation and wilderness preservation led him to push outward the boundaries of conservation philosophy. The "ratio" of utility to other conservation values shifted as Leopold matured. As the son of a hunter, successful furniture manufacturer, and active conservationist, Leopold understood from his earliest days the value of natural resources in meeting material human needs, and the responsibilities of stewardship that such dependency entails. He never forgot those early lessons and as an adult placed them within a broader context informed by ecology, ethics, aesthetics—and a revolutionary economics.

Leopold was never wholly comfortable with the utilitarian party line. Even in his headiest days as a young forester, he saw forestry as much more than the securing or processing of cellulose. "I have no ambition to be a tie-pickler or a timber-tester," he declared while still a student.[34] Among his first self-initiated chores after arriving on the Apache National Forest was the marking of boundaries for a proposed game refuge. The utilitarian view was surely pervasive in those dawning days of the Forest Service, but it was not monolithic.

By the time Leopold first began to define his philosophy of conservation, he had developed a personal set of premises and conclusions far broader in scope than those he was trained on. In an early effort to explain his views, "Some Fundamentals of Conservation in the Southwest" (1924), Leopold revealed a Muir-like frustration with the anthropocentric approach to conservation—and to life: "Most religions, insofar as I know, are premised squarely on the assumption that man is the end and purpose of creation, and that not only the dead earth, but all creatures thereon, exist solely for his use. The mechanistic or scientific philosophy does not start with this as a premise, but ends with it as a conclusion."[35]

Leopold's alternative was not to deny outright the utilitarian worldview, but to harness it to a decency guided by respect. "The privilege of possessing the earth entails the responsibility of passing it on, the better for our use, not only to immediate posterity, but to the Unknown Future, the nature of which is not given us to know. It is possible that Ezekiel respected the soil, not only as a craftsman respects his material, but as a moral being respects a living thing."[36] Human use of the earth and its material components was a given. But human use, if undertaken without consideration of its moral dimensions, threatened to become corrosive.

Leopold arrived at this attitude as much through his reading of the landscape as his reading of books. He had fifteen years of Forest Service fieldwork under his belt. His studies of overgrazing, vegetation change, soil erosion, and fire ecology in the Southwest provided him with sufficient evidence of the long-term results of shortsighted land use. Without that field experience, his reading could hardly have resonated so deeply. Leopold read Pyotr Ouspensky and William Cullen Bryant and Walt Whitman against a powerful background: the rimrocks of the Colorado Plateau, the extrusions of the Mogollon Rim, the side canyons of the Gila. From the backcountry, their ideas echoed back through Leopold:

> Possibly, in our intuitive perceptions, which may be truer than our science and less impeded by words than our philosophies, we realize the indivisibility of the earth—its soil, mountains, rivers, forests, climate, plants, and animals, and respect it collectively not only as a useful servant but as a living being, vastly less alive than ourselves in degree, but vastly greater than ourselves in time and space—a being that was old when the morning stars sang together, and when the last of us has been gathered unto his fathers, will still be young.[37]

Mindful of the limits of scientific reasoning and unrestricted by the commands of academic philosophy, Leopold allowed his intuitive sense of the vital and indivisible earth to inform (though not dictate) his conservation stance. He recognized the earth "not only as a useful servant but as a living being." The understated tension in that phrase would be a constant goad to him, leading ultimately to the synthesis of "The Land Ethic." Were Leopold not so constitutionally forward-looking, or so possessed of the naturalist's ingrained delight in the natural world, or so plain dogged in his commitment to conservation, the tension might have been depressive and draining. At times in his life, it was. In general, however, it served as a creative tension, driving him to understand the changing relationship between humankind and the earth in a rapidly industrializing time.

That that relationship need not be destructive—that society need not acquiesce in the impoverishment of native flora, fauna, and landscapes— were basic premises behind Leopold's efforts to establish game management. As noted above, Leopold was determined to counteract the trends by initiating the painstaking study of actual, on-the-ground needs of species. When he next tried to summarize his conservation philosophy in "The Conservation Ethic" (1933), his argument bore the mark of his detailed field studies. The measure of success in conservation was not mere efficiency, even long-term efficiency. "The real end [of conservation]," he wrote, "is a *universal symbiosis with land*, economic and esthetic, public and private."[38]

Flush with the promise of this new aim and new methods with which to pursue it, Leopold was already anticipating the extension of game management's principles to other areas of conservation work. Through active engagement with land and its wild components, people might make some progress toward that "universal symbiosis": "The average dolled-up estate merely proves what we will some day learn to acknowledge: that bread and beauty grow best together. Their harmonious integration can make farming not only a business but an art; the land not only a food-factory but an instrument for self-expression, on which each can play music of his own choosing."[39]

Such statements reveal the influence of the midwestern landscape on Leopold. Wildlife managers learned many of their first lessons working with small game populations on midwestern farmsteads, where "bread and beauty" could, with effort, grow well together. Leopold understood, however, that certain environmental values would be sacrificed if this formula were applied indiscriminately across the landscape—in the Gila Wilderness, for example, where bread, and beef, and timber, took a back seat to beauty and wildness. The explanation of this seeming contradiction lay in an appreciation of scale: bread and beauty grew best together on the continent—on the planet—as well as the back forty. The trick was to strike some balance in a world so increasingly blind to natural beauty, so antipathetic toward wildness, and so hungry for bread, that the environmental conditions necessary for balance were threatened.

This would be the lesson of the environmental dilemmas of the 1930s. Leopold saw aesthetic appreciation of nature not as a luxury for the elite, but as a birthright and an absolute social necessity. Only by raising the level of public sensitivity to landscapes, to the processes and functions that determined land health, could that health be maintained in the common interest. Wildlands, as noted earlier, played an important role in framing this idea, at one end of the land-use continuum. But the land ethic toward which Leopold was headed applied across the board.

An important milestone along the path—the place, in fact, where the phrase "land ethic" first appeared in Leopold's writing—was a 1935 address, "Land Pathology." After weighing the problems of relying simply on the profit motive in conservation, he considered the social, cultural, and historical reasons for conservation's too-limited successes. The divorce of utility and beauty, virtually institutionalized in the conservation bureaus and in society at large, played prominently in his argument. Conservation's sharp divisions and diverse interests reflected "the age-old conflict between utility and beauty."[40] Leopold rejected the notion that one had to choose sides.

> This paper proceeds on two assumptions. The first is that there is only one soil, one flora, one fauna, one people, and hence only one conservation problem. Each acre should produce what it is good for and no two are alike. Hence a certain acre may serve one, or several, or all of the conservation groups.
>
> The second is that economic and esthetic land uses can and must be integrated, usually on the same acre. To segregate them wastes land, and is unsound social philosophy. The ultimate issue is whether good taste and technical skill can both exist in the same landowner.[41]

Such integration, however, was increasingly difficult to achieve in an urbanizing society whose legacy of land use was nothing to brag about in the first place. Leopold saw clearly that the forces were pulling in precisely the wrong directions. "The unprecedented velocity of land-subjugation in America involved much hardship, which in turn created traditions which ignore esthetic land uses. The subsequent growth of cities has permitted a re-birth of esthetic culture, but in landless people who have no opportunity to apply it to the soil."[42] And if such tastes and traditions became compartmentalized in a nation's collective mind, they would sooner or later became compartmentalized on the nation's landscape. In the worst-case scenario, the segregation of ethics, aesthetics, and economics would work to the detriment of each. Leopold did not avert his eyes from the most disturbing effects:

> Parks are over-crowded hospitals trying to cope with an epidemic of esthetic rickets; the remedy lies not in hospitals, but in daily dietaries. The vast bulk of land beauty and land life, dispersed as it is over a thousand hills, continues to waste away under the same forces that are undermining land utility. The private owner who today undertakes to conserve beauty on his land does so in defiance of all man-made economic forces from taxes down—or up. There is much beauty left—animate and inanimate—but its existence, and hence its continuity, is almost wholly a matter of accident.[43]

Writing amid the Depression, Leopold was particularly sensitive to the proposition that "man-made economic forces" would automatically bring about the good life. "Granted that science can invent more and more tools, which might be capable of squeezing a living even out of a ruined countryside, yet who wants to be a cell in that kind of a body politic? I for one do not."[44] Conservation provided an important corrective, a counterforce that could begin to meet the inseparable material, emotional, and spiritual needs of people. In exploring this potential, Leopold had identified the ultimate consequence of the divorce of utility and beauty on the land: a compulsive devotion to increased efficiency and productivity, in increasingly and intensively modified landscapes, supporting a human population with little direct connection to land, content that it could "conserve nature" (or "protect the environment") by setting aside a few isolated scenic parks.

On occasion, Leopold hinted at the personal cost of being ecologically literate, at the sadness that came from "living alone in a world of wounds."[45] Yet he was not by nature a pessimist or cynic. It was always his style to realistically assess a situation, weigh options, make the best-informed choice, and press forward. As the insights of ecology seeped ever more deeply into Leopold's work through the late 1930s, his response continued to be positive and self-critical. Without letting down his wilderness guard—wildland protection remained a personal priority—he wrestled time and again with the very definition of conservation, regularly confronting "the age-old conflict between utility and beauty."

To Leopold, the first step in achieving "wise" use was to resist pat paeans to utilitarianism itself. In one of many articles Leopold aimed at farmers at this time, he wrote:

> Sometimes I think that ideas, like men, can become dictators. We Americans have so far escaped regimentation by our rulers, but have we escaped regimentation by our own ideas? I doubt if there exists today a more complete regimentation of the human mind than that accomplished by our self-imposed doctrine of ruthless utilitarianism. The saving grace of democracy is that we fastened this yoke on our own necks, and we can cast it off when we want to, without severing the neck. Conservation is perhaps one of the many squirmings which foreshadow this act of self-liberation.[46]

Leopold had no problem affirming nature's utilitarian value, but he insisted that that value be more carefully defined and bound to other values. At times he anticipated modern discussions of sustainable development: "This new science of relationships is called ecology, but what we call it matters nothing. The question is, does the educated citizen know he is only a cog in an ecological mechanism? That if he will work with that mechanism his mental wealth and his material wealth can expand indefinitely? But that if he refuses to work with it, it will ultimately grind him to dust? If education does not teach us these things, then what is education for?"[47]

To hold that utility was not the only or ultimate criterion in conservation was to imply that better ethical guidelines were needed to guide its expression. Leopold now saw the full scope of the conservation dilemma, although another decade would pass before urgency prompted him to compose "The Land Ethic." In the meantime, utility and beauty grew ever closer in Leopold's thinking. In formulating a "land aesthetic" that celebrated not the superficial appearance of natural objects and places, but their evolutionary history and ecological relationships, he extended traditional criteria of natural beauty to the point where they essentially merged with his sense of long-term utility based on land health.[48] The converse was equally valid: in exploring the practical value of long-term ecological health, Leopold came to appreciate more deeply the subtle workings of land. In 1938 notes on "Economics, Philosophy, and Land," he wrote under the heading "Esthetics":

> We may postulate that the most complex biota is the most beautiful. I think that there is much evidence that it is also the most useful. Certainly it is the most permanent, i.e. durable. Hence there is little or no distinction between esthetics and utility in respect of biotic objective.
>
> Esthetics is an aspect of argument about land, not of land. It is part of the package system. We segregate esthetics so as to give farmers none and women's clubs a lot. In actual practice, esthetics and utility are completely interwoven. To say we do a thing for either reason alone is prima facie evidence that we do not understand what we are doing, or are doing it wrong.[49]

For Leopold, the line segregating utility and beauty was now all but obscured. Ecology provided a view of land and natural systems too expansive to be contained by conservation as he had learned and practiced it. In applying that vision back to conservation, the old definitions of utility and beauty changed and blended.

World War II only added immediacy to Leopold's views. His postwar writings reveal richer shades of concern over the primacy of utilitarianism and the neglect of aesthetic values. Leopold's writing achieved a certain fullness—a mellowness hard-won in the struggle to *comprehend* conservation and a clarity remarkable even by Leopold standards: "The citizen who aspires to something more than milk-and-water conservation must first of all be aware of land and all its parts. He must feel for soil, water, plants, and animals the same affectionate solicitude as he feels for friends and family. Family and friends are often useful, but affection based on utility alone leads to the same pitfalls and contradictions in land as in people."[50]

Leopold's valedictory expression of the theme came in his final revisions of *A Sand County Almanac* in 1947 and early 1948. That some reconciliation of utility and beauty was at the heart of his intentions for the manuscript was clear from his words in his foreword: "We abuse land because we regard it as a commodity belonging to us. When we see land as a community to which we belong, we may begin to use it with love and respect.

There is no other way for land to survive the impact of mechanized man, nor for us to reap from it the esthetic harvest it is capable, under science, of contributing to culture."[51] Could our need to use nature and our interest in protecting nature be, in fact, reconciled? Not easily, and not quickly. But in the end Leopold was pragmatic enough to see that they *had* to be, and idealistic enough to believe that they *could* be.

◂◂ ▸▸

The preservation-versus-utility paradigm will not fade away in our considerations of conservation history, policy, and practice. Nor should it. But by focusing on it so exclusively, have opportunities for more honest conversations and more effective consensus—on sustainable use as well as protection—been lost? We may predict that a mature conservation/environmental movement will work across the entire spectrum of land-use types, from the wild to the semiwild to the cultivated to the settled to the urbanized, and will recognize the relevance of each to all the others.

In the past, Leopold's land ethic has been criticized for being so abstract and poetic as to lose meaning in its application. History has shown the value of its scope: only a broad, even poetic, statement could hope to span the full range of land uses and call all land users to attention. Only such a statement could embrace and hold the common ground between Muir and Pinchot. And although Leopold himself might look askance at such tributes, it is revealing that his name has been affixed to both a university center for sustainable agriculture (in his native Iowa) and a public wilderness area (in his wife Estella's native New Mexico).

Aldo Leopold endeavored to be a healing presence, stanching the flow from the psychic wound in American conservation, even in the American mind. He did so by pursuing shared goals wherever they existed, by using history to show the connections between people and land, by reaching beyond conservation proper for insight and reinforcement. In so doing, he maintained that society's choice is not in fact between utility and preservation, but between short-term exploitation and long-term well-being. It may be that the wholeness he sought came to exist more in his own soul than in the exterior landscape, but through his efforts he also helped to nudge that landscape—what he once termed "that great biota we call America"—toward a richer and more vigorous existence.[52]

5

Emergence of an Idea

Hardly any aspect of life is more characteristic
than its almost unlimited diversity. . . .
Every organism depends for its survival
on a knowledge of the diversity of its
environment, or at least on an ability to cope
with it. Indeed, there is hardly any biological
process or phenomenon where diversity is not
involved.
—ERNST MAYR (1982)

WHEN THE complete saga of conservation in the twentieth century is finally told, one of its main storylines will involve the path by which scientists, resource managers, policy makers, and citizens came to—or failed to come to—a fuller appreciation of life's diversity. In the closing decades of the century, the impact of human activity on biological diversity became a matter of increased global concern. Scientists began to examine more carefully the full extent of nature's variety, the relationship between diversity and the structure and function of ecosystems, and the myriad contributions of the earth's diverse life forms to human well-being. Philosophy, ethics, and religion, which Aldo Leopold in his day lamented had "not yet heard of" conservation, began to explore the role and responsibilities of humanity within the larger community of life.[1]

These trends redefined the context of conservation. The diminishing of diversity came to be seen as both cause and effect of environmental decline. A host of environmental phenomena—pollution and contamination of soils, waters, and air; accelerated rates of habitat loss, disruption, and fragmentation; desertification and deforestation in the tropics; degradation of soils and waters in agricultural landscapes; the worldwide spread of exotic invasive species, especially in island habitats; mismanagement and overharvest of wild plants and animals; the specter of global climate change—focused attention on biological diversity as an essential attribute of ecosystems. Conservationists revisited standard approaches to resource management with an eye toward their influence on genetic, species, and community diversity. In short, diversity came to be widely acknowledged as a basic consideration in all efforts to protect, manage, and restore ecosystems and their constituent species.

One indicator of this fundamental shift was the adoption of the term *biodiversity*, beginning in the late 1980s.[2] Some have seen the emergence of biodiversity—as a word and an idea—as the result of a self-conscious (and even self-serving) effort by biologists to gain greater stature within the political arena. According to this view, the term *biodiversity* became "a tool for a zealous defense of a particular social construction of nature that recognizes, analyzes, and rues [the] furious destruction of life on Earth." By this reading, biological diversity came to be of concern when biologists and ecologists launched "a determined and vigorous campaign" to promote a reconceived notion of what nature *is*, what is valuable within it, and what people should do about it.[3] In so doing (it follows), scientists stepped beyond their traditional role as rational and dispassionate students of the natural world, to become just one more special interest group vying for political privilege and influence.

This thesis begs for a more careful examination of the history of the concept of biological diversity in conservation thought and practice. The word *biodiversity* is new; knowledge of biological diversity, appreciation of its role in nature and in human affairs, alarm over its loss, and attention to the challenges of conserving it, are not. The dramatic surfacing of biodiversity as a core concept in the late 1980s tends to obscure the more mundane story of the steady, if fitful, identification of biological diversity as a concern in conservation over many decades. That history, in fact, is still being written.[4]

Human knowledge of biological diversity obviously has much deeper historic and prehistoric roots. One effect of the recent surge of interest in biodiversity has been a reassessment of the evidence from anthropology, paleontology, and paleoecology of traditional ecological knowledge, anthropogenic environmental change, and the resource management practices of native peoples. The record of past human impacts on biological diversity is decidedly mixed, involving extinctions and extirpations as well as relatively benign stewardship, varying in intensity over time and according to ecosystem type and taxonomic groups. Yet, in many if not most native cultures, social mechanisms evolved to reinforce an attitude of respect and reverence toward nature, to evoke nature's bounty, and to sanction appropriate human use of that bounty. The conservation movement might be characterized as modern society's conscious effort to develop and exercise analogous social practices and restraints in its relations with the nonhuman world.[5]

Appreciation of biological diversity is not hard to find among early naturalists, biologists, and proto-conservationists.[6] In *The Story of My Boyhood and Youth*, John Muir reveled in the memory of his arrival on the Wisconsin frontier, of "young hearts, young leaves, flowers, animals, the winds and the streams and the sparkling lake, all wildly, gladly rejoicing together!"[7] As a student at the University of Wisconsin in the early 1860s, Muir had his eyes opened when he received his "first lesson in botany": a fellow student showed him that the locust tree and pea vine are both legumes, demonstrating nature's "essential unity with boundless variety." "This fine lesson," Muir wrote, "charmed me and sent me flying to the woods and meadows in wild enthusiasm."[8]

While Muir was receiving his botany lessons, an ocean away, Alfred Russel Wallace addressed his colleagues in the Royal Geographical Society on the theme of biological diversity, its study, and protection. Wallace described plant and animal species as "the individual letters which go to make up one of the volumes of our earth's history" and warned against "extinction of the numerous forms of life which the progress of cultivation invariably entails." Wallace pled with his colleagues to promote research on nature's diversity and to assume the responsibility for stewardship that came with knowledge: "If this is not done, future ages will certainly look back upon us as a people so immersed in the pursuit of wealth as to be blind to higher considerations. They will charge us with having culpably allowed the destruction of some of those records of Creation which we had it in our power to preserve; and, while professing to regard every living thing as the direct handiwork and best evidence of a Creator, yet, with a strange inconsistency, seeing many of them perish irrecoverably from the face of the earth, uncared for and unknown."[9]

A year after Wallace's address, George Perkins Marsh published his first edition of *Man and Nature*. In his second chapter, "Transfer, Modification, and Extirpation of Vegetable and of Animal Species," Marsh surveyed the human influence on various kinds of living things. Arguing that people were in essence a "new geographical force" affecting the fate of species, Marsh cited examples of human impacts on plants, "quadrupeds," birds, insects, reptiles, fish, "aquatic animals"—and even "minute organisms" (or, as Marsh described them, "troops of artisans . . . these wonderful architects and manufacturers" of the earth). "All nature" he surmised, "is linked together by invisible bonds, and every organic creature, however low, however feeble, however dependent, is necessary to the well-being of some other among the myriad forms of life with which the Creator has peopled the earth." He concluded his chapter with the hope that we might "learn to put a wiser estimate on the works of creation." By "studying the ways of nature in her obscurest, humblest walks" we could "derive not only great instruction . . . but great material advantage."[10]

Such examples do not make the case that biological diversity was at the core of the conservation movement from its origins. They do, however, suggest that the story of biological diversity as an organizing concept in conservation is much older than the coining of the special term *biodiversity*. The idea emerged long before even the term *conservation* itself became widely used. The forces that ultimately precipitated the new terminology have a long and complicated history.

◂◂ ▸▸

In the 1940s, Aldo Leopold nominated the complexity of the land as "the outstanding scientific discovery of the twentieth century." He was not engaging in hyperbole. After thirty-five years as a professional forester, field biologist, and wildlife manager, he concluded that "only those who know the most about [this complexity] can appreciate how little we know about it."[11] In the face of this dilemma, he counseled a true conservatism:

"The last word in ignorance is the man who says of an animal or plant: 'What good is it?' If the land mechanism as a whole is good, then every part is good, whether we understand it or not. If the biota, in the course of aeons, has built something we like but do not understand, then who but a fool would discard seemingly useless parts? To keep every cog and wheel is the first precaution of intelligent tinkering."[12]

Since the 1980s, land stewards, biologists, agency officials, and advocates have regularly invoked these words. The passage was as clear an expression of the importance of conserving biological diversity as Leopold ever wrote. Its recent rise on the hit parade of Leopold's quotable quotes may be taken as an indicator that conservation as a whole has evolved closer toward the point where Leopold found himself in the 1940s.[13]

Prescient though he often was, Leopold did not always place high value on keeping "every cog and wheel." To the contrary, Leopold's awareness of biological diversity as an understanding attribute of landscapes and as a conservation concern grew only incrementally over his career. When he started out along his professional path as a forester in 1909, biological diversity was not part of forestry's professional lexicon, much less addressed in its curricula or management plans. By the end of Leopold's days, he would argue that maintenance of diversity was key to the healthy functioning of all natural communities and to the long-term fate of human activities within them. He would hold, too, that we bore a moral responsibility to sustain that diversity.

The trail that Leopold followed both foreshadowed and stimulated the same changes within the conservation movement as a whole. The term *biodiversity* obviously does not appear in Leopold's writings or those of his contemporaries. Conservation, however, has continually changed as knowledge of life's diversity has expanded. The circle of ethical consideration—the scope of conservation interest and concern—has continually expanded as well. Leopold was by no means alone on this path; he was, however, unusually disciplined in exploring and documenting it.

As early as 1915, the germ of the idea can be found in Leopold's earliest formal writings on game protection and management. As a young forester in Arizona and New Mexico, he urged his colleagues in the U.S. Forest Service to devote more attention to what had been a neglected responsibility: the active protection and management of wild game populations on Forest Service lands. In his *Game and Fish Handbook* (1915), Leopold's (and perhaps the Forest Service's) first publication on the subject, he made the case: "The breeding stock must be increased. Rare species must be protected and restored. The value of game lies in its *variety* as well as its abundance."[14]

At the time, concern about the fate of wild plants and animals had not expanded much beyond species that people hunted, fished, logged, or otherwise directly exploited. Yet, even within the limited sphere of game animals, Leopold held that "variety" was valuable, and worth preserving. His main goal was to convince his fellow foresters that the protection of game animals was part of their professional responsibility and deserved their attention; in so doing, he argued for "the perpetuation of every indigenous species" of game in the Southwest.[15] To that end, Leopold during these years organized sportsmen across the Southwest into local "game protective associations" to work for more effective state conservation laws and administration.

As a game conservation advocate, Leopold faced not only the indifference of other foresters, but competition from a group with far different notions of what conservation entailed: game farmers. In distinguishing his approach from those of the game farmers, he again stressed the importance of diversity. "The game farmer," he wrote in 1919, "seeks to produce merely something to shoot, while the Wild Lifer seeks to perpetuate, at least, *a sample of all wild life, game and non-game*."[16] Leopold probably did not coin the term "non-game." His early use of it, however, underscored the breadth of his outdoor interests. His personal commitment—and that of most conservationists of his day—may have focused initially on the protection of game animals, but ever since his boyhood in Iowa, the circle of his concern had included other wild creatures as well.

The circle, however, was not all-embracing. "Non-game," as then reckoned, included mainly songbirds and small mammals. The term certainly did not apply to those large predators and other creatures generally deemed "vermin." While calling for the perpetuation of "a sample of all wild life," Leopold hastened to add that "the advisability of controlling vermin is plain common sense, which nobody will seriously question."[17]

That "plain common sense" would be in fact called into question beginning in the mid-1920s, and Leopold himself would become one of the most
astute questioners. For the time being, however, he continued to rail
against "vermin" and "varmints," especially the wolves, grizzly bears, and
mountain lions that still held reign in the mountains of the Southwest. "It
is going to take patience and money to catch the last wolf or lion in New
Mexico," he declared in 1920. "But the last one must be caught before the
job can be called fully successful." [18]

While promoting the need for game protection, Leopold became
increasingly interested in other aspects of conservation in the Southwest.
In the early 1920s his official duties as a Forest Service inspector stimulated
his lifelong interest in processes of landscape change and watershed function. He also began his campaign for wilderness protection. Explicit in
Leopold's wilderness advocacy was his recognition of the opportunity,
lost in other regions, for large expanses of wild land to support native
"wild life" (and hunters thereof). Importantly, this encouraged Leopold to
stress the value not just of *species* diversity, but of varied *ecosystems* and
landscapes as well. In one of his wilderness advocacy statements from the
mid-1920s, he observed: "It is often assumed than only mountain lands are
suitable for wilderness areas. Why not swamps, lakelands, river routes, and
deserts also?" [19]

◄◄ ►►

In 1924, Leopold moved to Madison, Wisconsin, to become assistant director of the Forest Service's Forest Products Laboratory. He remained in
this rather sedate position for four years, devoting what extra time he could
afford to his dual causes of wilderness protection and game management.
In 1928, Leopold followed his true calling and left the Forest Service to
devote himself full time to game management.

The focus of Leopold's new work was the "Game Survey of the North
Central States," an ambitious effort to describe, on a state-by-state basis, the
status of game populations, habitats, and management activities throughout
the region. There was no precedent for such a large-scale, on-the-ground
assessment. Leopold's three years of field investigations, from 1928 to 1931,
provided his emerging theories of game management with a firm grounding

in firsthand observation. But it was as chair of the American Game Policy Committee that Leopold was able to effect the conceptual revolution in conservation. "The one and only thing we can do to raise a crop of game," an early version of the policy report stated, "is to make the environment more favorable. This . . . holds true for all classes of game at all times and places. It is the fundamental truth which the conservation movement must learn." In a concerted effort to expand the committee's purview, the draft report stated up front that "while this plan deals with game only, the actions necessary to produce a crop of game are in large part those which will conserve *other valuable forms of wild life.*"[20]

The final report of the committee proposed that "the public is (and the sportsman ought to be) just as much interested in conserving non-game species, forests, fish, and other wild life as in conserving game."[21] By this time, even predators had gained provisional admittance to the fold. Early studies of predation and population ecology had begun to change scientific understanding of the role of predators. Meanwhile, the zealous efforts of federal predator control agents in the national parks, forests, and other public lands had been called into question by scientists and conservationists.[22]

These changing ideas came into play most notably in the case of the Kaibab Plateau north of the Grand Canyon, where predator eradication had apparently contributed to an irruption of the mule deer population, with devastating effects on range conditions. The massive die-off of Kaibab deer in the winters of 1924–1925 and 1925–1926 remains one of the most important and controversial episodes in the history of wildlife ecology and conservation.[23] The episode had a lasting effect on Leopold and his contemporaries. The immediate impact was reflected in the policy report's recommendation that "no predatory species should be exterminated over large areas." The report further advised that "rare predatory species, or species of narrow distribution and exceptional biological interest or aesthetic value, should not be subject to control."[24] The circle of concern had expanded a further degree.

This phase of Leopold's work culminated with the publication of his textbook *Game Management* in 1933. *Game Management* offered students a generalized approach to its subject, built on a foundation of contemporary ecological theory and applicable to any species in any environment. It reflected the important influence of British ecologist Charles Elton. In his own 1927 book *Animal Ecology*, Elton had spelled out many of the basic concepts of ecology: environmental factors and succession, food chains and food "cycles," the niche, the "pyramid of numbers," population fluctuations and dispersal. Elton's dynamic approach to ecology had a lasting impact on Leopold's own scientific research, writing, and teaching.[25] In 1931 Leopold and Elton met at a conference in Canada—a critical moment, in retrospect, in the history of conservation biology, representing as it did the intersection of ecological theory and management technique in the interest of conservation.

Game Management, as its title suggested, focused primarily on game species. In its text, however, Leopold made it clear that game species were not his only concern, and that mere production was not his only goal. "The objective of a conservation program for non-game wild life should be . . . to retain for the average citizen the opportunity to see, admire and enjoy, and the challenge to understand, the varied forms of birds and mammals indigenous to his state. It implies not only that these forms be kept in existence, *but that the greatest possible variety of them exist in each community.*"[26]

He made the same point in his landmark concurrent article "The Conservation Ethic": "[The] idea of controlled wild culture or 'management' can be applied not only to quail and trout but to *any living thing* from bloodroots to Bell's vireos. . . . A rare bird or flower need remain no rarer than the people willing to venture their skill in *building it a habitat.*"[27] Leopold's expanding circle now explicitly included the plant kingdom and indeed all "living things." Even as Leopold was working to convince his contemporaries that game management could be a viable enterprise, he himself was moving beyond it.

✦ ✦

Leopold joined the University of Wisconsin in 1933. The new position gave him unprecedented opportunities to develop his research methods, management techniques, and conservation ideas, to share them with students, and to apply them to the land.[28] As director of research at the university arboretum, Leopold worked with colleagues in botany and horticulture (and a company of the newly mustered Civilian Conservation Corps) to restore tallgrass prairie and other plant communities on the arboretum lands—among the first experiments in ecological restoration.[29] Importantly, the work at the arboretum further bolstered Leopold's growing interest in, and concern with, the vegetative component of the landscape. His personal research and restoration interests found a new home in 1935 when he acquired the worn-out bottomland farm along the Wisconsin River that would become the setting for the first part of *Sand County Almanac*.

Meanwhile, the environmental dilemmas of the mid-1930s were raising complex questions among Leopold and his contemporaries in conservation, centered on the ecological functioning of land and the relationship between the land and human economic activity. Leopold was blunt in his diagnosis. "Society has developed an unstable adjustment to its environment, from which both must eventually suffer damage or even ruin. Regarding society and land collectively as an organism, that organism has suddenly developed pathological symptoms, i.e., self-accelerating rather than self-compensating departures from normal functioning."[30] Moreover, Leopold had begun to focus on the loss of diversity as both a factor in, and manifestation of, this pattern.

His convictions on the point came into sharp focus during his 1935 study tour of Germany. In his travels he saw conservation—of a sort— carried to its self-destructive extreme. Driven by the special interest in raising timber and deer, intensive management had simplified central Europe's forests, even while undermining the long-term productivity of the conifer plantations, the vigor of the deer herds themselves, and the health of the forests in general. Leopold noted the extreme loss of diversity, particularly among the preferred browse plants of the forest floor. The forests were "deprived of a certain exuberance which arises from a rich variety of plants fighting with each other for a place in the sun. It is almost as if the geological clock had been set back to those dim ages when there were only pines and ferns." He noticed a similar dearth of mammalian predators, raptors, and cavity-nesting birds in the neatly maintained forests. Not even moss could survive on the acidified and "impoverished" soils. Leopold declared, in one of his more compelling metaphors, "I never realized before that the melodies of nature are music only when played against the undertones of evolutionary history."[31]

Among its other effects, Leopold's experience in Europe raised his level of anxiety about the fate of rare and endangered species. In a 1936 article "Threatened Species," his first devoted exclusively to the topic, he called for concerted attention to vulnerable species of plants and animals. "It admits of no doubt that the immediate needs of threatened members of our fauna and flora must be defined now or not at all." As an example, he chose the grizzly bear. In so doing, he revealed how far he had come in his concern over the survival of large predators as members of "our national fauna." "No one," he wrote, "has made a list of the specific needs of the grizzly, in each and every spot where he survives, and in each and every spot where he might be reintroduced, so that conservation projects in or near that spot may be judged in the light of whether they *help or hinder* the perpetuation of the noblest of American mammals."[32]

While Leopold was overseas, a subtle but significant shift was occurring within the American conservation movement. Several of the leading conservation organizations had adopted the one-word term "wildlife" to describe the objects of their attention. Noting this shift, Leopold specifically challenged his colleagues to attend to previously neglected members of the biota, including predators, "rare plant associations . . . such as prairie floras, bog floras, Alpine and swamp floras," and "all wild native forms which fly at large or have only an aesthetic or scientific value to man."[33] He called upon "the new organizations which have now assumed the name 'wildlife' instead of 'game' . . . to focus a substantial part of their effort on these threatened forms."[34] In one of many outward indications of his commitment to the new focus, Leopold switched his own title from that of "professor of game management" to "professor of wildlife management."

In contrast to Germany's grim lesson in too-intensive land management, Leopold's bow-hunting trips to northern Mexico's Sierra Madre Occidental in 1936 and 1937 brought him into a landscape where the human influence on the land was relatively light. The soils and watersheds were intact. Most, if not all, of the native flora and fauna persisted, including mountain lions and wolves. The land's natural beauty and ecological functions were unimpaired. Leopold found it ironic that Mexico should present "so lovely a picture of ecological health, whereas our own states, plastered as they are with National Forests, National Parks and all the other trappings of conservation, are so badly damaged that only . . . [the] ecologically colorblind can look upon them without a feeling of sadness and regret."[35] In the Sierra Madre, Leopold later recalled, he realized that "all my life I had seen only sick land, whereas here was a biota still in perfect aboriginal health. The term 'unspoiled wilderness' took on a new meaning."[36]

And new importance. Leopold noted that the Sierra Madre's deer herds provided an example of "an abundant game population thriving in the midst of its natural enemies," with none of the manifestations of over-abundance so evident on the U.S. side of the border. Leopold wondered "whether the presence of a normal complement of predators is not, at least in part, accountable for the absence of irruption? If so, would not our rougher mountains be better off and might we not have more normalcy in our deer herds, if we allowed the wolves and lions to come back in reasonable numbers?"[37] Every region, he subsequently argued, should retain "representative samples of its original or wilderness condition to serve science as a sample of normality."[38]

⤙ ⤚

By the late 1930s, the implications of ecological science for conservation practice could no longer be ignored. Diversity lay four-square at the heart of the issue. In his 1939 address "A Biotic View of Land," Leopold stressed the point. He noted that technological prowess had allowed modern humans to make changes of "unprecedented violence, rapidity, and scope . . . in the composition of floras and faunas": "The larger predators are lopped off the cap of the [biotic] pyramid; food chains . . . are made shorter rather than longer. Domesticated species are substituted for wild ones, and wild ones moved to new habitats. In this world-wide pooling of faunas and floras, some species get out of bounds as pests and diseases, others are extinguished."[39]

In his address Leopold concluded that "the biota as a whole is useful, and [the] biota includes not only plants and animals, but soils and waters as well."[40] His circle of concern as a conservationist now included not only the entire biota, but the physical components of the ecosystem as well. This view of life, as noted in the last chapter, called into question the very foundations of conservation philosophy. For its first three decades, the conservation movement had placed the most direct and obvious utilitarian values above all others. Ecology suggested that an expanded range of values had to be weighed in (and for) the future. For game management, as well as forestry, agriculture, and other fields, it implied a need to recalibrate approaches. "A good wildlife program," Leopold suggested, "reduces itself, in essence, to the deliberate perpetuation of a *diverse* landscape, and to its integration with economic and cultural land-use."[41]

During this important period Leopold cautiously explored the relationship between biological diversity and environmental stability. By "stability" Leopold did not imply a static state; he had explicitly rejected that notion and the associated image of the "balance of nature" many years before.[42] Rather, stability for Leopold denoted a condition of dynamic equilibrium that contrasted with the "self-accelerating rather than self-compensating departures from normal functioning" that he saw in the American landscape of the 1920s and 1930s.[43] "What, in the evolutionary history of this flowering earth, is most closely associated with stability?" he asked in 1940. "The answer to my mind, is clear: diversity of flora and fauna." In making his case, Leopold stepped very carefully. "It seems improbable," he continued, "that science can ever analyze stability and write an exact formula for it. The best we can do, at least at present, is to recognize and cultivate the general conditions which seem to be conductive to it."[44]

Leopold's thinking on the diversity-stability relationship was part of his still broader exploration of the overarching theme of land health.[45] In one of many attempts over the last decade of his life to communicate these ideas, he defined conservation as "a state of health in the land. The land consists of soil, waters, plants, and animals, but health is more than a sufficiency of these components. It is a state of vigorous self-renewal in each of them, and in all collectively."[46] In short, retention of a diverse biota was essential to the "functional integrity" of the land and the human communities dwelling thereupon. "This leads to the 'rule of thumb' which is the basic premise of ecological conservation: the land should retain as much of its original membership as is compatible with human land-use. The land must of course be modified, but it should be modified as gently and as little as possible."[47] Keep, in other words, all of nature's cogs and wheels.

Keep biological diversity, Leopold argued, for the ecological benefits it provides—as conserver of soil and provider of fertility, filter of water and regulator of watersheds, defense against pests and pathogens, check against irruption. Keep diversity, too, Leopold consistently pointed out, for both its immediate and long-term economic benefits. Drawing upon the work of geographer Carl O. Sauer, he also noted the value—now widely recognized—of biodiversity as a pool of potential genetic resources. "The domesticated plants and animals which we use now," he wrote in 1944, "are not necessarily those we will need a century hence. To the extent that the native community is extinguished, the genetical [sic] source of new domesticated plants and animals is destroyed."[48]

But for Leopold there was more to be gained through the conservation of biological diversity than even the incalculable environmental and material benefits. Land, he wrote in his foreword to *Sand County Almanac*, also "yields a cultural harvest."[49] His own garnerings, gathered up in the *Almanac*, provided ample evidence of the bounty. *Sand County* may be read as one human being's revelry amidst diversity: Canada goose and paper birch, white pine and trailing arbutus, bottle gentian and pileated woodpecker, pine weevil, ruffed grouse, aspen, tamarack, showy lady's slipper, larch saw-fly, gall-wasp, cottonwood, winged elm, red dogwood, prickly ash, woodcock, hazelnut, bittersweet, shagbark hickory, hawthorn, basswood, bobwhite quail, poison ivy, ragweed, raccoon, sugar maple, white oak, cottontail, chickadee, barred owl, crow, jay, wood duck, gray squirrel, prothonotary warbler. Those were the offerings just of drab November in Wisconsin's sand counties.

A Sand County Almanac endures not only as a memorable documentation of the events of a year, but as a record of the journey of Leopold's life. That life was marked at every step by an expanding comprehension of the natural world and humanity's place within it. The land ethic that Leopold finally proposed was premised on a radical redefinition of land. It enlarged the boundaries of the community to include "the soils, waters, fauna, and flora, as well as people."[50] It regarded the other members of the expanded community as worthy of respect and care regardless of any obvious economic value. Leopold used the diversity in his home community of Wisconsin as an example: "Of the 22,000 higher plants and animals native to Wisconsin, it is doubtful whether more than 5 per cent can be sold, fed, eaten, or otherwise put to economic use. Yet these creatures are members of the biotic community, and if (as I believe) its stability depends on its integrity, they are entitled to continuance."[51]

It was Leopold's conviction that, by acquiring a deeper appreciation and respect for the diverse life forms that share the planet, the human community could also take an important step toward assuring its own future health and continuity. Leopold's was only one track along conservation's long trail, but the stages of work and thought through which he passed are in many ways the same stages that conservation in general has struggled through over the last century and a half. The story tells itself through the succession of labels. Forests. Game. Varmint. Wild life. Nongame. Rare. Wildlife. Land. Threatened. Endangered. Biodiversity.

6

Giving Voice to Concern

elegy: a song or poem expressing sorrow or lamentation, especially for one who is dead; a pensive or reflective poem that is usually nostalgic or melancholy; a short pensive musical composition.

ALDO LEOPOLD's essay "Marshland Elegy" begins with an announcement: at dawn on "the great marsh," sandhill cranes emerge from a silent fog, their calls increasingly resonant over "the listening land." When the essay was first published in the magazine *American Forests* in 1937, neither its readers nor Leopold himself fully realized that the essay itself *was* an announcement.[1] Through it, a new voice proclaimed its arrival. That voice would help transform the way we write and think about the natural world, and the human place within it.

In 1937 Leopold had not yet begun to envision the collection of essays that became *A Sand County Almanac*. He was, one could say, not yet the writer of *A Sand County Almanac*. Leopold was, of course, constantly writing. His pen had always been productive and provocative. By then his output of scientific papers, professional reports, editorials, policy statements, speeches, popular articles, and essays amounted to some two hundred publications.[2] Spare, balanced, and elegant in his prose, Leopold had long since earned a reputation as one of conservation's leading stylists.

But the language of "Marshland Elegy" was of another order, from another part of Leopold:

A dawn wind stirs on the great marsh. With almost imperceptible slow-
ness it rolls a bank of fog across the wide morass. Like the white ghost
of a glacier the mists advance, riding over phalanxes of tamarack, slid-
ing across bog-meadows heavy with dew. A single silence hangs from
horizon to horizon.[3]

This was not the language of science, or policy, or pedagogy, or philosophy, although strong undertones of these hummed in between the
lines. Rather, this voice carried a "certitude" (Leopold's word) not unlike
that of the cranes of which he wrote.

The lyric quality had long been present in Leopold's private writings—
in personal letters, field journal entries, unpublished fragments relegated to
the "cooler" of his desk. One could hear it in the sharp phrases with which
he spiked even his most technical articles. Occasionally it emerged in a
lighter piece of commentary or description. In "Marshland Elegy," the
expressive voice took over.

Earlier in 1937 *The Condor*, one of the leading ornithology journals
(and not one especially known for experimental prose), had published
Leopold's "The Thick-Billed Parrot in Chihuahua." Inspired by the *guacamaja* he encountered during his 1936 hunting trip in Mexico, "The
Thick-Billed Parrot in Chihuahua" was an unusually evocative account
for Leopold—and no doubt for the readers of *The Condor*. In it Leopold
directly addressed the relationship between scientific understanding and
the apprehension of beauty. Seeking to convey the "imponderable
essence" of the Sierra Madre, he focused on the riotous calls of the "rois-
tering" parrots. "As a proper ornithologist," he wrote, "I should doubtless
try to describe the call. It superficially resembles that of the Piñon Jay, but
the music of the piñoneros is soft and nostalgic as the haze hanging in their
native canyons, while that of the Guacamaja is louder and full of the salty
enthusiasm of high comedy."[4]

Emboldened by this breakthrough article, Leopold next turned to the
marshes of his home landscape and to the similarly evocative cranes. With
"Marshland Elegy," Leopold tapped more deeply into his creative sources
and found the tone that in its full refinement would distinguish *A Sand*

County Almanac. This voice emerges from the backdrop of Leopold's other writings as do the cranes from the glacial mists, "a far clear blast of hunting horns, out of the sky into the fog."

"Marshland Elegy" also marked a historical coincidence. Even as events in Leopold's life were shaping his new voice, the cranes were calling it forth. By the mid-1930s the sandhill crane had been extirpated from large portions of its former range in the United States after decades of indiscriminate hunting, wetland destruction, and conversion of its upland habitats to agriculture. Wisconsin's sandhill cranes were almost gone; Leopold and his students estimated that only about fifty breeding birds were left in the state. The whooping crane was in continual decline and would soon reach its nadir of just fifteen known individuals in all of North America. Even among committed conservationists, the extinction of the whooper was considered a foregone conclusion (despite the Migratory Bird Treaty of 1916, which provided protection for both the whoopers and sandhills).[5] If Leopold's emerging voice was solemn, even nostalgic, in "Marshland Elegy," solemnity was appropriate to the circumstances of the cranes and their diminished habitats—especially against the contemporary background rumble of dust storms, economic depression, and international anxiety. Leopold heard high comedy in the calls of Chihuahua's thick-billed parrot; he heard a song of lament and mourning in the bugling of Wisconsin's cranes.

Yet, through the essay itself Leopold sought to rise from solemnity to celebration: not yet to memorialize the cranes (as he would memorialize the grizzlies of Escudilla, the wolves of Arizona, and the passenger pigeons of the midcontinent), but to draw attention to a passing wonder: "When we hear his call we hear no mere bird. We hear the trumpet in the orchestra of evolution. He is the symbol of our untamable past, of that incredible sweep of millennia which underlies and conditions the daily affairs of birds and men." As the cranes stood at the edge of extinction, so Leopold stood in his essay at the brink of despair, too knowledgeable as a conservationist to hold unrealistic hopes, too unwilling as an admirer to let the cranes pass into oblivion unheralded. So he went into himself, and into his countryside, to a greater depth, finding a way to express simultaneously irony and awe.

⤛ ⤜

sandhill crane. A fragment of a once more extensive population of resident southern sandhill cranes, the subspecies was limited (then as now) to just one small site in southeastern Mississippi.

Leopold's 1929 survey report yielded the first published record of Mississippi sandhill crane numbers: "at least fifty birds, and possibly a hundred or more." He noted that, although the birds seemed to be in no immediate danger, "there has been no attempt at a refuge or other action to give them special protection." He urged that such action be taken "before rather than after some radical disturbance takes place." "It hardly needs to be argued," he added, "that their preservation is a matter of statewide, or even national, moment." This was among Leopold's earliest expressions of concern for the perpetuation of a specific nongame animal taxon.[11]

Later that year, Leopold compiled his Wisconsin game survey report. Although Wisconsin's few surviving sandhill cranes, like Mississippi's, were not considered game birds, Leopold nonetheless devoted special attention to them. According to sketchy reports, a few cranes still bred in Wisconsin's most remote marshes, where the species had managed to find refuge through the previous decades of market gunning, marsh-dredging, and peat fires. As in Mississippi, no special effort had been made in Wisconsin to protect the cranes. Indeed, museum scientists were still seeking specimens, an activity Leopold deemed "unnecessary" and "bad public policy." "Scientists," he wrote, "ought to know better than anyone else that the Wisconsin birds are probably not interchangeable with the general migratory stock, and that their removal means the end of the bird in this state." He urged that "everything possible be done to avoid the extermination of the local stocks," including protection of their habitat, more active enforcement of state and federal conservation laws, and research into the species' habitat needs.[12]

Leopold's Wisconsin report included a map indicating known occurrences of cranes. The points on the map were few, and Leopold would add only a few more in the following years—confirmed records from Wood and Green Lake Counties in 1929, Burnett County in 1930, Wood County in 1932, Jackson and Marquette Counties in 1933.[13] Most of these sites lay in the marshy "sand counties" along the Wisconsin River in central Wisconsin.

At the time, Leopold's attentions were focused on this region. Since the advent of European settlement, the forces of fire, dredge, plow, drought, wind, and weed had altered much of the sand counties' extensive wetlands, leaving a legacy of ecological degradation, persistent poverty, and widespread tax evasion. In response to the region's economic woes, several New Deal programs sought to stimulate redevelopment in the area, including restoration of its damaged marshes. Leopold was involved in this work as a technical advisor and in 1934 prepared a special article on the situation titled "The Wisconsin River Marshes." The article, a forerunner to "Marshland Elegy," described the impacts of European settlement on the region and outlined the many perplexing management questions that wetland restoration entailed. Among these: "What can be done to build up the remnant of breeding sandhill cranes? No one knows what they eat, or what is the weak spot in their present environment."[14]

Leopold himself did not observe cranes in Wisconsin until 1934. That spring his student Franklin Schmidt reported that "Aldo Leopold, Wallace Grange, and myself saw a pair with their young" at Shiprock Marsh in Adams County (another of the "sand counties").[15] On July 16 that year, Leopold and his brother Carl paused while returning from a fishing trip to investigate a report of breeding cranes at Endeavor Marsh outside Portage, Wisconsin. The marsh was almost level with nearby Buffalo Lake on the Fox River and so had managed to escape "the epidemic of ditch-digging and land-booming" that had overcome so many other Wisconsin wetlands. Interviewing older farmers near the marsh, Leopold learned that breeding pairs of cranes had been declining locally for decades, but that perhaps three pairs remained. One farmer directed Aldo and Carl to a known territory near an oak hummock in the marsh. "We went over there, and were standing under the oaks, scanning the marsh with glasses, when with loud trumpetings the pair flushed from the edge of the woods not a gunshot away. It was a noble sight."[16]

After these sightings, Leopold's interest in the cranes and their wetland haunts increased markedly. Several times that fall of 1934 Leopold observed migrating sandhills while hunting at Pilot Knob Marsh in Adams County. Through his birding club in Madison he organized a special evening seminar on sandhill cranes. He assigned several students to work on cranes in the field and in the library. Franklin Henika reported on the Great Lakes sandhill crane population at the first North American Wildlife Conference in 1936.[17] That same year Leopold's student Frederick Hamerstrom organized a "Central Wisconsin Crane Study" to assess Wisconsin's crane populations and describe their life history, habitats, and conservation needs. The lack of such basic information, Hamerstrom wrote, was "the chief reason for [the] casual treatment of so rare a bird."[18]

Leopold filled his "Sandhill Crane" file with miscellaneous notes on cranes from his readings and from his many correspondents.[19] His friend Herb Stoddard reported fifty breeding pairs of sandhills in the Okefenokee Swamp. George Bird, a colleague in the university's journalism department, assured Leopold that Florida's resident sandhill crane population was secure. Lawrence Walkinshaw, a dentist from Michigan who became his generation's premiere student of cranes, traded news with Leopold— field sightings, breeding site locations, museum records. A student reported on breeding cranes in Nevada. Migrating cranes seen at Endeavor Marsh. Seventy-five pairs observed on Malheur Lake in Oregon in 1936. Even a poem or two. Milton:

> Part loosely wing the region; part more wise,
> In common ranged in figure, wedge their way
> Intelligent of seasons, and set forth
> Their aery caravan, high over seas
> Flying, and over lands; with mutual wing
> Easing their flight; so steers the prudent crane.[20]

As information on cranes flowed into Leopold's files, two events further directed his attention to the cranes and their Wisconsin habitats. In April 1935 Leopold acquired his own piece of worn-out sand county land along the Wisconsin River, just a few miles south of the Endeavor Marsh where he had seen cranes the summer before. Henceforth he would have an even greater personal investment in the restoration of this region whose fate seemed so closely connected to that of the cranes.

Then, in the fall of 1935, Leopold embarked on his trip to Germany. Among his other observations, he noted the decline of Germany's breeding population of common cranes (which, like the sandhill, suffered from "drainage and highways").[21] Among the species of concern that Leopold listed in his 1936 article "Threatened Species" was the sandhill crane.[22] As noted in the last chapter, "game management" was rapidly expanding to

include a wider range of goals and a broader spectrum of species, a movement that Leopold led. The cranes, in turn, were leading Leopold.

↤ ↦

Leopold composed "Marshland Elegy" in the summer of 1937. To it he
brought the full force of the data, wonderment, and concern that had
marked his interest in cranes and wetlands over the previous four years.

The essay contains five sections. In a three-paragraph descriptive
opening, Leopold sets the scene and tone, bringing dawn to a crane marsh
through simple declarative sentences, building from silence to sound, from
timelessness to the present. A more predictable essay might then have
moved into straightforward natural history of the sandhill crane. Leopold,
however, tells us that he has other goals for the essay when in the second,
two-paragraph section he enriches the opening scene, adding layer upon
layer of evolutionary time and ecological complexity:

> The cranes stand, as it were, upon the sodden pages of their own history.
> These peats are the compressed remains of the mosses that clogged the
> pools, of the tamaracks that spread over the mosses, of the cranes that
> bugled over the tamaracks since the retreat of the ice sheet. An endless
> caravan of generations has built of its own bones this bridge into the
> future, this habitat where the oncoming host again may live and breed
> and die.

After this cross-sectional, multispecies view of crane habitat, Leopold
next focuses on cranes in the context of deep evolutionary time, stressing
that aesthetic appreciation of natural objects and processes is not diminished, but enhanced, through scientific understanding. "Our ability to perceive quality in nature begins, as in art, with the pretty. It expands through
successive stages of the beautiful to values as yet uncaptured by language.
The quality of cranes, lies, I think, in this higher gamut, as yet beyond the
reach of words."

Ultimately, one of the principal achievements of *A Sand County Almanac*
would be this recasting of notions of natural beauty, away from the conventionally "scenic" and toward the more subtle sense that comes with ecological and evolutionary awareness.[23] Leopold had introduced this theme in
previous writings, but made the point explicitly in "Marshland Elegy":

"When we hear [the crane's] call, we hear no mere bird. We hear the trumpet in the orchestra of evolution."[24] Against the evolutionary background, and with the special human ability to perceive and appreciate the depths of time, the silence of the crane-less marsh becomes all the more poignant.

In the remainder of this section Leopold turns to human history, referencing several of his recent readings. In *Game Management*, he had cited Kublai Khan's provisioning of cranes and other favored birds as a precedent to modern conservation techniques.[25] Leopold had also just read Bengt Berg's *To Africa with the Migratory Birds*. Berg's adventurous account of his quest to find the common crane's wintering grounds was published in 1930. The influence on Leopold is unmistakable. In "Marshland Elegy," for example, one hears overtones of Berg's description of his first encounter with cranes in the upper Nile:

> The cranes at last! Our proud handsome cranes from Europe, white-winged crowned cranes of Africa, lovely pearl-gray demoiselle cranes from the steppes of Asia, cranes in myriads scattered over the millet fields, flying phalanxes of cranes in the cloudless tropical sky, and cranes in countless multitudes on the banks of the White Nile.[26]

After reading Berg's lively book, Leopold seems to have felt freer to use the more colorful literary palette of "Marshland Elegy."

The heart of "Marshland Elegy" is the long fourth section in which Leopold provides a concise post-Pleistocene environmental history of the sand county marshes, detailing the succession of natural and human impacts on both wetlands and cranes. Leopold's forte throughout his career was his ability to unravel and reweave stories of landscape change based on an understanding of ecological cause and effect.[27] In "Marshland Elegy" he sketched this history not only for its own sake, but also as a way of conveying the contemporary plight of the crane.

In preparing this section, Leopold drew heavily upon his 1934 article "The Wisconsin River Marshes." The development of Leopold's literary voice can be measured by comparing the two texts. Here, for example, was Leopold's earlier description of the process of marsh formation in the sand counties:

[These marshes] cover about half a million acres in five counties. They consist of peat-filled basins which represent the deeper parts of an ancient glacial lake. The lake was originally formed when an arm of the glacier plugged the Wisconsin River at its previous outlet through the Baraboo Hills. In the course of centuries the lake gradually drained, choked with vegetation, and became a series of sphagnum bogs.[28]

The scene comes alive in "Marshland Elegy":

When the glacier came down out of the north, crunching hills and gouging valleys, some adventuring rampart of the ice climbed the Baraboo Hills and fell back into the outlet gorge of the Wisconsin River. The swollen waters backed up and formed a lake half as long as the state, bordered on the east by cliffs of ice, and fed by the torrents that fell from melting mountains. The shorelines of this old lake are still visible; its bottom is the bottom of the great marsh.

The lake rose through the centuries, finally spilling over east of the Baraboo range. There it cut a new channel for the river, and thus drained itself. To the residual lagoons came the cranes, bugling the defeat of the retreating winter, summoning the on-creeping host of living things to the collective task of marsh-building.

In such manner, Leopold animates history throughout the section, making the landscape not merely a stage but the play itself, in which the human and nonhuman players interact and change over time.

There is room for criticism here. Leopold's environmental history omits the region's native peoples. He posits an "Arcadian age"—after European settlement in the mid-1800s but before the drainage mania—when "man and beast, plant and soil lived on and with each other in mutual toleration, to the mutual benefit of all." Even granting the Edenic illusion, this interval was less an "age" than a passing moment. Nonetheless, Leopold's panoramic account illustrates what set him apart from so many conservationists (and historians) of his day: his irrepressible interest in the deep history behind conservation problems. This in turn suggested where to look for lasting solutions: to the land itself, and the changing human demands on it. Leopold's method of problem solving through the combining of history and ecology was rare in his day, and remains too rare today. As he stated concisely in the essay, "To build a road is so much simpler than to think of what the country really needs."

Leopold closes "Marshland Elegy" with a brief and sober paragraph. Just as he had led the cranes to the reader through glacial mists, he leads "the last crane" away:

> Some day, perhaps in the very process of our benefactions, perhaps in the fullness of geologic time, the last crane will trumpet his farewell and spiral skyward from the great marsh. High out of the clouds will fall the sound of hunting horns, the baying of the phantom pack, the tinkle of little bells, and then a silence never to be broken, unless perchance in some far pasture of the Milky Way.

The cranes' din, having risen with their approach, falls to silence as they retreat. In "sadness," the craneless marsh fades to black: the possibility of a craneless *world*, a place bereft of wonder and mystery, "adrift in history."

◄← →►

The innovations of "Marshland Elegy"—its introduction of Leopold's emerging literary style, its movement toward a more sophisticated conservation esthetic, its defining of an ecological-evolutionary framework for conservation, its early use of environmental history—would not be fully appreciated for years to come. At the time, Leopold's fine prose was sufficient to draw readers' raves. Owen Gromme, a wildlife artist whose fascination with cranes equaled that of his friend Leopold, wrote, "Only a man who has worked with these noble birds can possibly grasp the full import and depth of your written words. There is *no sound on this earth* that stirs the primitive in me like the indescribable rattle of the Sandhill Crane. Well, I guess that you understand. You said it all."[29]

Leopold and his students continued to amass information on cranes. The small circle of crane informants—Leopold, Gromme, Walter Scott, Lawrence Walkinshaw, Franklin Henika, A. W. Schorger, Fred and Fran Hamerstrom—traded information on the cranes of the upper Midwest, building a base of scientific information that might lend support to the population's recovery. In the spring of 1940, Leopold kept a close eye on a sandhill pair that had taken to the marsh near Leopold's land on the Wisconsin River. In his journal he recorded the pair's activities:

APRIL 15 Again heard cranes at daylight. . . . Gus [Leopold's German shorthair] put them out of Baxter's corn—2 beauties. They flew out low, rattling the marsh with protest, and alighted in the brush marsh just west of Baxter's oak island. Could they possibly be going to nest?

APRIL 16 Hear them at night and at intervals during the day. They are using the prairie below Barrows as well as across the river.

APRIL 18 About 11 AM heard cranes and saw a pair—probably the same ones seen April 15—were circling the hay meadow. Think they were going to light but they saw us and passed on north up Lake Chapman.

APRIL 28 Heard cranes call when Gus went hunting in Tom's marsh. Saw 1 bird fly out to the meadow where he alighted in the sedge near the edge of the mowed land and the ditch. His being alone makes us suspect a nest.

MAY 4–5 Explored Baxter's marsh to verify whether cranes still here. Again flushed a single bird on the north point of the timbered island. He (?) circled, alighted in same place, and then got nervous and crossed to brushy marsh east of island. I think there is now a nest and that the female is incubating.[30]

Leopold could not confirm the nest that year, nor any others in the years that followed. He and his family would, however, continue to see and hear a few cranes during migration. ("They sound like a frog with a sore throat," he once told his daughter Nina.) This gave hope that the cranes would in fact return as a breeding species in the area.

Such hopes were fragile, but not unfounded. Critical wetland habitat was being protected and restored in the nearby Sandhill State Wildlife Area in Wood County and the Necedah National Wildlife Refuge in Juneau County. With portions of the sand county marshes reflooded, field research underway, and wardens now alert to the species' status, the basic conditions necessary to recovery were in place. Faint anticipations of that recovery could be heard, at least in certain corners of Wisconsin. The October 1941 issue of *The Passenger Pigeon*, the bulletin of the statewide ornithological society, contained a note on breeding cranes near New

London in Waupaca County. "Under protection," the author surmised, "these fine stately birds are coming back."[31]

It was a somewhat optimistic prognosis. The sandhill crane population would recover slowly, a process delayed by a further wave of wetland drainage after World War II. The numbers grew very gradually through the 1940s, 1950s, and 1960s. Eventually, however, the birds that managed to hang on in the sand county marshes formed the core of a population that continues to expand a half century later, bringing the loud rattle back to marshes that had "once harbored cranes." Illinois reclaimed breeding cranes (one might say that the cranes reclaimed Illinois) in the late 1970s; eastern Minnesota followed in the mid-1980s and northern Iowa in 1992.

Meanwhile, Leopold's essay had its own continuing impact. Encouraged by its reception, Leopold began to write more in this new lyrical vein. In 1938 he started a regular series of articles on natural history and conservation aimed at farmers.[32] More fully developed essays soon began to appear in national conservation publications—"Conservation Esthetic" (1938) in *Bird-Lore*, "Song of the Gavilan" (1940) in the *Journal of Wildlife Management*, "Escudilla" (1940) in *American Forests*, "Cheat Takes Over" (1941) in *The Land*. These essays formed the nucleus for the collection that would eventually come together as *A Sand County Almanac*. The first title he considered for the incipient collection was "Marshland Elegy—and Other Essays."[33]

Leopold died fighting a grass fire near the family's shack in the spring of 1948. In the aftermath of the tragedy, many of Leopold's friends, colleagues, and students offered their own eulogies of "The Professor." Perhaps the most poignant of these came from Leopold's student Albert Hochbaum, writing from the marshes of Manitoba:

> Yesterday, as on all days since he touched our lives, we had some reason to think of Aldo Leopold, once or a dozen times. In my own case, I saw a small flock of Sandhill Cranes in Brown's Slough about noon, the first I had ever seen there; and at once there came to mind the time at the shack when he showed me my first cranes, and the half-dozen times since when we had seen cranes together. Yesterday, Aldo left our world.[34]

→← →→

The Chinese poet Tu Fu composed the poem, "Clear Evening after Rain," in the eighth century AD:

The sun sinks toward the horizon.
The light clouds are blown away.
A rainbow shines on the river.
The last raindrops spatter the rocks.
Cranes and herons soar in the sky.
Fat bears feed along the banks.
I wait here for the west wind
And enjoy the crescent moon
Shining through misty bamboos.[35]

We read such verse with commingled serenity and remorse. The words are of the moment; their tranquility endures all time, soothes and clarifies like the rain shower itself of twelve centuries ago. Regret comes with the realization that the poet's own sense of certitude is increasingly foreign to us. It belongs to another time. The experience of cranes, and soaring herons, and feeding bears, even bamboo—of the wild itself—as a normal and expected part of our world can no longer be so casually assumed. It was not even in Leopold's day. The observant poet can no longer simply evoke, or celebrate, or allude to wild places and their wild inhabitants. The world has experienced much loss, and the poet knows too much.

Leopold in 1937 might have wanted only to portray or commend the crane, but he had also to lament. When he composed his elegy, it seemed as if cranes could not be assured safe passage into the future—and so they cannot. Of the world's fifteen crane species, ten are threatened to one degree or another, and the conservation challenges they face are daunting. Yet, even as Leopold was composing "Marshland Elegy," casual assumptions about the persistence and disappearance of cranes, and of biological diversity in general, were beginning to be questioned. Leopold's writing contributed significantly to this change in attitudes and to growing concern over known and potential losses. In this sense, the cranes, and the voice that Leopold found to tell their story, helped to redefine the very task of conservation.

The last cranes have not yet retreated to "some far pasture of the Milky Way." The remaining wild population of whooping cranes survived its bottleneck and has slowly increased, standing (as of 2004) at just under two hundred birds. Captive whooping cranes have contributed to the species recovery effort, providing eggs for experimental reintroduction efforts now underway in Florida and Wisconsin. Wisconsin's sandhill cranes number at least ten thousand, enough to make them a more common thrill (and, in some circumstances, a threat to sprouting corn and seed potatoes). Elsewhere, the prospects for cranes are mixed. Two of the Siberian crane's three populations stand at the very knife-edge of extinction. The rare crane species of East Asia—the Siberian, white-naped, hooded, and red-crowned—face an array of threats, from wetland conversion to large dams to urban encroachment. Sarus cranes, the world's tallest flying birds, are under pressure due to habitat loss, pollution, and human disturbance in Southeast Asia and India. In Africa, once-abundant populations of blue cranes and crowned cranes have recently declined.[36]

But if there is continuity in the threats to cranes, there is continuity too in the conservation response. Not far from the Leopold property at the southern edge of Wisconsin's sand counties, the International Crane Foundation (ICF) has made its home since 1973. ICF serves as the nerve center of a global network of scientists and others dedicated to the conservation of cranes and their ecosystems. ICF researchers and volunteers now monitor Wisconsin marshes that were devoid of cranes just a few decades ago. Around the world they work with local conservationists to ensure that their own wetlands remain wild with cranes.

Leopold's "Marshland Elegy" has proven, so far at least, to inspire transformation. Its warning helped to stimulate its own corrective. Yet there is no assurance that the cranes will be able to soar above and beyond the current high wave of human impacts. In his day, the best Leopold could do at the end of his essay was to sound an ambiguous note—of history ending "in paradox," and the cranes "some day, perhaps" trumpeting their last farewell. Leopold left open the possibility that the sight of a crane, soaring in a clear sky after rain, may again be easily expected, and the elegies reserved for another, later geologic era.

7

Moving Mountains

His love was for present things, and these
things were present somewhere; to find
them required only the free sky, and the
will to ply his wings.
—ALDO LEOPOLD (1949)

LITERARY CLASSICS are the mountains of our minds. They shape us, subtly and continually. They cast long shadows. They provide access to higher realms. They make their own intellectual weather. We take them for granted; yet they so define our view of the world, and of ourselves, that we can hardly imagine the world without them.

The history of American conservation contains its own range of classics: Thoreau's *Walden*, Marsh's *Man and Nature*, Muir's *My First Summer in the Sierra*, Stegner's *Beyond the Hundredth Meridian*, Carson's *Silent Spring*, Abbey's *Desert Solitaire*, Berry's *The Unsettling of America*, to name a few high peaks. But conservation's literary landscape is rich in its variety and abundance, and holds many less-prominent but no less durable expressions. We return to their pages again and again, and always find in them something timeless, and something new.

Because mountains seem permanent, we tend to disregard the intense tectonic shifts and internal pressures that give rise to them. Behind every story is another story. *A Sand County Almanac* is no exception. The face of this particular mountain is still fresh. The very pebbles seem still to be settling. *Sand County* emerged from a time of economic instability, international conflict, rapid technological change, scientific revolutions, and widespread environmental deterioration. During these same years Aldo

Leopold strove to provide more solid foundations for conservation. His conviction was that conservation had to rest on a base that included not only the natural sciences, but also philosophy, ethics, history, and literature. *A Sand County Almanac*, as it turned out, was the final proof of his conviction.

⤛ ⤜

Future generations would have understood if by 1940 Leopold had begun to rest on his laurels—which were many. He was widely acknowledged as one of the nation's foremost conservation leaders. In particular, through the 1930s he had played a central role in establishing wildlife ecology and management as a viable field. "By 1940," Susan Flader and Baird Callicott write, "Leopold could survey from its pinnacle the profession he had done more than anyone else to create."[1]

Leopold served as president of the young Wildlife Society that year and used the opportunity of his presidential address in March to step back and put the recent advances into perspective. Leopold's message was at once restrained and challenging, practical and visionary. He began with a disarming admission: "We are attempting to manage wildlife, but it is by no means certain that we shall succeed, or that this will be our most important contribution to the design for living. For example, we may, without knowing it, be helping to write a new definition of what science is for. We are not scientists. We disqualify ourselves at the outset by professing loyalty to and affection for a thing: wildlife. A scientist in the old sense may have no loyalties except to abstractions, no affections except for his own kind."[2]

As the events of World War II unfolded, Leopold became increasingly disenchanted with the course of the modern scientific enterprise. Although himself a pioneer in a new scientific field, he saw the drift toward what he considered misapplied science as a grave danger. In his view, scientists themselves could not shirk responsibility for the trend. Already, in 1940, he was airing his concerns. In his presidential address he stated: "The definitions of science written by, let us say, the National Academy, deal almost exclusively with the creation and exercise of power. But what about the creation and exercise of wonder, of respect for workmanship in nature?"[3] This was not, Leopold insisted, a peripheral matter for the new wave of "wildlifers"; it lay at the very core of their work. Mincing no words, he warned that "unless we can help rewrite the objectives of science, our job is predestined to failure."[4]

Rewriting the "objectives of science" plainly took matters of wildlife conservation beyond the domain of science proper and into the realm of the arts and letters, ethics and philosophy. From his earliest days as a young hunter, aspiring ornithologist, and outdoor adventurer, Leopold tended to take this unified approach to conservation matters.[5] The same trait carried over into his professional life and accounted, in part, for his innovations as a young forester. In the heady days of the 1930s, as wildlife conservation was metamorphosing, he kept his intellectual margins broad, regularly drawing connections to other disciplines. Now, as one of the profession's respected elders, having seen it through its infancy and preparing it for its adolescence, he reasserted the point:

> Our profession began with the job of producing something to shoot. However important this may seem to us, it is not important to the eman-cipated moderns who no longer feel soil between their toes. We find that we cannot produce much to shoot until the landowner changes his way of using land, and he in turn cannot change his ways until his teachers, bankers, customers, editors, governors, and trespassers change their ideas about what land is for. To change ideas about what land is for is to change ideas about what anything is for. Thus we started to move a straw, and end up with the job of moving a mountain.[6]

How to move a mountain? Not quickly, and not easily. To develop new wildlife management techniques—to document food habits, conduct life history studies, improve census methods, understand how land use influences populations, and so forth—was the daily work of the rapidly growing cadre of wildlife students and researchers. To develop new modes of perception and a new philosophy of land use was the work of generations and had to include other areas of human endeavor. Having defined the technical foundations of the field in his text *Game Management*, Leopold now challenged his professional progeny not to neglect this more complex task: "I daresay few wildlife managers have any intent or desire to con-tribute to art and literature, yet the ecological dramas which we must dis-cover if we are to manage wildlife are inferior only to the human drama as the subject matter for the fine arts."[7] Even as wildlife ecology was gaining definition and confidence as a science, its chief scientist was advising its adherents to surmount "the senseless barrier between science and art."[8]

Had Leopold himself neglected the humanistic aspects of wildlife conservation, he would still be remembered as a highly effective thinker, scientist, teacher, and advocate. In his own view, however, his contributions to the profession would have remained incomplete. The necessary (and ongoing) task of integrating wildlife management within a more comprehensive conservation vision would have been further postponed. The arts and humanities had to help "rewrite the objectives of science." In articulating that need, Leopold established a very high standard for his colleagues. In meeting that standard with *A Sand County Almanac*, he provided an exemplary model.

◄◄ ➤➤

Chronology of *A Sand County Almanac*

January–February 1937	*The Condor* publishes Leopold's "The Thick-billed Parrot of Chihuahua"
October 1937	*American Forests* publishes Leopold's "Marshland Elegy"
March–April 1938	*Bird-Lore* publishes Leopold's "Conservation Esthetic"
November 1938	*Wisconsin Agriculturist and Farmer* publishes the first of Leopold's series of short essays on farm wildlife
Early 1941	Leopold discusses possible collaboration with his friend and student H. Albert Hochbaum
November 1941–January 1942	Alfred A. Knopf indicates interest in Leopold's collection of essays in initial exchange of correspondence
January 1943–June 1944	Leopold drafts and revises many essays; corresponds regularly with Hochbaum over the nature of the collection and Leopold's narrative stance
January 1943	*Wisconsin Conservation Bulletin* begins publishing short essays by Leopold
8 September 1943	Leopold drafts "Great Possessions"

January 1944	Leopold "working steadily" on the essays; working title for the collection is "Marshland Elegy—And Other Essays"
1 April 1944	Leopold drafts "Thinking Like a Mountain"
Late April 1944	Leopold meets Macmillan Company editor at the Ninth North American Wildlife Conference
6 June 1944	Leopold sends thirteen essays to Macmillan, under the title "Thinking Like a Mountain—And Other Essays"; sends the same essays to Knopf two days later
20 July 1944	Rejection letter from Macmillan Company
24 July 1944	Rejection letter from Knopf
24 August 1944	Knopf sends follow-up letter, with reviewers' comments, to Leopold
20 November 1944	Leopold writes to Hochbaum that he is "flirting with the almanac idea" for the essay collection
19 January 1946	Leopold forwards essays to the University of Minnesota Press; rejected two weeks later
April 1946	Leopold's correspondence with Knopf resumes
Fall 1946	Leopold undertakes extensive drafting and revision of essays
31 October 1946	Initial communication between Leopold and Oxford University Press
February 1947	Albert Hochbaum withdraws from the project
July 1947	Leopold overhauls structure of the collection; adopts new title ("Great Possessions"); composes "The Land Ethic"; drafts foreword
11 September 1947	Leopold sends the "new manuscript" to Knopf
14 September 1947	Leopold meets with Charles Schwartz in Saint Louis to discuss the manuscript and illustrations; Schwartz agrees soon thereafter to provide illustrations
Fall 1947–Winter 1948	Leopold continues to draft and revise essays

5 November 1947	Knopf rejects manuscript, suggests that the collection as a whole be recast
November 1947	Luna Leopold approaches Oxford University Press about publication of the collection; William Vogt simultaneously approaches William Sloane Associates
5 December 1947	Leopold revises foreword
19 December 1947	Leopold sends manuscript to Oxford University Press and to William Sloane Associates
4 March 1948	Leopold again revises foreword
14 April 1948	Leopold receives telephone call from Oxford University Press accepting his manuscript for publication; Oxford's acceptance letter is sent the same day
21 April 1948	Leopold dies while fighting fire on a neighbor's property
22 April 1948	Oxford writes to Leopold's student, Joe Hickey, expressing concern over the publication of the collection
April 1948–December 1948	Luna Leopold and Joe Hickey, working with other Leopold family members and students, oversee final editing and preparation of manuscript; after extensive discussions, the title is changed to *A Sand County Almanac and Sketches Here and There*
Fall 1949	*A Sand County Almanac* published
1953	Oxford University Press publishes *Round River: From the Journals of Aldo Leopold*
1966	Oxford University Press reissues the volume in an enlarged edition as *A Sand County Almanac with Other Essays on Conservation from Round River*
1968	Oxford University Press publishes original volume in paperback
1970	Sierra Club / Ballantine Books publishes enlarged edition in paperback

◄◄ ►►

In 1940 Leopold was fifty-three years old. He had not yet even begun to think about the collection of essays that became the *Sand County Almanac*. But he was on the trail, having published "The Thick-Billed Parrot in Chihuahua" and "Marshland Elegy." In his 1938 essay "Conservation Esthetic," Leopold rehearsed the point that he would later make in his presidential address: "Let no man jump to the conclusion that [he] must take his Ph.D. in ecology before he can 'see' his country. On the contrary, the Ph.D. may become as callous as an undertaker to the mysteries at which he officiates."[9] Through his literary endeavors, he found a new way to show others the country as he saw it.

Leopold plainly appreciated the need for antidotes to insensitivity. Advances in ecology were improving the ability of wildlife biologists to analyze and adjust the forces that influenced wildlife populations. Now, Leopold suggested, aesthetic awareness would be needed to enhance their ability to *perceive* and respond to the workings of the natural world, and of people within it. It was as if Leopold, having helped shore up wildlife management's scientific underpinnings, now felt freer to attend to its cultural and ethical bases.

In November 1938 Leopold produced the first of his short articles on farm wildlife for the *Wisconsin Agriculturist and Farmer*. Over the next several years, twenty-nine of these seasonal pieces would appear in the widely distributed periodical. (From 1943 to 1945 Leopold published a similar series in the *Wisconsin Conservation Bulletin*.) He would later include several of these, in revised form, in the *Sand County Almanac*. Importantly, in preparing these articles Leopold was obliged to communicate regularly with a broader audience than he had in the past. His growing experience as a college instructor during these years also seems to have increased his dedication to this task of raising the general level of public ecological literacy. "The citizen-conservationist," Leopold wrote in 1937, "needs an understanding of wildlife ecology not only to enable him to function as a critic of sound policy, but to enable him to derive maximum enjoyment from his contacts with the land."[10]

By the summer of 1941, Leopold had begun to think about collecting several of his essays into a volume. In November of that year, an editor at Alfred A. Knopf wrote to Leopold indicating interest in "a good book on wildlife observation . . . a personal book recounting adventures in the field." As the editor saw it, this book should appeal to lay readers while allowing the author the opportunity to offer "opinions on ecology and conservation."[11] As it happened, Leopold had already been discussing such a project with his graduate student H. Albert Hochbaum, a pioneering waterfowl biologist and skilled illustrator and writer as well. Hochbaum and Leopold were both burdened with their normal heavy workload but had agreed to work together as time allowed. Their intense, sometimes rocky, but mutually challenging collaboration over the next several years would prove critical to the ultimate tone of the collection as a whole.[12]

Leopold soon found himself with more time to devote to the project. As the United States entered World War II and students departed from the University of Wisconsin campus, Leopold's teaching and advising load ebbed. His pen was busy through 1942, but not until he received a follow-up inquiry from Knopf in April 1943 did he focus his attention again on the proposed collection. Over the next year, Leopold drafted and redrafted some of his most memorable essays. Among these, importantly, were several that drew upon the Leopold family's activities at the exhausted piece of farm property he had acquired in 1935. These essays (in particular "Great Possessions," an account of a typical morning afield at Leopold's shack) gave a much more personal tone to the evolving collection.

Of those few who were reading Leopold's draft essays, Al Hochbaum most deeply appreciated the task of self-reflection and self-expression Leopold had taken on. He recognized that Leopold had reached a turning point in his literary development. In one of many blunt but respectful exchanges between them during this period, Hochbaum encouraged Leopold in this new direction. "This series of sketches brings the man [Leopold] himself into focus. . . . As you round out this collection, take a sidewise glance at this fellow and decide just how much of him you want to put on paper."[13] Less than a month later, Leopold responded to Hochbaum's prodding with "Thinking Like a Mountain," his famous account of killing a wolf during his youthful days as a forester in the Southwest. Committed to the new direction his collection was taking, Leopold changed its working title from "Marshland Elegy—And Other Essays" to "Thinking Like a Mountain—And Other Essays."

As of June 1944, Leopold's manuscript included thirteen essays.[14] He sent these off to Knopf and to an editor at the Macmillan Company who had also expressed interest in Leopold's writing. Both publishers turned down the manuscript. Macmillan, citing wartime paper shortages, rejected it outright. Knopf's editor felt the essays were simply too varied in tone, length, and subject to hang together. The Knopf review, however, gave Leopold hope that, with extensive revision and additional essays, the stylistic and structural problems could be overcome. By the end of 1944, Leopold indicated to Hochbaum that he was playing with "the almanac idea . . . as a means of giving 'unity' to my scattered essays."[15] The earlier series of farm wildlife essays, which appeared monthly, seems to have prompted Leopold to consider the almanac format. In any case, this was the first mention of it in the context of the evolving collection.

Other professional obligations absorbed Leopold's time over the following year. Not until the war was over, another rejection letter received (from the University of Minnesota Press), and the connection with Knopf reestablished did Leopold return to his disparate batch of essays. In corresponding with Knopf in the spring of 1946, Leopold suggested that he might add several of the more "philosophical" essays he had published in professional journals—thus making the collection's stylistic inconsistency even more problematic. Knopf's skeptical but supportive editor pointed out the difficulty in "fitting together the pieces in a way that will not seem haphazard or annoying to the reader."[16]

This remained a quandary for Leopold through the remainder of 1946 and into early 1947. Once again other responsibilities (including a substantial influx of students home from the war) prevented him from focusing on his extracurricular writing. What little time he had to spare for the essays usually found him, before dawn, at his desk in his university office, wielding the pencils and yellow legal pads that he typically used in his later years. Leopold rarely wrote at the family's "shack" or elsewhere in the field, and his meticulous journals were filled, not with literary expression, but with detailed phenological records, field observations, and other scientific data. Although Leopold was unable to work on his manuscript with any regularity during this time, he intermittently drafted new essays and revised older ones. He continued also to wrestle with the essential dilemma of the collection: how to meld his descriptive field sketches, his ecological cautionary tales, and his statements of conservation philosophy into a coherent whole.

In the spring of 1947 the manuscript hung in limbo. Because of other commitments, Al Hochbaum had to withdraw as illustrator. Leopold, as the chair and sole faculty member of his academic department, was preoccupied with accommodating the booming student enrollments. And increasingly he was distracted by the painful facial spasms associated with trigeminal neuralgia (or, tic douloureux), with which he had been afflicted since late 1945.

Finally, in the summer of 1947, Leopold found time to devote himself exclusively to the essays. In this crucial period the essay collection (which Leopold was now calling "Great Possessions") assumed the form that its eventual readers would recognize. He divided the manuscript into three parts. In the first, he used the almanac format to bring order to the Wisconsin "shack" essays. In the second, he gathered his essays recollecting and interpreting other landscapes in his experience. In the third section he included four of his more abstract discussions on conservation themes, including his newly synthesized summary essay, "The Land Ethic."[17] Leopold drafted a lengthy foreword that provided autobiographical context for the essays.[18] With renewed hope, Leopold sent the overhauled manuscript to Knopf on September 11. Scheduled to undergo brain surgery just one week later, at the Mayo Clinic in Minnesota, Leopold had made his summer one of determined and uninterrupted concentration.

Knopf's rejection letter arrived in early November. The editors again found the collection "far from being satisfactorily organized" and its ecological argument "unconvincing." The book, they stated directly, was "unlikely to win approval from readers or to be a successful publication as it now stands."[19] Giving up on Knopf, Leopold allowed his son Luna to assume the role of literary agent. While Luna approached Oxford University Press, Leopold's colleague William Vogt brought the manuscript to the attention of William Sloane Associates (who would soon publish Vogt's *Road to Survival*).[20]

Although disappointed and frustrated by Knopf's rejection, Leopold responded quickly. Following Luna's recommendation, he secured a new

illustrator, Charles Schwartz, then working with the Missouri Conservation Commission. He rewrote the long foreword ("the better to orient the
reader on how and why the essays add up to a single idea") and in December 1947 sent the manuscript to the two new prospective publishers.[21] The
earlier rejections hobbled Leopold's expectations, but over the winter he
continued to draft new essays (including "Good Oak"). Leopold also
asked several of his closest friends and colleagues to give the manuscript a
careful review. In his memo he wrote, "What I need . . . is the most critical attitude you can muster. Which [essays] are the weak ones? What is
ambiguous, obscure, repetitious, inaccurate, fatuous, highbrow? . . . Is
there sufficient unity? . . . Have I omitted some idea you think I could do,
or included something I should better let alone?"[22]

As Leopold recuperated fitfully from his surgery, he awaited word from
the publishers. Both, as it happened, were reading the manuscript with
approval. Oxford responded first. On April 14, 1948, Oxford's editor Philip
Vaudrin called Leopold in Madison to inform him that they were indeed
interested in publishing his manuscript. They discussed plans for final revisions, with the goal of having the book available in the fall of 1949. One
week later, on April 21, Leopold suffered a fatal heart attack while fighting
a neighbor's grass fire near the shack. He was sixty-one years old.

After the shock of Leopold's death had eased, Luna assumed responsibility for seeing the manuscript through to publication. Working with
Leopold's students Joe Hickey, Bob McCabe, Fred and Fran Hamerstrom,
and other close colleagues of Leopold, Luna negotiated the final terms of
publication with Oxford Press. This team collaborated in making final editorial decisions. Several essays were added, shifted, or renamed, but most
of the alterations to Leopold's manuscript were minor. The team felt that
it was better to leave Leopold's work intact than to risk making inappropriate changes.

Luna Leopold did agree, reluctantly, to one significant change. Oxford
considered Leopold's manuscript title "Great Possessions" too obscure
and too Dickensian. Consultations among Oxford's editors, Luna, and the
editorial panel yielded several alternative titles, none of which seemed to
capture the book's characteristic tone of concern tempered by understated
irony, humor, and wonder. In the end, they chose for the title the heading

of the manuscript's first section, "A Sand County Almanac." Oxford Press published the book in the fall of 1949 under the full title *A Sand County Almanac and Sketches Here and There.*[23]

◄◄ ►►

This condensed narrative cannot convey fully the impact of contemporary events, professional experiences, and private interactions on Leopold's evolving vision for his book. It does, however, indicate how deeply devoted Leopold was to the project's overarching goal—so much so that he persisted through multiple rejections, continual questioning of its content and style, and a series of difficult personal challenges. That goal was nothing less than to breach "the senseless barrier between science and art"; to unite informed observation of the living world, through the lens of ecology and evolutionary biology, with enriched appreciation of nature's beauty and drama.

Leopold understood his literary effort as something more than an exercise in ecological aesthetics. Throughout the 1940s the trends in world events, human relations, and human interactions with the natural world weighed heavily on Leopold, as they did on many of his colleagues in the conservation movement. Careful reading of the *Almanac* provides ample clues that this was deeply a book of its times. From "Pines Above the Snow": "The 1941 growth was long in all pines; perhaps they saw the shadow of things to come, and made a special effort to show the world that pines still know where they are going, even though men do not."[24] From "Wilderness": "Ability to see the cultural value of wilderness boils down, in the last analysis, to a question of intellectual humility. The shallow-minded modern who has lost his rootage in the land assumes that he has already discovered what is important; it is such who prate of empires, political or economic, that will last a thousand years."[25] From "The Land Ethic": "In human history, we have learned (I hope) that the conqueror role is eventually self-defeating."[26] The value of the ecological perspective lay in its potential not only to enhance human awareness and appreciation of the natural world, but also to improve our chances of achieving "harmony with land"—Leopold's definition of conservation. And it might even have something to offer in our efforts to achieve more decent human relations.

Those chances seemed to be diminishing at the time. Already the post-war era was bringing forth unprecedented economic and technological changes. Science too was changing. Laboratory work, new quantitative methods, and reductionist approaches would soon overwhelm the field-oriented biology at which Leopold excelled. Leopold was defiant in his critique of the forces driving the scientific agenda. In a 1946 address to the Wisconsin Society for Ornithology he stated, "Science, as now decanted for public consumption, is mainly a race for power. Science has no respect for the land as a community of organisms, no concept of man as a fellow passenger in the odyssey of evolution."[27]

Leopold was equally forthright in criticizing his fellow professionals in conservation. He shared with his students his concern that conservation, too, suffered from the fallacy, "clearly borrowed from modern science, that the human relation to land is only economic. It is, or should be, esthetic as well. In this respect our current culture, and especially our science, is false, ignoble, and self-destructive."[28] Harsh words to cast upon the ears of listening undergraduates. Characteristically, Leopold lightened his message by pointing out the fringe benefits of ecological literacy: "I am trying to teach you that this alphabet of 'natural objects' spells out a story, which he who runs may read—if he knows how. Once you learn to read the land, I have no fear of what you will do to it, or with it. And I know many pleasant things it will do to you."[29]

Through *A Sand County Almanac*, Leopold sought to teach others to see the land, to recognize the wounds, and to savor the pleasures. By his very tone he conveyed his trust in their ability to do so, and to act upon what they saw, learned, and enjoyed. This human response was for Leopold the foundation upon which conservation finally rested. In his unassuming and idiosyncratic book of essays, Leopold showed that we may move mountains by allowing the mountains—and the skies, the oceans, the freshwaters, the marshes, the forests, the prairies, the tundras, the deserts, and all the lives, human and otherwise, they contain—to move us.

8

The *Secret* Leopold

*Biographies are but the clothes and buttons of
the man—the biography of the man himself
cannot be written.*

—MARK TWAIN (1924)

"ALDO LEOPOLD was a forester and wildlife ecologist who wrote *A Sand
County Almanac*, a collection of essays about the natural world and conservation. The book was published posthumously in 1949. *A Sand County
Almanac* went on to become one of the key texts of the environmental
movement. Leopold is closely identified with 'The Land Ethic,' the final
essay in the *Almanac*, in which he argued that people are part of the 'land
community,' and so bear moral responsibilities that extend beyond the
realm of the human to include the nonhuman parts of that community."

This would be a fair and accurate answer to the question "Who was
Aldo Leopold?" But is it a sufficient answer? To conservationists and historians, at least, the question is urgent. Leopold defined challenges that remain
at the core of conservation thought and practice more than five decades
after his death. The demands being made upon his legacy are increasing. At
the same time, the living memory of Leopold must inevitably fade as direct
connections to Leopold slip into the all-welcoming past. Paradoxically, it
will become both harder and easier to answer the question: "Who *really*
wrote *A Sand County Almanac*?" What we gain in detachment and critical
judgment, we lose as firsthand impressions grow dim.

These concerns are of more than just passing importance. We may
turn, for example, to an exchange in the January 1998 issue of the *Journal
of Forestry*, the field's premier professional journal. The cover featured a

photo of Aldo Leopold and beckoned with the question: "Has Leopold Supplanted Pinchot?" (i.e., as the guiding philosophical force behind American forestry). The lead article, by a forestry professor, offered "Another Look at Leopold's Land Ethic"—a harsh critique of the ideas in Leopold's famous essay. Its first sentence read: "Aldo Leopold's influence is based largely on a brief essay (20-odd pages), that outlines what he calls the 'land ethic.'"[1] The author's argument, and a counterargument by environmental philosopher and Leopold scholar J. Baird Callicott in the same issue, prompted intense discussion and led to further rounds of debate within the journal.[2]

The point here is not to comment on the play in this particular volley of critique and response, but rather to note that our knowledge of Leopold is, and must be, increasingly contingent not on the reality of the living, breathing human being, but on the received images and impressions of that reality. Leopold the human being belongs to the ages. Leopold the historic figure has been and will be shaped according to the ideas, questions, and requirements—as well as the fears, blind spots, and prejudices—of subsequent generations.

The sentence quoted above illustrates how time inevitably narrows the range of impressions of the rich, complex, multidimensional reality that is an individual human life. In the case of Aldo Leopold, awareness of his experience has largely been limited to his writings in *A Sand County Almanac* (or even, as in the above instance, just one essay within the *Almanac*). This has strongly shaped our images of Leopold. There is Aldo Leopold, who lived a life and, toward the end of it, wrote a memorable book. Then there is "The Author of *A Sand County Almanac*," a figure who for two generations has been a mirror to our relationship with the natural world and has borne the burden of our environmental hopes and fears. There is some confusion between the two.

◄◄ ►►

For readers, reviewers, and scholars, Aldo Leopold displays as many facets as there are perspectives. Consider the variety of fields that can—and do—legitimately claim Leopold as an important figure in their development: forestry, wildlife ecology and management, outdoor recreation, range management, sustainable agriculture, wilderness protection, conservation biology, restoration ecology, environmental history, environmental ethics, environmental law, environmental policy, environmental education, nature writing.[3] There are, in this sense, many Leopolds. But Leopold remains a compelling figure, and *A Sand County Almanac* an irresistible focal point, in part because these interests were so tightly fused in his personality and prose.

The Aldo Leopold that the most of the world knows, admires, and criticizes is really the late Leopold, and then only a part of that. Leopold's list of accomplishments was impressive long before he began work on the manuscript of *A Sand County Almanac*. He of course did not live to see his book published, to know its influence, or even to know its title. That his name and the book's title would become so tightly paired is a historical irony.

It becomes a matter of importance, then, to ask: How has public understanding of Leopold's work changed? What perspectives on his legacy do we inherit? The answers remain dynamic. Leopold's legacy is still being discovered by environmental professionals and the general public, and is revisited regularly by those who do know it. In retrospect, however, we can identify several general phases in the evolution of Leopold's public reputation. Those phases, in turn, tell us much about what various audiences have sought—or neglected—in the record of Leopold's life.

Leopold among His Contemporaries

We can start at the end of that life, as Leopold was pulling together the manuscript of *A Sand County Almanac*. It is useful to distinguish between Leopold's local and "more-than-local" reputation. Within Wisconsin, and especially at the University of Wisconsin, Aldo Leopold was a recognized figure, though by no means "famous." He had played an important role in many conservation policy initiatives at the state level beginning in the mid-1920s. In 1933 he joined the university, assuming the new and experimental Chair of Game Management within the Department of Agricultural Economics. Leopold was not an academic by background, and his field of expertise had yet to gain intellectual definition or professional acceptance. Securing wildlife ecology's foothold within academe would be one of Leopold's major accomplishments over the remaining years of his life.

For some time Leopold was, to quote Art Hawkins, one of his early graduate students, "suspect." Hawkins recalled that Leopold was "not part of the academic crowd" and "a real novice" in understanding the social ecology of the university campus.[4] In the words of another student, Frances Hamerstrom, he was "very thoroughly respected by a rather small, select group; in general, he wasn't even noticed."[5] By the late 1930s and early 1940s, when Hawkins and Hamerstrom worked most closely with him, Leopold had acquired a large circle of good friends and colleagues within Madison but led a relatively quiet academic life. By contrast, Leopold was very well known and highly regarded among his professional colleagues around the country. His national reputation had risen steadily over the decades, especially as wildlife management staked out its territory among the conservation professions in the 1930s.

His friend and student Al Hochbaum probably had the keenest sense of Leopold's status at the time. He wrote to Leopold in 1944: "If you will put yourself in perspective, you might realize that within your realm of influence, which is probably larger than you know, Aldo Leopold is considerably more than a person; in fact, he is probably less a person than he is a Standard."[6] After attending a conference of wildlife managers in 1947 Hochbaum wrote to Leopold, "For a long time the crowd has been more or less following (and sometimes objecting to) *rules* of wildlife management which you have prescribed. Now they are beginning to follow your *philosophies*, by and large without realizing whence they came. That is progress!"[7] Hochbaum had access to dimensions of Leopold's private and public persona that others missed, which in turn allowed him to offer the most trenchant criticisms of Leopold's *Almanac* essays.

During his lifetime, Leopold's professional reputation reflected his many qualities: a steady personality, a facility with words, his effectiveness as a teacher, the breadth and depth of his conservation philosophy, and especially the degree to which he matched word and thought with deed. Leopold was well aware of his prominence, and it is fair to say that he was quietly proud of it. At the same time, the older he grew—particularly in the last three years of his life, from the end of World War II until his death—the more he looked back on his accomplishments with a mature and self-confident modesty. He was certainly humbled by his own earlier mistakes, communicated most famously in the essay "Thinking Like a Mountain," in which he recounted his role in the extirpation of the wolf from the American Southwest.[8]

Leopold, however, was far from universally admired by his contemporaries. Among his peers Leopold was known as a hard-headed critic, though a fair, constructive, and thoughtful one. In the last decade of his life Leopold became increasingly blunt in his view of the direction taken by universities and government agencies. As noted in the last chapter, he was notably critical of the trend toward increasing disciplinary specialization and reductionism within the academy. In many ways, "The Land Ethic" itself was the ultimate expression of his position.

He was often entangled in thickets of controversy. The most prominent instance involved his role in Wisconsin's "deer wars," the drawn-out and vitriolic battles over the state's deer management policy in the 1940s. Leopold's determined advocacy of herd reduction made his name well known—and oft-blasted—among some segments of Wisconsin's populace (including especially hunters, antihunters, and resort owners). Leopold neither welcomed nor enjoyed the notoriety. Although decades of frontline conservation battles had thickened his hide, he now felt as viscerally as ever the difference between his view of conservation and that of "that collective person, the public."[9]

Leopold staked out unpopular or controversial positions on other issues. He remained adamantly active in the Wilderness Society until his death. He did not hesitate to raise his voice in opposition to indiscriminate wartime incursions into wild country, a postwar juggernaut of dam building, and what he saw as inappropriate uses of designated wilderness areas. The cause of wilderness protection had not yet achieved the wider public acceptance that would come with the Echo Park dam battle of the early 1950s. As America entered the era of postwar economic boom and political paranoia, Leopold occasionally found himself at odds even with old colleagues in the conservation movement over wilderness.

At the end of Leopold's life, then, his conservation work was well known, widely appreciated, and occasionally contentious, but he himself was little known outside of the professional conservation world. He was one of several leading voices from within the movement that in the immediate postwar years sought to communicate the importance of the science of ecology to a broader public. As the manuscript of *A Sand County Almanac* went to press, however, its author remained "very thoroughly respected by a rather small, select group."

Leopold Reaches a Broader Audience

A second phase in public awareness of Leopold began with the initial publication of *A Sand County Almanac* and extended roughly to the mid-1960s. During these years two conflicting trends played out. As the level of popular environmental awareness rose dramatically, the traditional conservation fields found themselves internally divided over the fundamental principles that Leopold and others had sought to define.

A Sand County Almanac helped to raise environmental literacy among the American public; conversely, readership of *A Sand County Almanac* grew along with that increasing awareness. This mutually reinforcing process can be traced back to the first reviews of the book. *A Sand County Almanac* was widely reviewed both locally and nationally, by readers familiar with Leopold and by those who learned of him for the first time through the book. Because of the confluence of events, many reviews served in essence as obituaries of Leopold, as reviewers used the occasion to reflect upon Leopold's legacy. The reviews of the day thus provide a fair picture of Leopold's public persona at the time of his death.

August Derleth, one of Wisconsin's leading literary figures, reviewed *A Sand County Almanac* for Madison's *Wisconsin State Journal*. Derleth knew of Leopold's conservation work and was well familiar with the Wisconsin landscapes described in the *Almanac*. Although he and Leopold were not themselves intimates, they shared many acquaintances. Derleth wrote in his review, "All genuine conservationists throughout Wisconsin and the Midwest generally realize that in the death of Aldo Leopold, Wisconsin lost one of its most able men in the field of conservation. Posthumous publication of his book offers ample evidence that his death deprived us *also of an author of no mean merit*. His book is one of those rare volumes to which sensitive and intelligent readers will turn again and again."[10] Derleth's phrasing is instructive. For most readers, Aldo Leopold would be known first and foremost, and often only, as an *author*; for Leopold's contemporaries, especially local contemporaries, Leopold was known primarily as a *conservationist*.

Many of the national reviews of *Sand County* were marked by a similar tone of surprise and delight, although most reviewers knew little if anything of Leopold's accomplishments. Lewis Gannett, in the *New York Herald Tribune*, wrote: "Aldo Leopold died fighting a neighbor's fire in the spring of 1948. I am sorry, for I should like to have known him. I do not recall ever hearing his name until I stumbled on this book; to read it is a deeply satisfying adventure. This was a man who wrote sparsely, out of intense feeling and long experience. You will find here no statistics about erosion, no screaming warnings to 'do something about the soil.' Aldo Leopold was primarily concerned with the importance of feeling something. He himself felt deeply, and his feeling gives a rich texture to this too-short book."[11] Gannett did not know about Leopold's years of devoted statistic-taking on erosion, his many forceful pleas for action, his constant assertion of the vital role of scientific research in conservation. Yet, for all that, Gannett was correct. In *A Sand County Almanac*, Leopold *was* "primarily concerned with the importance of feeling something."

New readers from beyond Leopold's personal or professional circles found something unusual in *A Sand County Almanac*. Its style was quite different from that of other prominent conservation books of the time, in particular Bill Vogt's *Road to Survival* and Fairfield Osborn's *Our Plundered Planet*. These two prescient books on the state of the global environment were chock full of statistics and warnings. Their authors read the future, and what they saw was not pretty. Both books gained a large, immediate, and influential readership. Leopold shared their grave concern—he had worked with both Vogt and Osborn, and had read and endorsed Vogt's book in manuscript—but he spoke in subtler tones. Leopold's book sold far more modestly at first, but steadily over the longer run. *A Sand County Almanac* continued to gain readers through the 1950s and into the 1960s. By the mid-1960s, some twenty thousand copies had been sold, mostly among dedicated conservationists and natural history enthusiasts.

The significance of the *Almanac*'s durability becomes clearer when viewed in relation to the second general trend in this period: the ambivalence with which even many conservation professionals regarded (if they regarded it at all) the path that Leopold and his like-minded colleagues had blazed. In "The Land Ethic," Leopold expressed concern over the growing division between those who "[regard] the land as soil, and its function as commodity production," and those who "[regard] the land as a biota, and its function as something broader."[12] The former were gaining a firm upper hand. "We are remodeling the Alhambra with a steam-shovel," Leopold lamented, "and we are proud of our yardage."[13] Leopold and his generation came to be seen as important, but old-fashioned, predecessors. The kernel of their legacy—the integration of the natural sciences and humanities in the service of conservation—fell under the heavy tread of the steam shovel.

Leopold and the Environmental Movement

That seed of that legacy, however, would prove hardy. A third phase in public appreciation of Leopold began in the mid-1960s and would last roughly into the mid-1980s. Paperback editions of *A Sand County Almanac*, published in 1966, 1968, and 1970 placed Leopold at the forefront of the new environmental movement. Rachel Carson's *Silent Spring* (1962), Stewart Udall's *The Quiet Crisis* (1963), and other books of the period created a growing critical mass of readers as *A Sand County Almanac* reappeared in its more accessible and affordable form.

As the paperbacks worked their way into the backpacks and reading lists of the baby boomers, a generation gap began to develop in perceptions of Leopold and the application of his ideas. On one side were the more senior conservationists, many of whom had themselves known and worked with Leopold or his contemporaries. On the other side stood the growing corps of younger (and more urban and suburban) environmentalists who knew of Leopold only through the *Almanac* essays. These younger devotees came to their environmental awareness as the landmark legislation of the era—the Wilderness Act (1964), the National Environmental Policy Act (1970), the Clean Air Act (1970), the Clean Water Act (1972), the Endangered Species Act (1973), the National Forest Management Act (1976), the Federal Land Policy and Management Act (1976)—redefined the context of the older conservation movement.

Older and younger readers alike invoked Leopold in support of their causes and adapted him in their approaches, but those causes and approaches did not always jibe. Underlying differences in (to cite just a few examples) the aims of resource management, attitudes toward hunting, appreciation of wilderness, and political styles and affiliations divided these audiences. Importantly, however, Leopold also served as a bridge across the generations. All were reading from the same book, a fact that would prove critical in the long run.

Leopold and the Reintegration of Conservation

Through the 1980s, the demographic shift continued to play out. Within the conservation professions, elders from the post–World War II generation approached retirement; older baby boomers rose through the ranks; younger baby boomers, trained after Earth Day, entered those ranks. Meanwhile, nonprofessional readers of *A Sand County Almanac* went about their lives in their communities, the paperbacks still residing on their bookshelves, the words still working their quiet influence.

By the late 1970s and early 1980s, changes in society, politics, and the environment itself cast Leopold's words in new light. Systemic environmental problems—vitriolic disputes over national forest management; water quality problems due to intensified agriculture; climate change and global-scale threats to biological diversity; incessant suburban sprawl; and on down the list of modern environmental dilemmas—demanded more systemic solutions. Such solutions came to be explored under the rubric of *ecosystem management, conservation biology, ecological economics, community-based conservation, sustainable agriculture* and other emerging fields and approaches.[14] These responses, while novel in name, often returned to the first principles of integrated conservation, as explored earlier by Leopold and his contemporaries. Leopold's intellectual stock thus continued to rise through the 1980s and 1990s.

We are still within this most recent phase, and it is difficult to read it with objectivity. Clearly, however, as waves of passion in the conservation and environmental movements have swelled and subsided, Leopold's legacy has remained robust. Why and how? The answer involves, of course, the historic record of his accomplishments and the quality of his writing and thinking. But it also reflects a welter of social and political forces that keeps

Leopold relevant and that invariably brings conservationists back to him—
more sober, perhaps, but more interested in the subtleties of his work. These
forces include:

*Continuing environmental degradation and the need for more effective
responses informed by ethics.* For those who see our fragmented approach to
landscapes, their resources, their biological diversity, and their human
communities as a root cause of environmental degradation, the search for
solutions leads back to the integrated view that Leopold articulated, especially in "The Land Ethic." Leopold's declaration of the ethical underpinnings of conservation has continued to gain attention and affect national
policy (through, for example, the shift toward ecosystem management in
the land management agencies and in many conservation organizations).[15]
Leopold regarded the lack of attention from philosophers and theologians
as "proof that conservation [had] not yet touched these foundations of
conduct."[16] The emergence of environmental ethics and the greening of
religion may now be regarded as evidence of progress.

The antienvironmental "wise use" movement. As the forces of opposition to conservation and environmentalism gained political power in the
1980s and 1990s, many younger environmentalists were compelled to
revisit their roots and to learn about (often for the first time) their connections to the older conservation movement. Likewise, more conservative
conservationists were also led to examine their political loyalties. For many
in this period, Aldo Leopold stood out as one who did not place his politics
before his conservation commitments. The relationship between political
conviction and conservation action has always been complex. In his writing Leopold does not come across as an ideologue, and in life he was not.
His has been a relevant and flexible voice during a period of intense politicization of conservation.

The erosion of community. During these years many commentators
have examined the sweeping changes that are transforming community life
in the United States and around the world.[17] Somewhere between the
shoals of unwarranted nostalgia and blind economic optimism lies (we
may hope) safe passage, but the route has been difficult to discern.
Renewed attention to communitarian values is an important part of contemporary social criticism. A parallel expression has emerged within con-

servation, emphasizing the need to *re-place* communities, to see them in terms of the biophysical environments in which they are embedded. "Community" was a key word in Leopold's lexicon, and the "extension" of community that Leopold advocated in "The Land Ethic" has accordingly assumed increased importance.

The interdisciplinary imperative. This pertains particularly to academia, where hyper-specialization and reductionism move on apace, the opportunities for "thinking time" shrink, and the selective pressures on success continue to intensify. Such trends tend to overwhelm efforts to maintain connections among the sciences, arts, and letters. Leopold's customary interdisciplinary approach carries authority here. He is a reminder of a time before the need to specialize was ratcheted up several additional notches, and a greater share of rewards still accrued to those whose training, teaching, and work were broad and diverse.

These forces—and others no doubt—have allowed Leopold's recent readers to see him in a new light, as one who perceived trends that would increasingly characterize American society and the American landscape through the twentieth century. The implicit messages in Leopold's essays, spoken amid the bugling of cranes and the songs of wild rivers, have become more explicit. Yet, new readers can still respond to the conviction Leopold felt to his very marrow: that the future of the human enterprise on this (and any other) continent is tied inextricably to the future of our landscapes and our wild coinhabitants.

⤛ ⤜

Since *A Sand County Almanac* was first published, most of its readers have remained unaware of the life that gave it shape, responding not so much to Aldo Leopold the person as to "The Author of *A Sand County Almanac.*" For the general reader, this is of small consequence; a worthy book stands on its own. The duty of the historian and biographer, however, is to fill in facts, weigh the text against the life, and surround the book with a sort of narrative *habitat.* Such scrutiny deepens our understanding of the creature itself—robbing it of some of its immediate mystery but providing a richer appreciation of its existence. With such perspective, we might see in our prior responses and images a little less of Leopold and a little more of ourselves.

What do we see when we reexamine "The Author of *A Sand County Almanac*"?

Leopold the Prophet

Leopold's daughter Nina Leopold Bradley, when asked about her father's conservation philosophy, has occasionally referred to "that poor old land ethic." It is a great deal to ask one essay, or book, or person, to bear the weight of society's need to transform its relationship with the natural world. Over the decades, a disproportionate amount of that weight has fallen upon Aldo Leopold.

Among Leopold's contemporaries were several who fully appreciated the depth of Leopold's conservation critique and first employed the all-but-inevitable tag of "prophet." Roberts Mann, a Leopold friend and superintendent of the Cook County (Illinois) Forest Preserve District, published an article in 1954 titled "Aldo Leopold, Priest and Prophet."[18] Ernie Swift, another friend and colleague who led Wisconsin's Conservation Department, followed in 1961 with "Aldo Leopold, Wisconsin's Conservation Prophet."[19] Historian Roderick Nash, in his classic 1967 study *Wilderness and the American Mind*, called his chapter on Leopold simply "Aldo Leopold, Prophet."[20] The trope has endured. Wallace Stegner, not one given to hyperbole, described *A Sand County Almanac* as "almost a holy book in conservation circles . . . one of the prophetic books, the utterance of an American Isaiah."[21] *A Sand County Almanac* continues to be referred to regularly as the "Bible" or "scripture" of the environmental movement.

The "prophet" image, whether one regards it as appropriate invocation, forgivable embellishment, or unnecessary overstatement, is revealing. Leopold reflected a strong social need. Any movement requires prophetic voices to give itself coherence and direction. Martin Luther King was the preeminent prophetic voice of the civil rights movement. There was no one equivalent iconic figure in the environmental movement. But environmental reformers could and did look back to find not only Leopold, but also John Muir, Henry David Thoreau, and, among contemporaries, Rachel Carson and David Brower, Sigurd Olson and Barry Commoner, Edward Abbey and Gary Snyder. They became the movement's "prophets." As conservation itself continued to evolve at the

turn of the twenty-first century, Leopold (among others) continued to fulfill the prophet *function*.

Leopold the All-Purpose Hero

One factor set Leopold apart even within the pantheon of environmental "prophets": he coupled the inspiration of his prose, thought, and advocacy
with the authority of his experience. Unlike the others, Leopold wrote from
a varied background in on-the-ground forestry, range and wildlife management, wilderness protection, and ecological restoration. He was a respected
figure in all these fields, and could speak their languages. And so Leopold
served another posthumous function: as an all-around, acceptable and accessible "conservation hero," able to appeal to a broad range of conservation
factions . . . as long as the deeper tensions within conservation lay dormant.

One of the more interesting variations on this image of Leopold
involved an unlikely source. The February 18, 1956, edition of the *Saturday Evening Post* featured a sketch of Leopold in a full-page advertisement
for the Weyerhaeuser company. The ad depicted Leopold on bended knee
with a vulnerable fawn under his protective watch, against a clearcut
mountainside in the background. Apparently Aldo Leopold by this time
was seen as a reasonable conservationist who could support, as the text of
the ad put it, *"true conservation* through the wise use and perpetuation of
industrial forest uses."[22]

This Leopold-as-conservation-hero motif reflected conservation's
growing mainstream constituency. By 1956, conservation, however pliable
its definition, had become acceptable across a broad demographic spectrum. As long as Leopold represented the kindly and constructive school
of *reasonable* conservation, even a major industrial force such as Weyerhaeuser could use his image in one of their prominent advertisements. It
could, for the time being, ignore the fact that Leopold was a dedicated
activist, a critical scientist, politically involved, and not one to shrink from
unseemly controversies over conservation policy.

Leopold the Radical Environmentalist

If Leopold's work and words helped lay the groundwork for a
broader, more popular, better funded, more respectable, mainstream social

movement, it also inspired a counterresponse. As environmentalism became more acceptable, it also became, in the view of others, more diluted. And so another reading of Leopold's legacy arose: Leopold as radical environmentalist and deep ecologist.

The most prominent example of this "redeployment" of Leopold came through the actions of the 1980s Earth First! movement. When Dave Foreman and his compatriots launched the movement, they drew upon Leopold in raising high the bar of compromise in conservation politics. Leopold's powerful image of the faltering "green fire" in the eyes of the dying wolf of "Thinking Like a Mountain" symbolized for this new generation of wilderness activists the loss of North America's wild places. "A militant minority of wilderness-minded citizens," they read in Leopold's essay "Wilderness," "must be on watch throughout the nation and available for action in a pinch."[23] Their philosophical standard-bearers in the deep ecology movement could point to "The Land Ethic" as a foundational document.[24]

Of course, counter-counterresponses ensued. Hence the disgruntled forester, grousing in the *Journal of Forestry* that Leopold was merely a "starry eyed . . . pipe-smoking academician." Another suggested that Leopold's pipe contained more sinister substances, noting that he, the reader, had "seen nothing that Aldo Leopold had to say that does not make me think that he was anything but the original pot-head."[25]

What do we learn from Leopold the Deep and Radical Ecologist? He reflected a growing polarity within the environmental movement. Prior to the 1970s, if one were engaged in environmental advocacy, one was likely an amateur, poorly paid (if at all), and engaged primarily out of a sense of public duty. By the mid-1970s, the scene was changing. Membership in the major environmental organizations was on the rise. The ranks of environmental professionals burgeoned. As paid staffs grew, professional expertise began to overshadow grassroots activism. Passion was nice, but a master's degree got you the job and respect. Yet, as the environmental professional class grew, the grassroots activists, driven by powerful social, political, and spiritual motives, hardly went away. The result, in a sense, was a splitting of Leopold's legacy. Suited professionals could see Leopold as a sort of master diplomat and spokesman, able to speak to all sides on environmental issues. Activists could see Leopold as a committed and deeply honest radical, whose message provided intellectual armor.

Leopold the Naïve Interloper

This category encompasses an entire suite of images. It refers to the response evoked as Leopold's interdisciplinary influence has come to be felt in disciplines not his own. This response may be traced in any number of fields; it will suffice here to examine it in philosophy, politics, and conservation itself.

That Leopold in fact made *any* useful contribution to philosophy is not a view that all have shared.[26] H. J. McCloskey, an Australian philosopher, suggested that "there is a real problem in attributing a coherent meaning to Leopold's statements, one that exhibits his 'Land Ethic' as representing a major advance in ethics rather than a retrogression to a morality of a kind held by various primitive peoples." Far from an advance in ethics, Leopold offered only a throwback to primitivism. Another regarded Leopold the philosopher as "something of a disaster, and I dread the thought of the student whose concept of philosophy is modeled principally on these extracts [from Leopold's writings]." Another reviewer saw "The Land Ethic" as "dangerous nonsense."[27] In short, for at least a few formally trained and credentialed philosophers, Aldo Leopold's adventuring in this field was hardly worthy of serious consideration.

How does Leopold fare among politicians and political theorists? Marginally better, actually, especially more recently. Because Leopold's conservation politics defied ideological pigeonholing, those searching for deeper political lessons have found his work in this arena instructive.[28] The same maverick quality, however, has also left Leopold open to easy criticism. Such criticism has come, on the one hand, from those who have preferred a more overtly political approach to environmental issues. Thus, in 1974, still in the wake of the initial high wave of environmentalism, a critic could disapprove of "the inadequate politics of Aldo Leopold." The author found Leopold's politics to be "wholly conventional, some would say naïve. From one point of view the wonder is not that he accomplished so much as a political operator, but that he accomplished so little. . . .

Again and again in his writing [Leopold] seemed on the verge of some sort of ideological breakthrough, but appeared to draw back from the brink of discovery. . . . In the political and administrative sector . . . this inexperienced administrator had little to offer for implementation of his 'land ethic' beyond a very traditional reliance on high-minded moral persuasion."[29]

If some saw Leopold's politics as naïve and deficient in the highly politicized context of 1970s environmental activism, others would see his approach in a new light as that context continued to change. A decade later, Leopold's biographer (i.e., this author) could receive inquiries from a conservative journal interested in an article on Aldo Leopold because they felt he was "an environmentalist they could live with." This is not as surprising as it may seem. Conservatives and libertarians can find much to agree with in "The Land Ethic." A core component of "The Land Ethic" is in fact Leopold's belief that governments simply could not assume or carry out all necessary conservation functions; that individuals had to assume greater responsibility for the health of the land; that, absent such responsibility, governments would *need* to step in. The editors evidently saw here an opportunity to explore these "conservative" elements of "The Land Ethic."[30]

Aldo Leopold's politics were not naïve. His sense of citizenship and civic responsibility was intense, and evolved along with the changing currents in the conservation movement.[31] That we can read his politics as conservative and progressive, naïve and sophisticated, personal and public, again tells us as much about ourselves as it does about Leopold. It suggests that we have yet to evolve a politics that can respond in a healthy and democratic fashion to complex conservation dilemmas; that we are still struggling to find, in Leopold's words, "mechanisms for protecting the public interest in private land"[32]; that we continue to paw among traditional political ideologies in search of solutions and find it very difficult to imagine where constructive alternatives may lie. For those deeply involved in the struggle to forge new relationships with the land, and among the people who inhabit it, Leopold's politics, far from being naïve or inadequate, remain instructive and encouraging.

The Leopold-as-naïve-interloper view has occasionally found currency within the conservation world as well. Many of Leopold's precepts were beyond the pale in his own day, and many remain so. The breadth of perspective he brought to conservation was highly unusual and those who inhabited one portion of the conservation spectrum could not always appreciate his view. The story was told, for example, of the joke that went around the hallways of Wisconsin's Conservation Department, about how to spell this word "aesthetic" that the Professor was always using. Leopold was both a specialist (in several fields) and a generalist. As the conservation professions advanced, it became very easy to look back and regard Leopold as a dilettante in these increasingly insular fields. Hence, for example, latter-day foresters who could ignore Leopold's credentials in the field and claim, in effect, that he wasn't a forester after all.

Another "subheading" in this particular category involves the problematic (for some) fact that Aldo Leopold was also a lifelong hunter. For this, Leopold has received his share of criticism from at least some anti-hunters, animal rights activists, and environmental ethicists. Conversely, conscientious hunters have held him high as a premier example of the ethically sophisticated and environmentally committed sportsman.

Leopold stepped up to this chasm in attitudes toward hunting regularly in his own lifetime. The chasm would grow only deeper in the years after his death. No less a figure than Rachel Carson, for example, had an outright disdain for the only Leopold, apparently, that she knew: the one of *Round River*, the collection of Leopold's hunting journal entries first published in 1953.[33] Carson's ethic was more closely aligned with Albert Schweitzer's "reverence for life" philosophy than with a Leopoldian land ethic. *Round River*'s portrait of Leopold the hunter was more than she could tolerate. The same response can be found, again, in a lambaste from the 1998 *Journal of Forestry* critique: "Leopold preached the extension of ethics to all fellow members of the land community, and he practiced killing them until the end of his life."[34] Suffice it to say that this critic chose the bluntest of rhetoric to address one of the most complex of human behaviors and one of the most sensitive issues in conservation—one that Leopold pondered carefully and consciously on a daily basis for decades.

These dismissals of Leopold by philosophers, political activists, and conservationists again track broad trends. In them we can read the impact of increased specialization and politicization in conservation, and in society at large. Divided into areas of special knowledge and special interest, conservation like other fields struggles to maintain connections between the present and the past, the abstract and the actual, the sciences and the arts, philosophy and practice. By contrast, Leopold's written record reveals a mind at ease with complexity, open to mystery as well as new data, and resistant to reductive tendencies in both science and politics.

Aldo Leopold had his share of flaws and made his share of mistakes. But he was also, by general consent of those who knew him, a decent and delightful person to know and work with, a highly respected leader in conservation, tolerant of human foibles, lacking in hidden demons. Such qualities may account for the challenge some have in "handling" Leopold. Modern readers, attuned to irony and sensitive to political subtexts, may find Leopold's personality an increasingly difficult kind to get a hold on. In facing our contemporary postmodern dilemmas, we may project them onto Leopold.

Two illustrative references. For years, a portrait of Leopold has hung on the walls of his home department of wildlife ecology on the University of Wisconsin campus. The artist chose to depict Leopold with cigarette in hand (an intermittent smoker, he however preferred his pipe to cigarettes). Graduate students—if not the genuflectors—have appreciated the incorrectness of that particular icon. Then there was the survey question in *Sierra* magazine. The editors asked readers to respond to the query, "Can you eat meat and consider yourself an environmentalist?" Among the responses: "Remember: Aldo Leopold ate meat, Adolph Hitler did not."[35] The past calls out to us . . . from the far side of the postmodern minefield.

Leopold the Ecofascist

Extreme examples of these images of Leopold may be found on the far fringes. Because Leopold has been a focal point for discussion of environmental ideas and strategies, he has occasionally been caricatured as an advocate of oppressive social and governmental actions to safeguard environmental quality. The reasoning is this: Leopold in "The Land Ethic" places the good of the community, the whole, the ecosystem, above the good of the constituent parts; he, therefore, would direct the whole to impose its will on the constituent members of that whole; he would, further, sacrifice individual freedom for the collective good. (The point, of course, is easily lost on such critics, i.e., that Leopold saw individual action

and responsibility, as articulated in "The Land Ethic," as a necessary anti-
dote to such eventualities.)

Many of these criticisms arise out of reasoned consideration of the difficult questions that Leopold's work—that conservation generally—that
modern life—poses. These arguments, well developed and thoughtful,
appear in academic journals and conference proceedings. So do effective
counterarguments.[36] Not all such exchanges, however, are so civil or reasoned. A 1993 letter to the editor of the *Iowa State Daily* criticized the mission of Iowa State University's Leopold Center for Sustainable Agriculture. Not content to question the institution, the letter writer attacked
Leopold as a "Nazi" and "racist," stating, "He believed in the superiority
of the Nordic race. He believed that population growth has to be stopped;
he rejected the sanctity of life and he scorned human beings so much that
he believed the population of a country could be managed like an animal
reservation."[37] Such rantings are not to be dismissed lightly. We have read
into Aldo Leopold not only our hopes and concerns, but our insecurities
and our fears.

There are, no doubt, other "Leopolds" that bear consideration. As
the taxonomy fills out, it reveals several basic tendencies that have historically marked much Leopold commentary and criticism. The most common, noted earlier, is to assume that Aldo Leopold existed only as "The
Author of *A Sand County Almanac*"; that it is unnecessary to take into
account other dimensions of his conservation career; that the historical
and personal context of the *Almanac*, however interesting, is of incidental importance. One may find this view among Leopold's devotees as well
as his detractors.

A second common tendency is to divorce Leopold's publications from
his practice. Leopold was a person of action as well as words, and the
dynamic between these two spheres of his life may be the most significant
of all his contributions. In his writing, he tried to define a workable standard for conservation to follow and to strive toward. But he worked toward
it himself, and thereby humanized it. The fingers that held the pen had dirt
under the nails.

A third tendency is to consider only that part of Leopold with which
one feels most comfortable or conversant, and to avoid regarding the

entirety of the person, his expertise, and his record. Hence, the critic who attends to only one of the several disciplines Leopold studied, or one of the professions he practiced. Evidence of this tendency can be found in many of the fields to which Leopold contributed, from agriculture and wildlife ecology to economics and ethics.

Finally, another tendency is to consider Leopold's work only up to a certain point in time. Hence, for example, the occasional wildlife manager who will read *Game Management* and appreciate it as the profession's founding volume, while ignoring or slighting the epic progression from *Game Management* (1933) to *A Sand County Almanac* (1949).

Leopold, in short, has been a mirror to our environmental responses. We see in him a succession of reflections over the decades since his death. In the years immediately after World War II, as awareness of widespread environmental problems increased, our fears grew apace. Leopold was a vehicle for understanding the human dimensions of these problems and imagining possible solutions. He cast warnings, as did others of the time, but tempered the warnings with wit, self-criticism, and poetry. In one essay after another, he leavened his conservation message not only through his expressions of love for "things natural, wild, and free," but also through his understanding of the human condition and human shortcomings (including his own).

As the environmental movement coalesced in the 1960s and early 1970s, many found Leopold's words inspirational. Leopold clearly recognized the harsh realities of environmental degradation, but provided a positive response. In the academic and policy arenas, he showed how the sciences, literature, history, and philosophy not only could be, but had to be, brought together to address problems and forge solutions. He contributed to the foundations upon which new, more integrated environmental policies and programs could be built.

Into the 1970s and 1980s, Leopold's words provided guidance not only for far-reaching policy changes, but in a sense for their complement: a well-tempered understanding that conservation problems could not merely be legislated or administered away, but had to be addressed from within—within our selves, communities, cultures, businesses, organizations, and institutions. The limits of purely technical, legal, or political solutions became apparent. Stated another way, readers found in Leopold's land ethic not just a rationale for short-term technical fixes or policy initiatives, but a guide to necessary longer-term social and cultural changes.

Finally, it seems of late that readers have increasingly responded to the degree of personal commitment that they find in Leopold. Leopold, although acutely aware of global conservation dilemmas, avoided the mire of despair. One of his most notable character traits was his capacity to face difficult conservation problems squarely, and to address them constructively despite overwhelming odds. This trait marked his literary endeavors as well, and never more so than in completing "The Land Ethic." Despite serious health problems and other difficult personal circumstances, he found the internal resources to pull together "The Land Ethic" and complete his collection of essays in the summer of 1947. That strength of character rests between every line of *A Sand County Almanac.*

◄◄ ►►

Aldo Leopold's life provides a unique medium through which to address recurring issues, debates, developments, and trends in conservation. And because Leopold was in many ways his own sharpest critic, his ideas have resisted fossilization. His insights cannot serve if they are regarded as inert museum specimens. His legacy, to remain vital, must be able to grow and evolve, tolerate dissent, resist dogma, and welcome criticism.

As noted at the outset, the immediate connections to Leopold's legacy will inexorably fade. Fortunately, students of Leopold's work have testimony from many primary sources to draw upon. Alfred Etter, who studied with Leopold, penned in 1948 one of the more sensitive accounts. It appeared as an obituary and described a day afield with Leopold. Etter's account captured well Leopold's personal qualities. At the family's shack, wrote Etter, "[Leopold] tried to piece together answers to the questions which Nature so often tempted him to solve. From pads of moss or patches of quack grass he learned a piece of history. From a tangle of ash logs a suggestion of some principle dawned upon him. From a broken pine a brief diagram of the balance of the forces in the environment was devised. Above all, this farm was a place where his children could learn the meaning of life and gain confidence in their ability to investigate small problems and discover things which no one knew."[38]

Such historic accounts of Leopold's way of thinking and observing and conducting himself provide some immunity against distortion. Paul Errington, another contemporary, spoke to this, again in a 1948 obituary: "Let no one do [Leopold] the disservice of fostering Leopoldian legends or Leopoldian dogmas. Knowing him as I have, I can say that he would not wish these to arise from his having lived. . . . I can imagine his gentle scorn at the thought of anything like elaborate statuary in his memory, while despoliation and wastage of the land and its biota continue as usual."[39]

Readers returning to Leopold will no doubt continue to find their own growth reflected in his words. Not uncommonly, students who first encountered Leopold through *A Sand County Almanac* in their idealistic youth return to its pages years later to find the earlier inspiration enriched by a more subtle wisdom. Leopold for many has become the proverbial parent who has "grown *so much smarter* since *I* was young." But he is also a baseline. Readers will look to see what Leopold missed, what he could not anticipate, what we still need to work on.

A fine example of the "reread Leopold" can be found in a 1988 essay published in the *North Dakota Quarterly*. The author, Patrick Nunnally, recalled that he had first read *A Sand County Almanac* in the politically charged 1970s, when he was fighting wilderness battles in the southern Appalachians. He later moved to Iowa, where he found himself interacting more regularly with farmers. He also found himself asking what Leopold had to offer under those quite different circumstances. Nunnally recalls returning to the *Almanac* and finding new appreciation of its value:

> [Leopold] establishes a grounding, a framework for conversation, without foreclosing much in the way of intelligent reflection and inquiry. It seems to me that I formerly used Leopold to end conversations: "This is what Leopold says, and that is the final word." Instead, I look to him now to keep me focused and to keep me reminded of the larger conversation and stakes of which individual land protection discussions are a part. . . . He still has value as a source for quotations—he writes better on this subject than nearly anyone else who has tried, and his particular phrases ring better than any of my own. But it is more important to me now that he provides exemplary inquiry to complicated problems, with

more than one viable position but only one best position. What formerly I cited as received dogma, now, I hope, I can use as wisdom of a thinker who has preceded me in the land conservation debate.[40]

This is the better-balanced view of Leopold that we can anticipate. Finally, more than a half century after Leopold's death, we may appreciate his continuing influence without having to make him over into a demigod or a devil, a hero or a threat, without having to regard him as naïve, radical, old-fashioned, or prophetic. This is the kind of critical attitude that pays due honor to Leopold by reflecting not merely our desires or our fears, but our growth.

Facing Forward |

PART THREE

9

Inherit the Grid

*The culture of a nation by general consent,
would, I suppose, be regarded as its greatest
heritage, but a heritage perhaps equally
worthy of being cherished is the land surface
which a nation occupies. The culture to a
large extent must have been influenced by
the character of the land surface, and in
any event culture and land surface are
interwoven, and interact in countless
directions difficult to unravel.*

—REGINALD G. STAPLEDON (1935)

*Ecological design is the careful meshing of
human purposes with the larger patterns and
flows of the natural world and the study of
those patterns and flows to inform human
purposes. . . . When human artifacts and
systems are well designed, they are in
harmony with the larger patterns in which
they are embedded.*

—DAVID W. ORR (1994)

WE FACE a sharp bend in the road. Behind us lies the landscape we inherit.
Before us lies the landscape that, in due time, we will bequeath. Looking
back, we can see important flaws in the relationship between people and
land. Looking ahead, we can see a need to reform that relationship, but find
it hard to know just how we might alter our direction, shift our momentum,
and adjust our speed. We seek a more careful "meshing" (to use Orr's

word) of our human communities and natural systems, but we have no sure map to guide us.

Lacking explicit directions, we peer ahead, advance with deliberation, and make forays. We ask: what kinds of knowledge and experience do we need to bring together in any given place to address issues of environmental quality, landscape aesthetics, economic sustainability, social justice, and community cohesion? We begin to combine perspectives, ideas, and data from diverse fields—ecology, restoration ecology, conservation biology, economics, geography, landscape architecture, public health, land-use planning and design, architecture and the allied arts. History offers a caution: we need to know how and why we arrived at this point.

We need, as well, to understand our context. If, as Orr suggests, sound design requires that "human artifacts and systems" fit well with "the larger patterns in which they are embedded," then a clear view of those larger patterns is essential. But our artifacts and systems themselves can cloud the view. Architectural historian Vincent Scully writes, "The relationship of manmade structures to the natural world offers . . . the richest and most valuable physical and intellectual experience that architecture can show, and it is the one that has been most neglected by Western architectural critics and historians. There are many reasons for this. Foremost among them, perhaps, is the blindness of the contemporary urban world to everything that is not itself, to nature most of all."[1] Scully extends and responds to his own complaint:

> Most human beings of the developed nations live in an environment that is almost entirely manmade, or think they do so. Hence the major contextual questions of modern architecture have come to be those having to do with the modification of existing manmade environments by new structures. But underneath all the complexity of those urban situations *the larger reality* still exists: the fact of nature, and of humanity's response to the challenge—the threat, the opportunity—that nature seems to offer in any given place. It follows therefore, that the first fact of architecture is the topography of a place and the way human beings respond to it with their own constructed forms.[2]

In considering past and future landscapes, we need to amend Scully's observation only slightly. Not only have our urban structures been inattentive to the "larger reality"; so, too, have patterns of settlement and land use generally. Subdivisions, suburbs, edge cities, towns, farms, ranches, managed forests, and semiwild lands are also "manmade environments," though less obviously so than the skyscraper and city block. They too are constructed forms within the landscape. Recently, environmental historians, ethicists, and conservation biologists have reexamined even wilderness—or at least our received idea of wilderness—as a human construction.[3] Meanwhile, our understanding of "the larger reality" of nature continues to expand and change. Since the mid-1980s, ecologists have increasingly recognized the dynamism of natural systems and the need to respect ecological processes in all conservation and resource-management activities.[4]

Here, then, is a task. We need to step back, away, apart from the artificial order in which our lives are embedded. We need to read well the character of the earth and know how culture has influenced our view from within. We need to see ourselves living amid varied scales of time and space. We need to find "border crossings": places where we can move between, and connect, the cultural and the natural.

The lenses through which we see landscapes, and ourselves within them, vary from place to place and culture to culture. In much of North America, we perceive—and manage, and modify—the landscape through the superimposed system of rectangular land surveys, with its grid of township and range lines, that was instituted in the late 1700s. Where the grid system predominates, it has profoundly shaped landscapes and the patterns of life within them. "It is the grid," writes John Brinkerhoff Jackson, "not the eagle or the stars and stripes, which is our true national emblem."[5]

Yet the very pervasiveness of the land survey system can hinder our appreciation of it. As Hildegard Binder Johnson notes in her book *Order Upon the Land*, "most Americans and Canadians accept the survey system that so strongly affects their lives and perception of the landscape in the same way that they accept a week of seven days, a decimal numerical system, or an alphabet of 26 letters—as natural, inevitable, or perhaps in some inscrutable way divinely ordained."[6] In our efforts to devise more sustainable land-management and landscape-design practices, we need to grasp fully the historic impacts of the survey system and the constraints and opportunities they entail. Wes Jackson writes, "The grid and property lines and what they mean must be factored in, almost as immutable givens, as we begin our journey to become native to the place. Those lines are likely to last as long as there is a United States."[7]

To factor in the grid—what it signifies, the impact it has had—we first need to gain some perspective on it.

We are attracted to places where Earth's "larger reality" can be sensed. Old forests—even the threatened fragments that remain—can still lift us beyond the human scale and put us in our place. Those who dwell among mountains have ready access to open country. It draws people to the modern American West as ardently as the halt are drawn to Lourdes (and with much the same hope for healing).[8] Those who dwell near oceans and other wide waters are also blessed with built-in access to larger realities, and mysteries: the visible arc of the far horizon, the creatures of the deep, the tidal pull of the moon.

For dwellers of flatlands and inlands, however, a sense of the enveloping order can be hard to come by. No swelling sea, no grand vistas, no vaulting trunks and shafts of light to lift the eyes to greater proportions. Johnson writes that, in our most *extreme* Midwest of straight roads, furrows, and ditches, "all forms seem to be hardened into plane geometry. . . . Enthusiasm over nature's roundness can be stirred only by the spectacle of clouds under the dome of the sky."[9] In flatlands, a feeling for magnitude and ultimate context must come to us through filters: rectangular crop fields, straight county roads that meet at ninety-degree angles, strip developments that cling to the grid lines like detritus to a storm grate.

Yet, even within neatly ordered, buttoned-down landscapes, the larger reality of wild nature cannot be completely ignored or repressed. Where to find it?

From an odd corner, memory whispers a hint: seventh-grade English class, suburban Chicago, Miss Fitch presiding. Or trying to, anyway. The rowdy adolescents under her care were none too attentive to begin with, and she had begun to lose control. One afternoon, in an effort to get into our heads and strike a spark of critical thinking, Miss Fitch pulled out the classic brainteaser. "Okay, listen. . . . You're standing in the door of your house at Point A. You walk a mile *due south* to Point B. Then you turn right and walk another mile *due west* to Point C. And then, suddenly, you see a WILD BEAR! So you turn right, and race one mile *due north*, where you arrive safely back home." Dramatic pause. "What color was the bear?" The expected bewilderment all around. I recall trudging my triangular way around those imaginary stations, and actually arriving at the answer. Distraction, however, ruled. It was not the logic of the problem that entranced me, but the daydream vision of a great bear wandering through arctic mists. Before I could raise my hand, some classmate screamed from the southern latitudes of my consciousness: "WHITE!"

The ostensible point of discussion that afternoon had more to do more with methods of deductive reasoning than with finding our place in the world, or the role of mystery in illuminating reality. Yet, however unintended, the latter lessons snagged. "Nature is not a place to visit," Gary Snyder writes, "it is *home*."[10] Let the White Bear signify the presence of the wild in our home, and of our home in the yet larger wild place—the wild that we banish to odd corners of our classrooms, our memories, our landscapes, our selves, the wild that can offer guidance if we are ready for it. Aldo Leopold understood the value of these wild presences and places. They "give definition and meaning to the human enterprise." We return to them again and again, he wrote, "to organize yet another search for a durable scale of values."[11] And when we turn back to the cultural enterprise, to the more humanized part of the landscape, we find ourselves, and our place, changed. With pragmatic consequences. "The lessons we learn from the wild," Snyder observes, "become the etiquette of freedom."[12] The better we know the larger reality, the better we might know how to act within it.

◄◄ ►►

About 70 percent of the land in the continental United States—all but the thirteen original states, Maine, Vermont, West Virginia, Kentucky, Tennessee, and Texas—is delineated according to the land-survey system. The system was developed originally under the Land Ordinances of 1784 and 1785, the Northwest Ordinance of 1787, and the Land Act of 1796, and modified through later acts and policies.[13] Under the survey, all lands in the nation's public domain were to be measured and divided along survey lines whose coordinates would, in Johnson's words, "always run north-south and east-west with complete disregard of the terrain. This unconditional rule [made] it possible for the survey to be continuous not only in concept but in practice over thousands of square miles—the most extensive uninterrupted cadastral system in the world."[14] Eventually, the survey's grid would cover more than three million square miles of land.

Developed under the influence of eighteenth-century European rationalism and Enlightenment-era science, drawing upon (or at least resembling) diverse precursors, applied and polished according to Thomas Jefferson's political vision, the survey system was well suited to its central task: the efficient distribution of lands whose indigenous peoples were being dispossessed of their tenure, among newly arrived inhabitants for whom individual land possession was a bulwark against the inequities of European land tenure and a stabilizing keel for the embarking democracy. "It is not too soon," Jefferson wrote from France in 1785, "to provide by every possible means that as few as possible shall be without a little portion of land. The small landholders are the most precious part of a state."[15] Among the "possible means" was the land survey system.

The original land ordinances established the principles and methods of the survey: adoption of the nonvarying gridwork of survey lines as the fundamental model; subdivision of the western territories into square townships (first envisioned to be ten miles square, later amended to seven, and finally six, square miles); further subdivision of the six-square-mile blocks into thirty-six square sections of 640 acres (one square mile) each; consecutive numbering of the sections; reservation of one section (#16) in each township for a public school; careful mapping and description of the surveyed lands; appointment of surveyors and geographers to undertake and direct the survey; and the auctioning off of the lands so defined.[16]

So began the process that would transform the face of the continent. "Across the public lands," Wallace Stegner writes, "the General Land Office imposed a grid of surveys upon which the small freeholds of the ideal agrarian democracy could be laid out like checkers on a board."[17] With strict Euclidean geometry and Cartesian coordinates in mind, and compasses, stakes, and Gunter's chains in hand, the government surveyors began laying their lines at the "Point of Beginning" in the uncharted wild lands of eastern Ohio. The work that began along the banks of the Ohio River on September 30, 1785 would continue to the shores of the Pacific. "The result," John Hildebrand observes in *Mapping the Land*, "was the landscape as a work of political imagination."[18]

Not, that is, as a foundation for social, economic, and environmental sustainability. The sciences behind the survey, after all, were mathematics and geometry, not geology, botany, zoology, the natural sciences of the day—much less in the *integrating* natural sciences of ecology, biogeography, and evolutionary biology, which were only faint premonitions in the Age of Enlightenment. The survey, in abstracting the earth, might indeed extend across the continent to the far Pacific. Despite "insuperable obstacles," nothing would stop it—not the continent's great rivers, or thick forests, or mucky wetlands, or treeless prairies, or sweeping plains, or abrupt plateaus, or high deserts, or bold mountains.[19] For that matter, not native uprisings, or civil wars, or land speculators, or corrupt officials, or land rushes, or lumber, mining, and railroad barons. All fell before, within, and under the grid. In the laying on of lines, order and perfectibility, precision and control—or at least the illusion of these things—could be maintained.

Up to a point.

For the methodology of the land survey contained an inherent, original flaw. The survey aimed to render square townships on the land, with their eastern and western boundaries laid out along parallel north-south longitudinal meridians. But—as English teachers and polar bears can teach us—the meridian lines are not in fact parallel. They converge as they move away from the equator and toward the earth's poles, where they finally intersect. In reality, the survey's two-dimensional "squares" are not (and cannot be) squares at all. Technically, they might be described as "arched isosceles trapezoids in three-dimensional space." If the survey were extended to the poles, the trapezoids would become triangles. In short, one simply cannot construct and stack identical, flat, square townships on a round earth. Or, as one student of the survey system put it, gridding the surface of the planet is "like trying to wrap a grapefruit with graph paper; there has to be a fold somewhere." [20]

The convergence of the meridians could not be ignored. The grid might extend unencumbered by climate, geology, hydrology, slope, aspect, soil type, flora, fauna, and native tradition. Resurveying might be required as waves washed away sandbars, rivers gained and lost oxbows, landslides reshaped hills, or volcanoes created new land. Corners might be cut and lines skewed through the fatigue, error, or bribery of the surveyors. None of these called into question the attempt to fit an artificial order upon the natural order. But this one ultimate "natural feature"—the curvature of our earthly orb—could not finally be dismissed.

In the beginning, nonetheless, it was. The Land Ordinances of the 1780s did not address the problem. Nor did the Land Act of 1796. Not until 1804 did Surveyor General Jared Mansfield and his stalwart surveyors begin to work out . . . not exactly a *solution*, but a *technique* to cope with the flaw. The problem was addressed not by reconstituting the survey or reconsidering its basic principles, but through a series of pragmatic steps described in the surveyors' field manuals over the first half of the 1800s. The key innovation was the designation of regular "correction lines" that allowed the grid to be adjusted slightly by shifting its lines. The General Land Office's 1855 manual instructed the surveyors to establish correction lines "at stated intervals to provide for or counteract the error that otherwise would result from the covergency of meridians."[21] The technique could not solve the unsolvable problem; all it could do was shift the gridlines to compensate for it.

Johnson notes that, while most deviations from the grid are invisible to casual observers, the hard corners produced by correction lines are more readily seen. Across the broad landscape of the American earth, one may find what she calls "this right-angled curiosity." "Offsets through correction lines. . . . can be seen from the air because of the sharp angles they produce on north-south running section roads. On the ground they make for awkward driving, even in the twentieth century. . . . On good modern roads, corners have often been replaced by a curve."[22] We might wish to protect some of these anomalies. They might remind us of our own illusions of perfectibility. They might show us that the earth remains, despite the order we impose upon it, whole, round, and essentially wild—beyond, in the end, the willful impulse of immodest human intentions.

⤙ ⤚

Before me lies a sharp bend in the northbound road. I park along the wide grassy shoulder, fifty yards before the country road takes a ninety-degree dogleg turn to the east. A driving wind from the northwest carries the first serious chill of the fall. High pressure has also brought bright emphatic clouds. Behind them the falling sun shines resplendently. Braving the gusts, strewn flocks of mallards plummet into the field on the west side of the road, joining those already feasting on the dross of the just-harvested corn. At least a thousand birds forage in this field alone, moving methodically among gaunt remains of the summer's crop, vacuuming waste kernels.

I turn up my collar to the wind and stride north to the traffic sign, its black arrow pointing east against the yellow background. Take heed, motorists, or carom among solid oaks in the woodlot straight ahead.

Turn east. In the adjacent field, the farmer combines his corn, moving in concentric rectangles; now he approaches the far corner. The road goes straight east for a hundred yards, where another sign directs the traveler to take another ninety-degree turn, left, to head north again.

Proceed one hundred yards to the second corner. At the bend, there is activity in the branches of scrawny Chinese elms. Migrating juncos have just arrived. Some have taken to this particular spot for food and shelter from the wind, in the lee of the woodlot. A dozen birds flit from elm branch to ground, working just the thin strip of shoulder between the pavement and the roadside brambles. Like the mallards, the juncos are dining on waste corn. In this case, however, the corn has spilled over centrifugally from trucks negotiating the sharp ninety-degree curve. Close inspection reveals that the laws of physics and ecology remain intact: the corn kernels, and hence the juncos, are predominantly in the shoulder of the outer, not the inner, curve of the road.

Pause at the corner. Off to the side of the road, a yellow stake hides among the elms. A small sign mounted at its top reads:

WITNESS POST

Please do not

disturb nearby

S	M
U	A
R	R
V	K
E	E
Y	R

At the base of the post, a small aluminum shield marks the section corner.

Round the corner and face due north. Walk on. The woodlot on the left is great with oaks. The brawniest, an expansive bur oak four feet wide at breast height, dates from a time before survey markers, farmers, roads, and corn arrived in the savannas, when the Sauk and Fox and Ho-Chunk watched mallards fly among the interstitial wetlands.

Stop. Reverse course. Head back around the bend in the road.

Along the way I try to ignore, but then finally acknowledge, my civic responsibility. I pick up a can from the roadside. And another. And another. Soon my hands are full. But—good fortune!—an empty plastic ice cream bucket has also been deposited. I retrieve it, and soon fill it with cans liberated from the clutch of rhubarb, foxtail, and vetch. Maybe the bend in the road forces drivers to slow down, making it easier to toss cans. A systematic survey of many roadsides and correction line corners would provide valuable data. My own one-hundred-yard transect yields the following numbers:

Litter Type	Quantity
Busch Light	11 cans
Miller	2 cans
Budweiser	2 cans
Busch (regular)	1 can
Pabst	1 can
Mountain Dew	1 can
7-Up	1 can
Pepsi	1 can
La Croix Spring Water	1 plastic bottle ("naturally sourced")
Homemade jelly (grape)	1 jar

Thus, the first index to local beer-diversity, and a wealth of new research topics and speculation. Was a carload of passengers finishing off a twelve-pack of Busch Light even as the driver rounded the bend? Why Pepsi and no Coca-Cola? Had Coke's marketers missed this township in the battle for domination of the global cola market? And what's with that grape jelly? An agitated grandmother burning the curves of rural Wisconsin?

Walk again past the feasting mallards, one mass hopscotching another through the corn stubble.

Return to my Point of Beginning.

Before moving on, pay due respect: face true north again.

→← →→

The flaw in the survey was not fatal. For all practical purposes, the surveyor's makeshift correction lines sufficed. The grid triumphed. Where the grid was laid, we now live the world through it. It defines property. It orders the streets of cities, towns, and suburbs. It turns in on itself in subdivisions and cul-de-sacs. It dictates how we walk to school and drive to work. It guides buses, trucks, limousines, ambulances, and hearses. It shows our neighbors where to stop and tells our politicians where to campaign. It directs our backhoes, tractors, manure spreaders, plows, and combines. Our cows lie down in its green pastures. It drains water from some lands, spreads it out over others. It fixes the borders of lands we deem special enough to include in parks. It bounds our public forests and wildlife refuges. It delimits Indian reservations. Ironically, even wilderness came to be defined by the grid: when in 1924 Aldo Leopold and his colleagues in the Forest Service first traced the boundaries of the Gila Wilderness Area, they did so along survey lines.[23]

Although the grid's influence was and is ubiquitous, its triumph was not absolute. Johnson's *Order Upon the Land* is an extended study of one region, the intricately dissected coulee country of the Upper Mississippi River, where one may view "the tension between the efforts of surveyors to put a conceptual order upon the land and the country's natural configuration of hills and valleys."[24] Close examination of the grid's deviations in such places might reveal just what angle of slope, what curve of river, what depth of wetland mud, was required to give the surveyors pause and nature precedence.

One can observe other manifestations of the "tension." Angled street corners where Chicago's diagonal thoroughfares, following ancient beach ridges, game trails, and Indian paths, intersect the city's postsettlement latticework of streets. Center-pivot irrigation systems on the high plains that, due to some wrinkle in local topography, leave pie wedges of unwatered land during their circumambulations. The weird artificiality of the Four Corners of Arizona, New Mexico, Colorado, and Utah. The way Camelback Mountain blots out the otherwise uniform nighttime grid of bright Phoenix streetlights.

Such places underscore the point. The triumph of the grid, and the tenacity of the surveyors, remains mind-boggling. The consequences, for ecosystems and human communities alike, are pervasive. In organizing the way Americans have defined, distributed, possessed, exchanged, and used land, the grid has thoroughly modified the gene flows, populations, species, and communities of life in the landscape. No one has tried to review the myriad ways in which the land survey has affected the continent's flora and fauna. Even listing the mechanisms of influence would be an exhausting exercise. Just the broader categories would include encouragement of rapid agricultural development and urbanization; facilitation of habitat conversion and fragmentation; construction of roads, highways, fences, and other artificial barriers and corridors; segregation and concentration of particular land uses; various direct and indirect effects on the quality, quantity, and distribution of water; and the division of land into multiple, exclusive jurisdictions.

Examples of the grid's impact on biodiversity can be found at all levels of biological organization:

Genetic. Many of the structures that follow grid lines—roads, fences, ditches, hedges, windbreaks, shelterbelts, telephone and cable lines—serve as barriers to or, alternatively, corridors for the dispersal of organisms and the exchange of their genetic material. Roads in particular have been shown to have differential impacts on invertebrates, and on small and large mammals, depending on road width, type, and frequency of traffic. One multiyear study in a Kansas grassland, for example, found that cotton rats and prairie voles rarely crossed a three-meter-wide dirt road.[25]

Population. By directing construction of roads and other landscape features, the grid has encouraged the spread of some plant and animal populations, restricted others. In the forests of the upper Great Lakes, for example, the density of gray wolves has been found to be inversely proportional to the density of roads. In this region (where roads often follow section lines), wolves rarely occur in areas where the density of roads exceeds 0.9 linear miles per square mile.[26]

Species. The grid has had lasting impacts on the distribution of plant and animal species. For example, during the decades following European settlement of the mixed-grass prairie of Oklahoma, Kansas, and Nebraska, Osage orange was widely planted as a windbreak hedge plant (usually along the straight field borders) outside its presettlement range. This in turn allowed the eastern fox squirrel, which favors the Osage orange's softball-sized fruits, to increase its area of habitable territory by moving beyond wooded riparian zones and into the uplands.[27]

Community. The grid's demands have also altered the composition and function of plant and animal communities, both aquatic and terrestrial.[28] I regularly use County Road A, which heads north along a section line. The road neatly bisects a small, shallow pothole, less than an acre in size. To build the road around this tiny refuge for arrowheads, muskrats, and migrating buffleheads and grebes might have required a jog of fifty yards to the east or west. Now the road has become a lesson in disrupted hydrology. The compacted soils of the roadbed have changed the surface and groundwater flow. The western half-moon of wetland drains a somewhat larger catchment than the eastern. The western half holds more water through the summer; the eastern half tends to dry up.

Landscape. The effects of the grid are apparent in any landscape where it has influenced land use. For example, few factors have been so effective in galvanizing support for forestry reforms in recent decades as published images of the stark borders between clearcuts and forested lands in the American West.[29] The impact of such artificial habitat edges on the biodiversity of forest interiors has been a central focus of research in conservation biology since the early 1980s. These edges often follow the survey lines, dividing private and public forestlands as well as public land jurisdictions (i.e., national parks and national forests). In the Pacific Northwest, checkerboards of mountain forests and clearcuts mark where the Northern Pacific Railroad long ago received alternate sections of federal land.

Ecosystem. The grid brought change to entire ecosystems. The tall-grass prairies and oak savannas are among the most extensively altered ecosystems on the continent, with estimates of their loss and conversion exceeding 99 percent.[30] As William Cronon remarks in *Nature's Metropolis: Chicago and the Great West*, few other regions in the United States were better suited to the application of the federal land survey system. "By imposing the same abstract and homogeneous grid pattern on all land, no matter how ecologically diverse, government surveyors made it marketable. . . . The grid turned the prairie into a commodity, and became the foundation for all subsequent land use."[31]

In addition to its direct impacts, the grid, through the patterns of land use it facilitates, affects biodiversity by disrupting biological and ecological processes, including migration, colonization, seed dispersal, herbivory, pollination, parasitism, predation, fire, and flooding. William Romme has described, for example, how elk migration in LaPlata County, Colorado, "is becoming more difficult and dangerous for both elk and humans as their traditional movement corridors become obstructed by subdivisions and strip development along highways."[32]

The grid's pervasive effects on human communities and the character of civic life is well beyond the scope of this essay, but deserves discussion. It is no understatement to say that the continuing evolution of our social and political landscape cannot be understood apart from the grid upon which it quite literally rests. Farm economies and communities grew out of the grid; those same rural economies and communities have been depleted by the economies of scale the grid encourages. Many a Main Street was laid out along the grid line; many a Main Street has, in turn, declined through grid-abetted sprawl and rational calculations of, for example, optimal Wal-Mart placement. Only recently have commentators begun to consider the connections between the political economy the grid has engendered and the fraying strands of community life.[33]

What can we say, in sum, of the enduring effects of the land survey and its grid? The very extent of the survey and its impact on American history, ideas, and land trivializes any list of attributes. Let us mention, however, a few overarching consequences.

A tentative inventory would include the grid's many positive and long-celebrated features. Jefferson and his contemporaries devised the system with the best of intentions. The efficient process of surveying provided foundations for the nation's burgeoning wealth and its experiment in self-government. The survey gave definition to millions of freehold farms. The yeoman farmer, keeping fertile the ground of American democracy, was, in Wallace Stegner's words, "a kind of Jeffersonian hope more than he was a Jeffersonian fact."[34] Nonetheless, the availability of land opened opportunities for individual enterprise on an unprecedented scale. It grounded the very idea of democracy. The beneficiaries included not only the innumerable waves of farmers and other immigrant settlers, but veterans of the nation's wars, beginning with the Revolutionary War.

Concentration of land ownership, wealth, and political power might have been far worse without the survey. Had the older metes-and-bounds system of surveying been followed, property disputes might have been pandemic in the new nation. Setting aside momentarily that which cannot be ignored—the alienation of the continent's native inhabitants—Americans have generally been able to avoid conflicts over land possession through the survey's clear definition of property.[35] Through the setting aside of the "school reserve" sections and the eventual establishment of land grant colleges under the Morrill Land Grant Act of 1862, Americans enjoyed extraordinary access to public education. From a conservation perspective, the original survey notes and maps provide invaluable records of the land at the time of European settlement and serve as an essential source for mapping, ecological analysis, and restoration.

On the other side of the ledger are the forces that the grid directed, and with which conservationists, architects, landscape architects, economists, and planners (among others) must now contend. The survey abstracted reality. Its standardized treatment of land overwhelmed the particularities of place. It promoted land fraud, speculation, and exploitation across the continent. For generations, it encouraged the adoption of the hard utilitarian view of land as commodity, rather than (in Johnson's words) "a common good under the stewardship of its owners" or (in Aldo Leopold's words) "a community to which we belong."[36]

The land survey magnified and deepened the distinction between public and private land, and hence between public and private interest in the use of land. For our inability to bring into harmony these interests—not to mention the interests of the prior inhabitants, future generations, and other species—we continue to pay mightily. "Too much rectilinearity, tied to efficiency, in our daily environment has been an American misfortune," Hildegard Binder Johnson concluded.[37] The grid, of course, did not breathe these forces into being. Economic doctrines, land policies, and traditions of faith, philosophy, commerce, and science contributed as much, if not more, over many centuries. But the grid did give these forces exceptional opportunity to express themselves.

We inherit a grid that is simultaneously real and metaphorical. It has shaped materially our system of land use and our way of thinking about land—about the natural, the wild, the humanized, the civilized. It holds our memories and our lives and our plans. At the same time, it signifies our adherence to, and the imposition of, an abstract construction of the human mind. We have looked to the lines first, not to the land upon which the lines were laid. In this light, we can see that one of the functions of an evolving land ethic is to help us now to read in between—and across—the lines.

◄← →►

Our inheritance of the grid is a given. The question is: what will we do with it? We can neither uncritically celebrate, nor deny, its impact. If we unconditionally embrace what it has made of us and of our society, we become thoughtless patriots. If we unconditionally denounce what it has made of us, we fall into self-hate, availing nothing.

In any case, there is no return to a pre-grid world. Moreover, there is no assurance that ways of life beyond North America's grid are any better "fitted" to the land or more conducive to a sustainable future. Other humanized landscapes around the world developed, too, before ecology and evolutionary biology provided us with an alternative view of the land, its history, its "membership," and its workings. Other lands lacking the grid have nonetheless been even more thoroughly converted than North America's, leaving only the smallest patches of wildness. North Americans have inherited the grid, but it is of recent enough vintage that it still contains much residual wildness. For now.

The grid was designed to allow land tenure to be quickly and efficiently modified. It has done that. If it continues to do so in the same way, it is easy to see what lies ahead: ever more intensively used, simplified, and commodified landscapes. We are speeding on toward a wholly domesticated, extremely mechanized, and not necessarily civilized landscape. There is, however, still time to change direction. We can choose to build beauty, diversity, community, and wildness into the grid. We can accept the inheritance with new awareness, with a sense of responsibility, and with grace.

How can conservation biology, landscape ecology, and landscape design aid in this task? Part of the answer lies in understanding previous efforts to reconcile the dictates of the grid with a more humane and naturalistic vision. The tradition of such efforts is as old as the land survey itself. Vernon Carstensen notes, for example, that in 1785, George Washington and other farmers "foresaw and complained about" the influence that the straight lines and rectangular properties would have on the size and shape of fields and thus on tillage methods.[38]

The traditional 160-acre family homestead that the survey established worked reasonably well for settlers coming into the moist Midwest. But over the latter half of the 1800s, as European settlement advanced into the Great Plains and the West, the limitations of the traditional homestead under more arid conditions became apparent. In *Beyond the Hundredth Meridian*, his study of the life and career of John Wesley Powell, Wallace Stegner writes:

> [The] firmly fixed pattern of settlement, of which the rectangular surveys and the traditional quarter-section of land were only outward manifestations, though in some ways determining ones, began to meet on the Great Plains conditions that could not be stretched or lopped to fit Procrustes' bed. . . . The rectangular grid of the General Land Office could easily leave all the water for miles within a few quarter-sections, and the man who obtained title to those quarters could control thousands of surrounding acres. Instead of rectangular parcels, therefore, Powell proposed surveys based on the topography, letting farms be as irregular as they had to be to give everyone a water frontage and a patch of irrigable soil.[39]

Through the 1870s and 1880s, Powell recommended a series of land reforms in the West based on the essential reality of aridity. It was the most significant challenge to the grid's primacy that had yet been made. Powell included proposals for political organization of the arid lands along natural watershed divisions, and for cooperative management of the region's range and water resources. Such ideas sought to encourage a system of land tenure based not on the polarity, but the complementarity, of public and private interests in land. The momentum, however, of the "firmly fixed pattern of settlement" proved irresistible. Powell's visionary proposals fell dormant.

Yet, within a few short years the impetus behind Powell's recommendations would begin to counter history's momentum. The efficiencies of the grid—in alliance with settlement patterns, market forces, speculative pressures, land policies, and new technologies—stimulated exploitation of the nation's timber, water, soil, mineral, and range resources on an unprecedented scale, which in turn would trigger the Progressive Era conservation movement. In this sense, it was within the grid itself that the seeds of conservation policy germinated. By fostering irresponsible land use on an epic scale, the grid underlay the emerging movement.[40]

Even as forestry supporters, national park advocates, and game protectors pursued conservation in the nation's hinterlands, others attempted to amend the grid in urban settings. As early as 1869, Frederick Law Olmstead and Calvert Vaux introduced curvilinearity into the plans for the Riverside community near Chicago. In the decades that followed, according to Johnson, "the opposition against rectangular planning was tied to a back-to-nature movement that produced two major 'substitutes for nature' on the American scene, landscape parks and suburbs."[41] Even larger scale projects were undertaken. Early in the twentieth century, for example, civic leaders in Chicago created the chain of forest preserves that still rings the city (and that protects some of the Midwest's most important remnants of prairie and savanna ecosystems).

The underlying importance of the watershed as a landscape unit—in contrast to the superimposed sections and townships—was reaffirmed during the 1930s as the national movement for soil conservation gained force. It manifested itself on the land, as contour plowing, terracing, and strip cropping introduced curves into the grid; and in communities, as landowners organized themselves in soil conservation districts. At Coon

Valley in western Wisconsin, farmers controlling ninety-two thousand acres of private land participated in the Coon Creek Erosion Control Demonstration Project, recognized as "The First Watershed Project of the Nation."[42] Aldo Leopold supervised the wildlife management component of the project. For Leopold, the experience provided a powerful lesson in the necessity of coordination in land conservation: "Each of the various public interests in land is better off when all cooperate than when all compete with each other. . . . The crux of the land problem is to show that integrated use is possible on private farms, and that such integration is mutually advantageous to both the owner and the public."[43]

Leopold's own intellectual evolution can be interpreted in part through the grid. He was accustomed, through his training and career as a forester, to working with the grid on the ground. His early attempts to define principles of game management were carried out largely in the Midwest, where clean farming was monotonizing the biota of the typical farmstead. Leopold proposed to diversify the habitat for wildlife on farms through what he called the "interspersion of types." Such interspersion of land use types (pastures, crop fields, woodlots, old fields) created "edges" that could enhance populations of bobwhite quail, cottontail rabbits, and other small game species on the farm. In *Game Management* he reduced the technique to a neat formula: "The potential density of game of low mobility requiring two or more types is, within ordinary limits, proportional to the sum of the type peripheries."[44] Leopold's faith in such formulaic answers was soon tempered by his increased appreciation of the complexity of ecological processes and human impacts, and by the need to redefine land as more than a mere collection of isolated and independent "resources." He peered through the grid to see the land itself as the evolving expression not just of our land survey and land tenure systems, but of our scientific understanding, our history and politics and our economics, our aesthetics and our ethics.

Although the din of postwar development fervor overwhelmed Leopold's call for a land ethic, new ways of thinking about land were emerging. Coincident with the advent of environmentalism in the late 1960s, Johnson notes, planners began to adopt land-use regulations that aimed to "loosen the hold of the survey pattern on real estate development and lessen the powerful influence that the existing cadastral system had on urban planning." For example:

> An architect in Barrington, Illinois, observed that subdivision based on soil information could "minimize a variety of problems which application of a rigid arbitrary gridiron system of design ignores or accentuates." At the time of these debates and observations much of the urban-rural fringe was already frozen into the survey pattern by streets, utility installations, and lots. As a countermeasure, town planners used soil maps, which follow the lay of the land, rather than the gridiron pattern.[45]

This liberalized approach also marked the pioneering work of Ian McHarg. In *Design with Nature* (1969), McHarg demonstrated the power of using superimposed graphic data on soils, water, vegetation, and other biophysical features of the landscape in large-scale design and planning projects.[46]

Broadly speaking, these and other efforts to respond to the grid aimed to correct its perceived aesthetic, social, political, environmental, and even spiritual deficiencies. Yet, integrative though they often were, they still tended to address particular parts of the landscape—soils, waters, forests, parklands, rangelands, wildlife, suburban lots, urban neighborhoods, transportation corridors—with only incidental attention to the entire landscape mosaic, the broad spectrum of living things, and the ecological processes that characterized the place. Even so welcome a concept as "green space" lacked a certain vitality, a sense of the evolutionary and ecological drama transpiring within and between those "green spaces." They might as well have been covered with Astroturf.

⊷ ⊶

By contrast, new concepts from conservation biology, landscape ecology, restoration ecology, and other fields have looked anew at these spaces. On the premise that it is wiser to recognize and respond to the order in the land than to impose an abstract order *upon* the land, they offer new approaches to planning. They attempt to build connectivity, dynamism, community coherence, and wildness back into landscapes where fragmentation and control were not merely collateral results, but purposeful goals.[47] They evoke a new aesthetic, one that may help to ease the old tension between utility and beauty in conservation.[48]

This work may be seen at different scales. At the level of the building site, architects and designers are incorporating ecological design principles and sketching the outlines of a "sustainable architecture." These efforts are marked by their emphasis on context. In *Designing with Nature*, Ken Yeang describes the need to see the project site as more than just "a physical and spatial zone":

> Many of the current design approaches that claim to be "green" do not show a thorough understanding of the earth's ecosystems and their functioning. In an ecological design approach, the concept of the environment has to be regarded as much more inclusive, encompassing not only the physical (inorganic) milieu of the building but the biological (organic) milieu as well. In most building projects, we . . . find that the architect or the designer has completely omitted any consideration of the biological components of the project site's ecosystem.[49]

This affirmation of embeddedness is no small advance and calls for a new kind of genius. Even Frank Lloyd Wright's masterworks, for all their inspired indebtedness to the shapes and lines of midwestern prairies and Appalachian falling waters, dealt little with the actual prairie and stream ecosystems themselves.

At a larger scale, landscape ecologists are showing how the spatial arrangement of land types affects their composition and function.[50] Similarly, one of conservation biology's central tasks since the early 1980s has been to investigate how biodiversity at all levels responds to the spatial arrangement and temporal dynamics of land mosaics. Increasingly, this information is being used in conservation planning for both protected areas and private lands. Planners increasingly recognize the full value of parks and refuges, trails and open space, waterways and riparian corridors, groundwater recharge areas—the total "green infrastructure" of the communities where they work. The advent of geographic information systems (GIS) technology has powerfully extended Ian McHarg's basic approach to landscape-level planning. GIS and other new technologies now allow conservationists to synthesize relevant field data involving, for example, hotspots of species diversity, distribution of rare and endemic species, and the siting of protected areas, as well as human infrastructure.

At still larger scales, ecosystem management and community-based conservation attempt to plan, not according to abstract lines, but to the native character of whole ecosystems, human communities, and geographic regions. In this, they can be considered recent incarnations of John Wesley's Powell's unorthodox recommendations for the aridlands.[51] They seek to overcome boundaries between disciplines, agencies, interest groups, and political jurisdictions in the stewardship of shared lands and resources. They try to address the root causes, and not just the symptoms, of ecosystem dysfunction. These approaches remain unproven and even contentious. Still, they hold the potential to reweave, in more enduring patterns, the fabric of thought and life with respect to place.

Attempts to inherit the grid with conservation goals in mind have thus been considered at scales from the local to the regional to the continental.[52] All are experiments, using new ideas, data, and techniques. Yet in them we hear echoes of the hopes and dreams that the land survey was created to serve over two centuries ago. For even as we inherit the grid, with all of its benefits, costs, and unforeseen consequences, we also inherit the aims its Enlightenment authors hoped to ensure in devising it: an active and democratic citizenry, an equitable share of wealth, a stake in the land, expanding opportunities, durable communities, a home place. The difference is that we can and must see this legacy in a different, larger, more complex context.

⋖ ⋗

So, how *do* we turn this corner? How do we get from here to there? How can we fit ourselves realistically into what Gary Snyder has called "the Big Watershed."[53] Nature has given us ecological systems that we understand and appreciate in new ways. History has bestowed upon us political systems and boundaries that evolved before ecology transformed our view of land. The natural and political systems operate at different scales of time and space. The pace of change within and between them varies. Hence confusion, and the sharp bend in the road before us.

Our task is to work with our natural and cultural legacies based on a realistic assessment of the situation. We need more than a merely romantic rebellion against the aesthetics of the gridded landscape. We need well-grounded ways of dealing with the social, economic, aesthetic, and environmental costs that are now, because of the grid, inherent in the landscape.

To negotiate the turn successfully, we will need to slow down, look around, watch for signs, and admit the world's nonlinearity and complexity, its beauty and mystery. We will need to consult the White Bear of the North.

We should not underestimate the task. There are major obstacles ahead: deeply ingrained land-use traditions bolstered at every turn by economic and political incentives; globalizing economies that undermine care for the local; extreme views of private property that have everything to say about rights and nothing to say about responsibilities; the drag of the already built; inherent degrees of scientific uncertainty; the constant challenge of crafting interdisciplinary solutions in a disciplinary culture; ethical systems that have only begun to extend our notions of community beyond the human circle; the persistent loss of native knowledge and traditions.

A sobering prognosis. We are led on—by the push of history and the pull of posterity. We go forward out of necessity and responsibility. On the journey to become native to this place, each generation takes its turn, and prepares a path for those who follow.

10

The Once and Future Land Ethic

I have purposefully presented the land ethic
as a product of social evolution because
nothing so important as an ethic is ever
"written."

—ALDO LEOPOLD (1949)

THIS SENTENCE, appearing near the end of "The Land Ethic," is arguably the most important Aldo Leopold ever wrote. With these words he acknowledged the limits of his own efforts to frame a large and complex idea. He understood that such an ethic could form and evolve only "in the minds of a thinking community."[1] The author of the essay "The Land Ethic" did not, and could not, "write" the land ethic. No one person could. And *everyone* could.

Which is not to say that Leopold did not pour himself into "The Land Ethic." His essay distilled a lifetime of observing, reading, writing, thinking, experimenting, blundering, and always asking the next question about the very meaning of conservation.[2] In it Leopold sought nothing less than to redirect the conservation movement by blending knowledge and insights from the natural sciences, history, literature, ethics, economics, aesthetics, and public policy. It was the culminating expression of Leopold's intellectual, professional, and spiritual growth.

Yet Leopold recognized the contingent nature of the land ethic— perhaps because the idea evolved continually in his own thinking, in varied landscapes. In any case, by explicitly framing his idea as the "tentative" expression of one member of a thinking community, Leopold opened wide the discussion. The land ethic might have gone down in history as the idiosyncratic expression of a mid-twentieth century naturalist, scientist, and writer. Instead, with his self-abnegating assertion, Leopold liberated the land ethic. He gave his readers a stake in the idea, and a responsibility to develop it. He invited other voices to join the conversation, thus ensuring that it would remain vigorous. Each of us as individuals, as members of different communities, and as participants in a broader culture, may help to "write" the land ethic.

What forces will shape the land ethic in the future? How must the concept of a land ethic evolve in order to thrive and provide guidance to conservation in the twenty-first century? There are, of course, innumerable answers to these questions. It is possible, however, to identify at least some overarching challenges a land ethic will need to meet to remain vital.

The land ethic will need to embrace, and be embraced by, new constituencies. How can the land ethic be nurtured within diverse and constantly changing human communities, with different traditions and relationships to land? Aldo Leopold's land ethic reflected the social realities of his time and place. Looking ahead, it is not difficult to predict that as our societies, economies, and demographics change, so will our environmental concerns. This will redefine what conservation is and how we pursue it. It will call for a blending of varied cultural traditions and values, with priorities that do not always mesh, and that may well be in conflict.

Fortunately, such openness and inclusiveness is in greater evidence now than perhaps at any time since Leopold's day. Conservation crosses cultural divides in a way it did not in Leopold's generation, with increasing appreciation of the complicated connections between healthy landscapes, communities, and identity.[3] Community-based approaches to conservation require that people be invested with responsibilities for decisions that affect the quality and sustainability of their home landscapes. Educational programs and new technologies provide access to information in ways that did not exist even a few years ago. Faith communities throughout the world have looked to their traditions for affirmation of environmental values. The environmental justice movement has opened opportunities for honest conversations on shared concerns—in much the same manner that Leopold tried to do in "The Land Ethic."

As these trends continue, the effort must involve more than merely communicating *the* land ethic *to* new constituencies. Rather, it will require

expanding the "thinking community" and encouraging people to understand themselves and their stories through their relationships to land. To
neglect such diverse voices is to leave, in Lauret Savoy's words, a "strength
. . . only partially realized." By contrast, when voices join, new worlds are
made possible: "Perhaps then we might fully imagine and comprehend
who and what we are with respect to each other and with respect to this
land. What is defined by some as an edge of separation between nature and
culture, people and place, is where common ground is possible."[4]

*The land ethic will need to respond to emerging scientific insights and shift-
ing scientific foundations.* How will the land ethic adapt to the insights that
flow from the natural sciences? Leopold's land ethic rested upon a solid
foundation of interdisciplinary science, but that foundation is itself subject
to continuous intellectual evolution. Over the last half of the twentieth
century revolutions occurred in every field of natural science, including
geology (especially plate tectonic theory), climatology, oceanography,
marine biology, hydrology, limnology, paleontology, biogeography, sys-
tematics, genetics, wildlife biology, forestry, and the agricultural sciences.
These revolutions have rumbled on beneath the surface of the land ethic.
If it is to stand, the land ethic must be supple and flexible.

In particular, the land ethic will need to reflect advances in the fields of
evolutionary biology, biogeography, environmental history, and ecology.
Over the last several decades, evolutionary biology and paleontology have
recast our understanding of ancient, "deep time" extinctions. We have a
much clearer picture of the impact of the human diaspora out of Africa on
the world's landscapes and biotas over the last hundred thousand years,
including the period of Pleistocene extinctions that "set the stage" for
today's living world.[5] Island biogeography and environmental history
have revealed the broad patterns of change that have shaped biotas, landscapes, ecosystems, and cultures over more recent centuries and decades.[6]
In ecology, emphasis has shifted away from the classic "balance of nature"
idea to a better-informed "flux of nature" paradigm that accounts for the
dynamic nature of ecosystems.[7]

In response to these changes, and others yet to come, conservationists
will need to incorporate the lessons of environmental history and sort out
the biological impacts of human activities at various scales of time and

space. This has already been happening in conservation biology, restoration ecology, and other fields. But the land ethic is not just for scientists. Conservation-minded citizens must also become familiar with these scientific advances to critically understand such issues, for example, as species invasions, fire management, aquifer depletion, and emerging diseases.

The land ethic will need to extend across, and recognize connections within, the entire landscape. How can the land ethic help to revive and strengthen bonds of common interest within the landscape and within conservation? Leopold's work focused on the health of wild, semiwild, and rural lands. His ethic spanned a broad range of conservation interests. But changes in society, the economy, and the landscape itself have undermined that fragile unity. Conservation's constituency has fragmented, as evidenced especially in increased polarization between urban and suburban environmentalists and rural people who own and work land. That fragmentation has been aided and abetted by those with special interests in particular parts of the landscape. Conservation, by contrast, is all about protecting the public interest in the beauty, diversity, and health of the landscape as a whole.

In his more expansive moments, Leopold tried to stretch his notion of a land ethic beyond those parts of the landscape he was especially interested in. In lecture notes from the 1940s he wrote,

> There must be some force behind conservation—more universal than profit, less awkward than government, less ephemeral than sport; something that reaches into all times and places, where men live on land, something that brackets everything from rivers to raindrops, from whales to hummingbirds, from land estates to window-boxes. I can see only one such force: a respect for land as an organism; a voluntary decency in land-use exercised by every citizen and every land-owner out of a sense of love for and obligation to that great biota we call America. This is the meaning of conservation, and this is the task of conservation education.[8]

Leopold was not alone in such expressions. In "The Land Ethic" he was indeed speaking on behalf of a community of conservation scientists, thinkers, and advocates who found common cause, and assumed a common responsibility.

There was no past golden age when conservation united people across social, economic, and political divides. However, there have been periods when the conservation consensus was unusually strong: the early years of the Progressive movement, the "dirty thirties," the Earth Day awakening of the early 1970s. Unfortunately, such consensus seems to emerge only in response to environmental crises—widespread deforestation and wildlife destruction, extensive soil erosion, unchecked environmental contamination and pollution, depletion of the earth's ozone layer. The question is: must it always be so? Or can conservation go on the offensive and provide a positive vision of the public good to be gained through environmental stewardship?

To do so, conservationists will have to assume many chores: linking concern for wild lands and the more developed parts of the landscape; forging a renewed movement for the conservation of private lands; recognizing, as Wes Jackson has noted, that "if we don't save agriculture, we won't save wilderness"[9]; bringing urban and suburban dwellers into conversations about conservation; taking seriously the connections between land, fresh water, and the marine environment. The land ethic cannot meaningfully endure if the fragmentation of interests prevails. It will flourish if it makes connections.

The land ethic will need to be extended to the aquatic and marine realms. How can the land ethic fully embrace water resources and aquatic ecosystems, and encourage an "ocean ethic"? We are terrestrial creatures with terrestrial biases. Only with time have even conservationists come to appreciate the essential connections between groundwater, surface waters, and atmospheric waters, and between water as a vital ecosystem component and a basic human need.

Leopold explicitly included water in his definition of "land" and devoted significant professional energies to understanding human impacts on watersheds and aquatic systems.[10] Aldo's son Luna, a renowned hydrologist and conservationist in his own right, defined the essential point: "Water is the most critical resource issue of our lifetime and our children's lifetime. The health of our waters is the principal measure of how we live on the land."[11] The headlines give regular notice of increasing pressures, locally and globally, on the quality, quantity, distribution, and uses of water and the health of aquatic ecosystems. These pressures are sure to increase in the century ahead and will inevitably raise issues of access, equity, and justice. Understanding water connections and articulating an ethic to guide the protection and careful use of water are urgent tasks not only for conservationists, but society at large.[12]

Until recently, conservationists have lagged in their attention to the oceans. With the popularity of Rachel Carson's ocean books and Jacques Cousteau's films in the 1950s and 1960s, marine conservation began to enter public consciousness. Although cetaceans, sea turtles, and other groups of organisms focused concern on the oceans, only in the 1990s did conservationists begin to consider more systematically the status and needs of marine resources, biodiversity, and ecosystems. Once again, however, consensus has come only in the wake of acute disasters—depleted fisheries, highly disrupted marine food webs, expanding "dead zones," the global spread of aquatic invasive species, intensified coastline development, the widespread degradation of coral reefs, mangrove swamps, estuaries, and other sensitive marine communities.

The conservation of marine biodiversity and the need for an "ocean ethic" now appear to be gaining the attention they have long required. New organizations have formed to raise awareness of marine conservation issues. Conservation biology has entered the marine realm, helping to establish marine protected areas and develop (hopefully) more sustainable, ecosystem-based fishing regimes.[13] For communities whose economies, livelihoods, and cultural identity depend on marine resources, sustainability is no vague abstraction. As the song goes, "No more fish, no fishermen."[14]

In this century, we will either remain mere consumers of the seas' bounty or become true caretakers of marine communities. Marine biologist and conservationist Carl Safina writes, "People who think of themselves as conservationists carry a concern for wildlife, wild lands, habitat quality, and sustainable extraction as part of the collective ethic, their sense of right and wrong. It is high time to take these kinds of ideas below high tide, and a sea ethic is the perfect vessel in which to begin the voyage."[15] The vastness, complexity, and mystery of the oceans have allowed us to postpone that project. The longer we delay, the more difficult the voyage will be.

The land ethic will need to confront directly the challenges posed by human population growth, and contribute to the shaping of a parallel consumption ethic. How can the land ethic help to address the pressures arising from human population growth responsibly, respectfully, and effectively? Will we recognize and act upon the connections between ecosystem health and resource consumption? These have always been among the most politically and economically vexing issues in conservation. They are the eight-hundred-pound gorillas whose presence we would just as soon not acknowledge.

But with the human population now over six billion, the interrelated trends of continued population growth and intensified resource consumption cannot be avoided. For decades—indeed, since Thomas Malthus's day—warring ideological camps have debated the relationship between population growth, economic development, and environmental degradation. Because the issue involves fundamental assumptions of economic philosophy, and cuts so very close to the political bone, the moments of consensus have been rare and elusive. The rapid growth and movement of the human population over the last century has no precedent in human history, and our inherited ethical systems provide too little guidance in response.

If the land ethic has any special contribution to make, it may be to draw attention to the land itself; to steer the discussion away from raw ideology and toward careful consideration of the quality of life, human and otherwise, over the long run. If there is to be any consensus, it will have to grow out of the realization that population and consumption are necessarily connected: environmental change is a function of both our numbers and our ways of life. Neither factor in the equation can be ignored. At present we tend to ignore both.

In the 1920s, Aldo Leopold pointed out the need for honesty in addressing consumption patterns and choices. He wrote, "A public which lives in wooden houses should be careful about throwing stones at lumbermen, even wasteful ones, until it has learned how its own arbitrary demands as to kinds and qualities of lumber help cause the waste which it decries. . . . The long and short of the matter is that forest conservation depends in part on intelligent consumption, as well as intelligent production of lumber."[16] His point extended beyond just forestry and wood products: conservation and consumption were, and are, connected. As forester Doug MacCleery has framed it, a land ethic that ignores those connections amounts to "half a loaf."[17] We need the whole loaf. "Intelligent consumption," were we to achieve it, would defy the assumptions of both modern hyperconsumer culture and of that brand of environmentalism that prefers to avert its eyes from the impacts of personal consumer choices.

The land ethic will need to help reform the traditional economic worldview to include conservation concerns in a meaningful way. Can the land ethic have deep and meaningful impact on the human economic enterprise? This is the 750-pound gorilla. For all the discussion of sustainability in recent decades, conservation has had a hard time gaining a full hearing within the dominant schools of neoclassical economics. Especially with rapid globalization and technological change driving economic development, conservation receives scant attention in the salons of high finance and international trade.

Is there room, in the long run, for true reconciliation of economic and ecological worldviews? Is there any safe way out of our current addiction to the quarterly earnings report to a sincere commitment to the seventh generation? Leopold worded his own views with extreme care: "We abuse land because we regard it as a commodity belonging to us. When we see land as a community to which we belong, we may begin to use it with love and respect." Leopold thus held out the possibility of *loving and respectful use.* But he took no comfort in the early expressions of the post–World War II economic boom. He saw a society "so obsessed with its own economic health as to have lost the capacity to remain healthy."[18] He did not live long enough to see the obsession become the norm.

In framing the land ethic, Leopold joined a long line of economic dissenters in the conservation tradition, stretching from George Perkins Marsh to Henry George to E. F. Schumacher to Herman Daly. That line took a new turn beginning in the 1980s. Economists operating under the banners of ecological economics and sustainable development began to challenge economic orthodoxy.[19] Although they have not yet convinced their disciplinary colleagues of the need to see the human economy as a "wholly owned subsidiary" of the global ecosystem, they have forced the boundaries of the

conversation outward. They have explored new ways to value nature, redefine capital, and build conservation-based economies.[20] Many a battle yet to
come will be framed reflexively according to shopworn jobs-versus-the-
environment myths. But conservationists are gaining new tools with which
they can not just wage the battle, but dispel the myth.

*The land ethic will need to engage, and find acceptance within, diverse dis-
ciplines, vocations, and professions.* How can serious consideration of the
land ethic be encouraged beyond its core devotees in the natural sciences,
environmental and conservation groups, and resource management professions? An effective land ethic will require commitment from a wide
spectrum of fields and occupations. Architects, designers, engineers, planners, artists, builders, bankers, clergy, teachers, doctors, farmers, manufacturers, business owners: all have an impact on land and the way people
regard land. All may benefit from the innovative thinking that arises when
land is regarded as more than just raw material or scenery.

In one of his lesser-known classic articles, "The Role of Wildlife in a
Liberal Education" (1942), Leopold included a simple graphic of food
chains to illustrate the "lines of dependency . . . in an ordinary community" of Wisconsin. One chain extended, rather conventionally, from rock
to soil to ragweed to mouse to fox. Another, however, linked rock to soil
to alfalfa to cow to farmer . . . to grocer . . . to lawyer . . . to student;
another branched off, going from cow to farmer . . . to implement maker
. . . to mechanic . . . to union secretary. Leopold's point was that to think
of "the wild community [as] one thing, the human community another"
was erroneous.[21]

When human communities are reconceived along such lines, all members have a role—and an interest—in formulating a land ethic. And new
connections are made. It becomes possible, for example, to think of ecologically informed design, sustainable architecture, and the "green infrastructure" of cities. It becomes important to think of the relationships
between individual and public health, the environment, and biodiversity. It
becomes prudent to plan and account for true costs, with the ecosystem in
mind. It becomes exciting to teach, and learn, across disciplines. The land
ethic becomes not just a rationale for protecting nature, but a means of
enriching community life.

The land ethic will need to promote awareness and critical thinking among young people. How can the land ethic, in the face of rapid changes in education and in society, encourage curiosity and critical judgment among students? In "The Land Ethic" Leopold noted the dilemma educators face. "Despite nearly a century of propaganda," he noted, "progress [in conservation] still consists largely of letterhead pieties and convention oratory." He agreed that more education was needed. "No one will debate this, but "is it certain that only the *volume* of education needs stepping up? Is something lacking in the *content* as well?"[22]

Propaganda was not to be confused with education. The quality of conservation education depended, in part, on a positive understanding of land as a dynamic community, which in turn depended on "an understanding of ecology." But, Leopold lamented, "this is by no means co-extensive with 'education'; in fact, much education seems deliberately to avoid ecological concepts. An understanding of ecology does not necessarily originate in courses bearing ecological labels; it is quite as likely to be labeled geography, botany, agronomy, history, or economics."[23] At the heart of the matter: modern education divides the world into subjects, disciplines, and fields, while effective conservation education requires an appreciation of relationships. We need, in David Orr's words, to "connect thought, words, and deeds with our obligations as citizens of the land community."[24]

Environmental education has made great strides over the last quarter century. Has the effort succeeded merely in exposing students to "correct" attitudes, or has it given them the tools to think, feel, and act with clarity and independence? It is a tough but necessary question to ask. For the land ethic to endure, students (of all ages) will need to be emotionally and intellectually engaged in the world around them. In a world where distractions reign, they will need to acquire the wisdom of their places: the rocks and weathers, soils and waters, plants and animals, origins and histories, people and cultures. And it will need to be more than a chore; it has to be an unending adventure.

The land ethic will need to provide encouragement and guidance for expanded community-based conservation projects. How can the land ethic more effectively encourage local responsibility for land and stimulate cooperative measures to protect, restore, and sustain land health? "A land ethic," Leopold wrote, "reflects the existence of an ecological conscience, and this in turn reflects a conviction of individual responsibility for the health of the land."[25] As Leopold recognized, individuals can act upon that conviction in various ways: as landowners, consumers, voters, students, parents, employees. Community-based conservation provides one more avenue through which individuals may act: as neighbors sharing a place.

The conservation movement has seen an explosion of innovation and energy at the local level, at home and around the world. Nongovernmental, community-based organizations—conservancies, watershed groups, land trusts, neighborhood associations, and a wild array of alliances, co-ops, partnerships, coalitions, projects, and councils—have transformed the social landscape of conservation. While there are older precedents to these efforts, the rise of community-based conservation is a new and potentially powerful force for change on the land and in civil society. It does not replace either individual or governmental action; it supplements them, providing new opportunities to reclaim common ground and enhance the public interest.[26]

The magnitude of our conservation needs, and the limits of both individual and governmental action in meeting them, are such that community-based projects must continue to expand. But it will be no small challenge for these organizations to stay on course, sustain themselves, resist provincialism, and incorporate solid science in their work.[27] The community-based conservation movement is one of the most hopeful recent indicators that the land ethic is alive and well, and dispersing into new fields. In the decades to come, the health of that movement will be a gauge of our overall societal commitment to the land.

The land ethic will need to build upon its roots in the American experience while remaining adaptable in other settings. How can the land ethic continue to grow if it was, and is, the product of a specific time and place? The land ethic, as Leopold framed it, emerged in response to particular landscapes, cultural traditions, and historical circumstances. It is an achievement to be proud of, and defended with vigor. Just as the American people have struggled, so painfully, to free themselves, from the original sin of slavery, so have we at least begun to emancipate ourselves from what Donald Worster has described as our "fanatical drive against the earth."[28] Much damage, to be sure, has been done—to the American land, and to ourselves in the process. We have much yet to do to redeem past losses, and to prevent new wounds. But in the last century we have also created a national ethic to provide guidance along the way.

Meanwhile, the land ethic has outgrown its American origins. It has done so in different ways. Over the last half century, especially, the land ethic has contributed to the emergence of a global environmental ethic (through, for example, the decade-long international effort to draft the Earth Charter).[29] It has crossed borders to influence the conservation policies of other nations. It has changed the way scientists, resource managers, policy makers, advocates, and business leaders are trained, regardless of location. But it has also inspired local conservation efforts in communities worldwide.

Still, the land ethic as conceived by Americans cannot be simply "transferred." Ethics cannot be exported, only evoked. Even within the United States, the land ethic continues to evolve in varied ecological, cultural, and historical contexts. It sets high goals—in Leopold's language, safeguarding "the capacity of the land for self-renewal" and protecting "the integrity, stability, and beauty of the biotic community"[30]—but no one prescribed path. To thrive, the land ethic will need to tell the stories, sing the songs, and dance the dances of people in their own home places.

≺≺ ≻≻

These needs (and no doubt others) will shape the land ethic in unpredictable ways in the century ahead. Other realities will surely influence our land ethic conversations. To name a few: climate change, continued international tensions and cultural conflicts, the transition beyond oil-based economies, global patterns of trade and development, and population growth and migration. But as members of the "thinking community," and citizens in a democracy that itself faces crucial challenges, we are obliged to continue "writing" the land ethic, not only with words but on the land. That process has a long history on this continent, and around the world. It began long before Aldo Leopold wrote his "tentative summary." It will continue as long as we care about people, land, and the connections between them.

11

Home, Land, Security

Come, I will make the continent indissoluble. . . .
I will make divine, magnetic lands. . . .
I will plant companionship thick as trees along
  all the rivers of America, and along the shores
  of the great lakes, and all over the prairies. . . .
    —WALT WHITMAN (1892)

I

In "For You O Democracy," one of the signature poems in *Leaves of Grass*, Walt Whitman bore witness to a land that in his day was both ripe with potential and riven with social and political discord. How, these days, shall we read Whitman? Should we yearn nostalgically for the young republic, so full of promise, that he surveyed? Should we scoff knowingly and ironically at his naiveté, his happy vision of a land characterized by civil "companionship" and the self-governing capacity of its citizens? Should we dare hope that such a democracy might yet emerge so apparently late in the national ball game? We may question even the notion of a national or continental poet: Who, we may ask, is *he* to speak for *me*? Then there is the hardest question of all: Who cares?

If, however, notions of responsible citizenship, general welfare, and national vision retain any currency, we can turn again, for perspective, to Whitman's democratic vistas, the places where he found a sense of the unity and shared adventure of America. In "Crossing Brooklyn Ferry," he gathered up the generations:

It avails not, time nor place—distance avails not,
　I am with you, men and women of a generation, or ever so many
　generations hence. . . .
　What is it then between us?
　What is the count of the scores or hundreds of years between us?[1]

While "Facing West from California's Shores," he gathered up the globe, and the mystery of our undetermined destiny:

Long having wander'd since, round the earth having wander'd,
Now I face home again, very pleas'd and joyous,
(But where is what I started for so long ago?
And why is it yet unfound?)[2]

Between the continent's borders—the Atlantic and Pacific shores—Whitman saw a land whose natural abundance would finally give rise to a vigorous democracy. "All the vast materials of America" would produce a more robust body politic; the vivid landscapes of the New World would bring forth "the new society at last, proportionate to Nature." Those phrases are from "Song of the Redwood-Tree." In those preforestry, pre-conservation days, Whitman could rationalize the loss of the great red-woods under the "crackling blows of axes," and could celebrate the "Clearing of the ground for broad humanity, the true America, heir of the past so grand / To build a grander future."[3]

Americans may still share (although seldom articulate) Whitman's perception that the health of this democracy is somehow tied to the state of the soils, waters, forests, mountains, and prairies.[4] But we are no longer universally secure in our devotion to the old formula: nature transformed = society fulfilled. Even as Whitman's great work was achieving its final form, that simple formula was coming into question. Whitman's ninth and last edition of *Leaves of Grass* was published in 1892, as President Benjamin Harrison was establishing the nation's first forest reserves.

The decades since have witnessed the transformation of North America on a scale Whitman could not have imagined, and the emergence of a conservation movement that has served, in essence, as mediator between the body politic and the land upon which it rests. Conservation, through all its phases of development, has elaborated an essential insight that even the visionary Whitman may have undervalued: land provides not merely the "vast materials" and setting for the experiment in democracy, but is in fact the proving ground of that democracy's success. "The landscape of any farm is the owner's portrait of himself," Aldo Leopold wrote.[5] In the end, the landscape of America is our portrait of ourselves.

America's political adventure is embedded deeply within an ecological and evolutionary context. The nation is, in Wallace Stegner's words, "the unfinished product of a long becoming."[6] In becoming who and what we are, we have divided and bounded ourselves and the land in ways that reflect the epochs in our history, the conflicting values we have inherited, the varied goals to which we have aspired, the many forces that shape our individual and social condition. How shall we regard these physical, political, and cultural boundaries? How do they shape our efforts to live carefully and respectfully with each other, with the land, with the creatures that share the land and the processes that characterize it? These questions lead inevitably toward consideration of the oldest and most fundamental challenge that we as social creatures face: can we harmonize self-interest and the common good? Stated otherwise: can we successfully mesh the self-interest of free individuals and the well-being of those entities within which the individual exists—the family, neighborhood, town, county, state, nation, tribe, the aquifer, watershed, salmon run and flyway, landscape and atmosphere? If so, what will it take?

Before venturing answers to such questions, we should try to define the core issue that Whitman pondered. What was it, he wondered, that we "started for so long ago?" And "why is it yet unfound?"

◄+ +►

We would all frame our answers to those questions differently. But every answer, it seems, revolves around, and sooner or later resolves itself in, matters of *security*. We draw boundaries to provide security, and we assume they will. But as doubts and evidence to the contrary grow, more questions arise. What is it we are trying to *secure*, in both senses of the word: what are we trying to *obtain*, and what are we trying to *safeguard*? And how well have our boundaries served us in the effort?

A case study. My friend Thorsten lives in an urban neighborhood of single-family homes. He enjoys city life, although he occasionally drops hints about a move to the country, where he might stretch out, indulge his aptitude for tinkering, and reconnect with his more rural childhood. That he has not yet felt the need to make such a move is due in part to the glories of his backyard. Under a canopy of birch and white pine, the former owner of the house, a professor of botany at the nearby university, nurtured a rich mixture of native woodland wildflowers. For each of the twenty-odd years since Thorsten acquired the house, he has savored his seasonal inheritance of bluebells, trout lilies, dutchman's breeches, and trillium.

One midwinter day, a neighbor removed several cottonwoods from the lot next door. The neighbor was building a new garage and widening the driveway between their houses. But, having intended to remove just two trees, the neighbor ended up clearing the entire side of his lot. Thorsten immediately realized that the project threatened his endowment of shade- and moisture-loving plants.

As the winter days lengthened, and the sun's daily arc expanded, the ecological status quo shifted incrementally, inexorably. Faced with the dilemma, and no place to transplant, my friend made the best of the situation. An electrician, he has long needed more garage storage space himself. In his own remodeling project, he managed to provide refuge for at least some of the threatened wildflowers. The final tally: one new garage; one remodeled garage; a boon for local contractors; a diminished diversity of plants, colors, connections; the dwindling of a late professor's legacy; a shaken sense of certainty in the spring.

Just one of countless backyard dramas, but it suggests the complexity of our larger dilemma. If a shared sense of place, value, and expectation is so elusive at home, how can we expect to find it at larger geographic scales, where the spectrum of needs and values is so much broader? Difficult as it is to be stewards of our own backyards, how shall we be so in our watersheds, our ecosystems, our nation, our earth? Can we "make the continent indissoluble"? Is there any hope, in truth, of securing the common good across boundaries? Can we agree on what the common good is? Can we agree that there *is* a common good? Is there even a *we*?

◄► ►►

Increasingly we seek personal and national security not in Whitman's "companionship" of neighbors, but in isolation, behind boundaries. Analogously, conservationists once rested secure in the knowledge that once the boundary of the public park or forest or wildlife refuge was declared, the life within it would dwell forever in safety. But history, ecology, and conservation biology have shown how illusory this sense of security can be. In fact, boundaries, if not understood in terms of both their *content* and their *context*, can undermine security in any lasting sense.

The American view of security was deeply conflicted even before the wrenching events of September 11, 2001. For proof we need only look into the fearsome mirror of television advertisements, at an iconic image of the 1990s: through a typical landscape of western grandeur, a large and expensive four-wheel-drive vehicle effortlessly negotiates a series of obstacles— falling boulders, tumbling logs, slick waters—before arriving safe at home, behind a heavy-duty fence. Then the tag line: this vehicle provides "a little security in an insecure world." Hidden darkly under the sophisticated words and imagery is the same old anxiety that Whitman identified. Despite our extravagant economic success (or maybe because of it), we are vulnerable. Meanwhile, the very notion of security has shrunk to the mean dimensions of the sport utility vehicle's well-upholstered interior.

Modern though such expressions of anxiety are, the concern for security obviously has deep biological roots, a long human history, and a venerable place in mythologies worldwide. In the Western tradition, we may trace it back to the expulsion from Eden, and the loss of security that came with self-awareness, curiosity, and the apprehension of mortality. There was security in that primeval paradise, but just one bite from the fruit of the wrong tree rendered it, one might say, unsustainable.

The word "paradise" was first used by Xenophon to describe the walled gardens of Persian kings and noblemen—segregated islands of beautiful space, abode for the blessed and righteous, embedded within but differentiated from wild, profane nature. In some connotations (the Oxford dictionary tells us), "paradise" referred to an oriental park or pleasure ground, "esp. one enclosing wild beasts for the chase."[7] Within the garden walls, wild nature—from which the garden emerged, and upon which the garden yet depended—could be ordered. It could become symbolic, separated from the larger reality, yet providing connection to it.

It is not so great a leap from the walled gardens of Persian estates, with their imported and impounded lions, oryx, and bustards, to a midwestern backyard plot of trillium and bluebells. Expelled from paradise and bearing the burden of original sin, Westerners have ventured forth, seeking security and freedom in Edens new. The notion found literally fertile ground on the shores of the New World. In the democratic American context, the search for Eden has been, in Donald Worster's words, "the key environmental idea, and at once the most destructive and most creative. . . . America, we have believed, is literally the Garden of Eden restored. It is the paradise once lost but now happily regained. . . . That mythic belief in Eden restored lies at the very core of our peculiar national identity. It is the primary source of our self-confidence and our legendary, indefatigable optimism. . . . We are still a people in love with our prolific Garden."[8]

Love and caring are all bound up in the matter of borders. Loving the Garden, but wanting to possess a piece of it, the new Americans divided and bounded it in new ways, altering profoundly the place of its prior human and nonhuman inhabitants.[9] Much was gained—for some—in the process. The bounding of the land afforded its new possessors security against the arbitrary authority of states and sovereigns. The surveying and distributing of land offered an alternative to concentrated land ownership and the endowment of a land-rich elite. Individuals and corporations gained opportunities to build private wealth. And when such opportunities were abused in the extreme, a national conservation movement emerged in response. The bounding and reserving of public lands provided at least temporary respite from the impacts of unfettered greed and hubristic resource management.

Through it all, much too was sacrificed. Worster writes, "Confident of having regained paradise, complacent and blissful in its midst, we have lost much of what we have most loved."[10] The search for what we lost continues. It brought Whitman to the far edge of the continent, to ask on behalf of all those who "round the earth having wander'd. . . . Where is what I started for so long ago? And why is it yet unfound?" Where might one finally find security, freedom, *paradise*—if not in California, then *where?*

In the domestic sphere we increasingly seek our paradise, as did the Persian nobles, in enclaves. The sign of our times is the one at the entrance to yet another "gated community," for those who can afford to purchase some safety and refuge. Building walls against the profane and uncontrollable threats of crime, poverty, congestion, pollution, noise and ugliness, new ideas and messy realities, we flee not west into the Pacific Ocean, but back inward to the open land at the edge of town, the planned neighborhood, the subdivision with a view, the clean place of security "in an insecure world."[11]

What of the larger sphere of the natural? Many environmentalists have proceeded on the assumption that wildness segregated is wildness saved. Sometimes the strategy of establishing protected areas has been followed in full confidence of its effectiveness; sometimes because it was the best or only strategy available at the time; sometimes because it was and remains necessary. But there is no ultimate security for wild things and wild places behind boundaries.[12] In a strictly biological sense, that illusion was suspect at least as long ago as the 1940s. Aldo Leopold noted in *A Sand County Almanac* that "many animal species, for reasons unknown, do not seem to thrive as detached islands of population." He noted, for example, that the national parks would "not suffice as a means of perpetuating the larger carnivores" or herbivore herds, and "are certainly too small for such a far-ranging species as the wolf."[13] We now have a much better handle on the reasons why wildlife populations respond as they do to changes in their home ranges and ecosystems. We no longer assume that refuge borders can provide sufficient security. Nor do we regard refuges as separate from the ecosystems or social systems in which they are embedded.[14]

We have arrived at a point where ancient yearnings for security meet modern ecological realities. Our science and our stories, and the testimony of our own eyes and ears, inform us of a deficiency in the landscape. Wendell Berry has defined clearly these connections among security, conservation, and community:

> There are two ways by which individual success and security can be made (within mortal limits) successful and secure: they must rest on a sound understanding and practice of economic justice; and they must involve and be involved in the success and security of the community. . . . If we are looking for insurance against want and oppression, we will find it only in our neighbors' prosperity and goodwill and, beyond that, in the good health of our worldly places, our homelands. If we were sincerely looking for a place of safety, for real security and success, then we

would begin to turn to our communities—and not the communities simply of our human neighbors, but also of the water, earth, and air, the
plants and animals, all the creatures with whom our local life is shared.
We would be looking too for another kind of freedom.[15]

Ultimately, for us in our social lives, but also for our prized protected
places and biodiversity generally, security cannot be found in simple
sequestration; it must entail good relations. The *content* of all gardens, no
matter how well-walled, no matter how successfully isolated, managed,
and fortified, is connected to and influenced by their *context*—obviously,
by elemental processes involving sunlight, temperature, topography,
bedrock, soil, air, fire, water, and plant, animal, and microbial life; but also
by human political, economic, and demographic forces. There is no security for biodiversity, or in the long run for people, if our interests as individuals and communities are harshly segregated. In the words of Paul
Johnson, "a nation that ends up with urban islands on one side, and islands
of wildland on another side, and a vast sea of food and fiber factories in
between, is not a geography of hope."[16]

Our boundaries, especially the boundaries of public lands and protected
areas, present a complex paradox. Our protected places were originally established to promote the possibility of better *integration* of the public and private
spheres. As Worster notes, "The conservation movement emerged out of
discontent with an intensely private approach to land ownership and rights.
It has been an effort to define and assert broader communitarian values, some
idea of a public interest transcending the wants and desires of a strictly individualistic calculus."[17] Americans as a democratic people chose, and still
choose, to draw boundaries and delineate public parks, forests, refuges, grasslands, marine reserves, and wilderness areas in order to conserve their natural features and to balance public and private interests and values.

Now, a century into the conservation movement, conservationists are
seeking to resolve this paradox, and to embark on a new conservation strategy. Boundaries have served historically (and remain necessary) to conserve the wild. Now, for different reasons but toward the same end, the
spaces need to be reconnected and linkages made—linkages not only in the
landscape, but between the landscape and ourselves. To secure nature's

legacy of beauty and biodiversity for the future, we need to address the impact of boundaries, and of our individual "wants and desires."

Can we overcome boundaries in pursuit of the common good? The question can be read in diametrically opposite ways. On the one hand, it seems hopelessly idealistic to consider the possibility. The question might as well be: can we become better *people*, more cooperative, more far-sighted, more considerate—better "companions" in Whitman's sense, better dwellers on the land? On the other hand the question can be coldly realistic: given the fact that people will *always* be too self-interested and shortsighted, too ornery and individualistic, too oblivious to nature's complexity, are there nonetheless steps we can take to minimize our unintended consequences and maximize our shared benefits?

However read, the question revolves around the same basic ecological fact of life: we, our selves, are surrounded, and we are permeable. We exist *in situ*. Self-interest and public interest are bound together in complicated ways. In the long run we can be secure only to the degree those bonds are recognized and respected. Self and surrounding cannot be severed. Individuality not only does not negate, but positively requires, a context, a world with which to interact. Whitman, champion of American individualism, understood this. So did Leopold: "All ethics so far evolved rest upon a single premise: that the individual is a member of a community of interdependent parts. His instincts prompt him to compete for his place in the community, but his ethics prompt him also to co-operate (perhaps in order that there may be a place to compete for)."[18]

◄← →►

Conservationists seek to secure—to obtain and to safeguard—the health of land and water and biotic and human communities. To do so, we need to convince others to care about not just the safe cultural spaces we build for ourselves, and not just the islands of wildness that we think we have protected, but all the places that provide us with our livelihoods and life support, our context and our identity. In this expanded space we may seek not only security but vitality for ourselves and for wild things. We may find ways to live that do not strain but strengthen "companionship."

Why now? Because it is necessary for our own good and the good of the life around us. Because science, history, and ethics suggest that we need to think and plan in new ways for the future. Because many conservationists are weary and hope that the work of caring can be made more enjoyable, more humanizing, if we don't have to holler across boundary lines (or hire lawyers to do the hollering). Because, in the process, we might just help to revive the neglected arts of democracy: reasoned debate, honed thought and open inquiry, tolerance, resistance to demagoguery, a living sense of history.

Conservation operates under both ecological and social mandates. We might once have accepted the fallacy that activities promoting the well-being of people and of the land could be pursued without reference to each other. But garden walls are porous and the illusion of security is plain. We risk continuing degradation of both biological diversity and human communities, and those losses are connected. When it comes to the good of life, and of people as a subset of life, we have a lot in common.

II

September 10, 2001, is a fine day in Wisconsin: clear, warm, and dry, daily life shifting from the ease of summer to the routines of autumn. Crops ripening, grasses browning, leaves yellowing, early flocks of ducks and geese moving through.

I am flying from Madison to Saint Louis, Missouri, where fifteen hundred members of the American Zoo and Aquarium Association, the AZA, are gathered from around the country for their annual meeting. George Rabb, director of Chicago's Brookfield Zoo and a respected elder in the zoo world, has invited me to join a panel discussion about the protection of wild animals and wild places. For three decades George has been a leading advocate of the idea that zoos can and should play an important role in conservation. Our session is scheduled to begin at nine o'clock on the morning of September 11.

Our jet descends into Saint Louis over the brown and braided channel of the Mississippi River. The portside passengers enjoy, on the mellow afternoon, an unobstructed view of the Gateway Arch on the river's western bank. The conference theme is "Where the Rivers Run Wild." The Father of Waters below us might no longer run unobstructed, but beyond the levees, amid the ripe cornfields and bottomland forests of Illinois and

Missouri, the old oxbows, like broken neurons, carry fragmented memories of the Mississippi's wilder days.

⫸ ⫷

Headquarters for the meeting is the Adams Mark Hotel in the heart of downtown Saint Louis, astride a central axis of American symbol, memory, and law. A quarter mile to the east flows the Mississippi, halfway along its route from Lake Itasca to the Gulf of Mexico, its waters joined by the Missouri River just upriver. Across the street, south of the hotel, is the Jefferson National Expansion Memorial. The Gateway Arch rises more than six hundred feet above the greensward between the hotel and the river. Underground, beneath the Arch, is the Museum of Westward Expansion. The Memorial's grounds extend to the west to include Saint Louis's storied Old Courthouse.

Just upstream, near Hartford, Illinois, Meriwether Lewis, William Clark, and the Corps of Discovery overwintered in 1803–1804 at Camp River Dubois, at the outset of their epic expedition. Jefferson had foreshadowed his charge to the Corps in his 1801 presidential inaugural address, when he pronounced the people of the United States blessed in "possessing a chosen country, with room enough for our descendants to the hundredth and thousandth generation." The United States—"kindly separated by nature and a wide ocean from the exterminating havoc of one quarter of the globe"—would find peace and prosperity in its beneficent setting.[19]

Jefferson's continental vision of American nationhood required that the European powers be vacated from the West. On April 30, 1803, American and French diplomats meeting in Paris put their names to the Louisiana Purchase, and 828,000 square miles of land came into American possession, at a price tag of $15,000,000. Three cents an acre. "The most significant real estate transaction in the history of civilization," as the saying would go.

Communications across the oceans and continents took time. Until papers were signed, the river remained the boundary line between the European powers and the American republic; between the Old and New Worlds; between a crowded Europe composed of nations in seemingly continuous conflict, and a spacious American union that Jefferson trusted would consist of "good neighbors *sharing* territorial boundaries in perpetual peace."[20]

Ratification of the treaty and the complicated transfer of jurisdiction were still playing out when the Corps of Discovery arrived at Saint Louis in December 1803. The governor of Upper Louisiana could not allow the Corps to proceed beyond Saint Louis without official clearance from his superiors. With winter coming on, the Corps set up camp on the eastern side of the Mississippi.

Finally, on December 30, 1803, the United States took possession of Louisiana. A transfer ceremony took place in Saint Louis on March 4, 1804. In May, the Corps was able to resume its westward journey. On May 14, Clark noted in his journal: "I set out at 4 oClock P.M. in the presence of many of the Neighbouring inhabitents, and proceeded on under a jentle brease up the Missourie." Two and a half years later, on September 23, 1806, the Corps "decended to the Mississippi and down that river to St. Louis at which place we arived about 12 oClock. we Suffered the party to fire off their pieces as a Salute to the Town. we were met by all the village and received a harty welcom from it's inhabitants."[21]

Jefferson's motivating vision looked ahead to the conversion of the continent's "immense regions of fertile and uncultivated lands."[22] With the east at his back, Jefferson cast his gaze not only westward, but northward and southward as well. In a well-known letter to his successor James Madison, Jefferson saw the domain of the nation extending inexorably to include even Cuba and Canada. Then, he ventured, the nation would have realized "such an empire for liberty" as had never been "surveyed since the creation."[23] Jefferson's words contained all the ideals and ambitions, concerns and contradictions inherent in the man and the nation. With the Louisiana Purchase accomplished and its lands well guarded, Jefferson felt upon leaving the presidency that he had left the nation "in a reasonable state of security against any probable attack." [24]

Facing the Gateway Arch across the grounds of the national monument stands the Old Courthouse, its Greek Revival proportions dwarfed by the Arch and other modern structures. The land where the courthouse sits was donated by its owner in 1816 with a powerful easement attached: the grounds were to be "used forever" as the site of the county's courthouse.

Construction of the existing courthouse began in 1839. Its walls could speak volumes: debates on sectional strife and immigration; meetings to arrange assistance for victims of Ireland's potato famine; gatherings of slaveholders to demand "protection of slave property against the evil designs of Abolitionists and others"; slave auctions to settle estates; Thomas Hart Benton calling in 1849 for the building of a transcontinental railroad; Ulysses S. Grant in 1859 freeing William Jones, a slave he briefly owned.

It was in the Old Courthouse in 1847 and 1850 that the slave couple, Dred and Harriet Scott, sued for their freedom. Their third suit, brought in 1854, was heard in another building, now gone, where the north leg of the Arch now sits. Their case rested on a simple geopolitical fact: Dred Scott had crossed the boundary between bondage and freedom. For more than eight years, Scott lived with his owner in free Illinois and Wisconsin Territory. The Missouri Compromise of 1820 had prohibited slavery in the new states and territories of the old Northwest. On one side of the Mississippi River, Dred and Harriet Scott were property. On the other side they were human beings.

It was the third suit, decided against Scott, that the U.S. Supreme Court reviewed in 1857. Seven of the nine justices held that Scott had no rights as a free person. In his majority opinion, Chief Justice Roger Taney stated that Dred Scott, by virtue of his status as a slave—as mere property—was not a U.S. citizen, had in fact never been free, and had no standing before the courts. Further: the Missouri Compromise was unconstitutional and the federal government had no business prohibiting or restricting slavery. In affirming the primacy of the property rights of slave owners over the human rights of slaves, Taney's opinion put the match to the tinderbox of civil war.

In the Old Courthouse in 1872, Virginia Louisa Minor traversed another boundary. Minor, a leader in the National Woman Suffrage Association, sued the Saint Louis registrar (one Reese Happersett) for refusing to register her to vote in the presidential election that year. Minor based her case on citizen rights guaranteed under the first sentence of the Fourteenth Amendment: "All persons born or naturalized in the United States, and subject to the jurisdiction thereof, are citizens of the United States and of the State wherein they reside." Minor claimed that, as a person and citizen, she enjoyed certain legal protections and privileges, among them the right to vote. Missouri's constitution and laws, she argued, illegally limited the right to vote to male citizens, and denied Minor her guaranteed rights.

Minor lost her case in the circuit court, on the first floor of the Old Courthouse. She lost her appeal to Missouri's supreme court, on the second floor. The case moved to the U.S. Supreme Court in 1874. In a unanimous decision, she lost. In the opinion of Chief Justice Morrison Waite, the Fourteenth Amendment did not define the "privileges or immunities" of citizens. Women may have been legal citizens of the United States, but individual states retained the authority to decide who could vote within their borders. U.S. citizenship, in short, did not ensure suffrage. The court's decision deflated the suffragists' hope for judicial recourse. Their energies shifted toward securing the vote through amendments to state constitutions and the U.S. Constitution itself. A women's suffrage amendment was presented to the U.S. Congress in 1878, but would not finally be ratified for another forty-two years.

In Saint Louis, Dred Scott and Virginia Louisa Minor challenged boundaries of race, gender, section, citizenship, rights, and freedom. At the confluence of great rivers and historical forces, Jefferson's "empire of liberty" confronted its internal tensions and sought to carve new channels. The planting of Whitman's companionship, "thick as trees along all the rivers of America," was to remain the incomplete work of generations.

◄◄ ►►

My room on an upper floor of the hotel faces east. I awaken just as sun rises over Illinois. The plan is to meet the other panel speakers for breakfast before our session. I have just enough time for a short outing before breakfast—and I need it! I have had no time to think about my remarks for the morning and want to clear my head. As day comes on I walk out of the hotel lobby and across Memorial Drive, river-bound, across the lawn of the memorial, threading the Arch.

The Arch is being restored. Construction crews are just stirring into action near the south leg. At the base of the north leg I stand agog, as any first-time visitor must, at the sweep of the thing. Where Eero Saarinen's great catenary curve meets the ground, it gains, literally, its human touch.

Forty years of the laying on of hands have lent a patina of tarnish to the stainless steel skin. I add my touch.

From the east side I look skyward, squinting. The whole face of the structure burns yellow-orange with morning light. I find relief from the intense gleam in the long shadow that falls over the lawn, the hotel, the Old Courthouse, over Saint Louis and Missouri and the West.

Crossing Sullivan Boulevard to the levee, I pause for a moment to orient myself here at the core of the continent, trying to conjure some words for later in the morning. I am distracted by the dragonflies cruising through the morning mist over the Mississippi, and by mallards squabbling in the water.

I linger as long as I can at the riverbank, then turn back toward the Arch and the hotel. At the south leg, the construction crew has fired up the generators and begun the workday. Saint Louis stirs around its center now as sidewalks fill and traffic thickens. Still wondering what I am going to say in our session, I walk back across the landscaped grounds to the hotel and our breakfast meeting.

Our plenary gang has gathered. Three of the panel speakers are venerable silverback males in the zoo and conservation world:

... George Rabb, who has called us together. George's career with the Brookfield Zoo began in 1956, and he has served as its director since 1976. For seven years George also headed the Species Survival Commission of the World Conservation Union, the international network of conservation scientists, agency officials, and nongovernmental organizations. Under George's guidance the commission expanded to include some seven thousand volunteer scientific experts and conservationists in 190 countries. Through dozens of active working groups, these volunteers provide technical advice for conservation projects around the world.

... Bill Conway, for thirty-seven years the director of the New York Zoological Park—the Bronx Zoo—and the driving force behind establishment of the Wildlife Conservation Society (WCS) at the zoo. Bill, in fact, is a native of Saint Louis and began his career at the city's zoo in 1945. Under his leadership the WCS has served as a catalyst in conservation programs around the globe, involving many of the earth's most threatened species and spectacular landscapes. Along with George, Bill has led the movement to redefine zoos as conservation research and education centers, and to link zoos to field conservation projects.

. . . And Peter Raven, our host in Saint Louis. As one of the world's preeminent botanists, Peter has been a tireless voice for the study, appreciation, and protection of the earth's biodiversity. As director since 1971 of the Missouri Botanical Gardens in Saint Louis, Peter has built that organization into a world leader in plant research and conservation. As home secretary of the U.S. National Academy of Sciences and president of the American Association for the Advancement of Science, he put issues of biodiversity conservation and sustainability before scientists, citizens, and political leaders at home and around the world.

George has called on other voices to fill out the panel: Simon Stuart, a British ornithologist and ecologist, and one of the world's leading experts on endangered species assessment and conservation policy; Monique Harden, an attorney from New Orleans who has worked on behalf of communities facing threats from industrial pollution, setting important precedents in the environmental justice arena; and Karen Lips, a field biologist who is a leading expert on the worldwide amphibian extinction crisis, and who has also been especially active in assisting Central American conservation scientists in their work.

George has us introduce ourselves and leads the conversation. Peter Raven had opened the conference with a wide-ranging address on global conservation challenges. Our task is to respond to Peter's remarks and stimulate those at the conference to think broadly about biodiversity conservation and the contributions that zoos can make to the cause. With our varied backgrounds, we have a wide field to run in, and our breakfast conversation jumps readily from theme to theme.

I still have no prepared notes. As the others around the table offer their thoughts, I surreptitiously jot down a few points on conservation and education and history and geography. I write down the phrase "teachable moment." I key in on this teachable *place*, this theater of convergence, and on several fortuitous events.

I will say something about the Gateway Arch, and Thomas Jefferson, and westward expansion, and the Old Courthouse, and the native flora and fauna of the midcontinent, and the native nations of the Mississippi and Missouri River basins.

I will note that in just three days, on September 14, we will mark the centennial of Theodore Roosevelt's presidency. I will say a few words about Roosevelt's passion for birds and his formative experiences on the high plains of the upper Missouri in the 1880s and 1890s. I will speculate that TR might even have observed whooping cranes during his ranching days.

I will share the news about the first ultralight-led migration of captive-reared whooping cranes from Wisconsin and Florida, which is just about to commence—an extraordinary moment in the long-term effort to recover the species.

I will end with a few words about the conservation movement growing and changing; about working through communities at home and abroad; about connecting people with the wild world; about the role zoos can play in weaving conservation into our daily lives and our home places.

⤙ ⤚

We adjourn and move toward the hotel elevators. Our session is to begin in a few minutes in the main ballroom on the second floor. I leave before the others in order to get to the dais and use the precious minutes to polish my notes.

Leaving the elevator, I am stopped by a couple in the corridor.

"Did you hear about what happened in New York?" the man asks.

"New York? No. What's up?"

"Plane crashed into the Trade Center. It's incredible!"

Outside the ballroom, the news spreads quickly among the several hundred people gathered there. In the first moments of disbelief, colleagues confer and hug. I see George and tell him the news. Focused as he is on beginning our session, he does not initially grasp the magnitude of the news.

The full scope of the attacks soon becomes apparent, and shock sets in.

For some minutes, people sit or mill about the ballroom. The AZA leaders struggle to get more information. I sit alone at the head table, trying to focus on my notes but somehow knowing that I will not need them. The conference technicians patch in an audio feed of the television broadcasts, and try to project the images onto the two large screens flanking the speakers' platform. At the front of the room, Peter Raven and the AZA leaders confer. A pall overcomes the group. In the large but tight-knit family of the AZA, tears flow easily and comfort is given in small groups around the room.

Minutes later, the technicians succeed and the images appear.

The conference organizers announce that the session is cancelled and ask everyone to stand by for further announcements. In the large ballroom, in this big river city, in the heart of the continent, we sit in uncertain alarm, waiting to learn more about the extent of the attacks, thinking of our friends and families in New York, Pennsylvania, and Washington, and who knows where else.

For a while, I sit alone. The compounding succession of television images and news flashes plays out. I notice George Rabb consulting with Peter Raven and Bill Conway. These three people, I think to myself, have done as much as any people on the planet—as much as could be asked of anyone—to build a healthier, more just, more secure world. Amid the complacency of the last two decades, they have labored ceaselessly to bring people together around a broader vision for the future, built upon international cooperation and shared responsibilities to future generations and the rest of creation. These are leaders. And already they know that a new era has dawned, one that threatens all they have cared and worked for.

George joins me. We sit together and silently watch the most horrific and incredible moments of the morning unfold. There are no words for this.

I cannot escape a feeling, which I finally share with George. I recall projects I had worked on in Eastern Europe, and times I had shared with conservationists there as the region achieved democracy. I had the privilege of seeing Jefferson's "empire of liberty," not in the mad rush for territory, resources, influence, and dollars, but in the faces of people free to debate and challenge authority and work passionately for the lands they loved. I have always treasured the experience, but never more so than this morning.

And yet, simultaneously, deep frustration wells up, which I also share with George. As the minutes pass, a window of opportunity slams shut. The period of promise that opened with the lifting of the Iron Curtain is now ending as the Twin Towers fall. A decade in which a radically fresh view of the future might have been nurtured and taken hold is abruptly closing. The 1990s were a sweet moment when, in the wake of the Cold War, leaders in every sector of society might have stepped forward and built, across ideological boundaries, a new global, national, and local vision of land stewardship and restoration, economic opportunity and sustainability, community health and reconciliation. That potential has been frittered away, squandered in the self-interest, excesses, and distractions of the 1990s. The losses of this moment signify a larger and longer-term loss, tragic and unfathomable, to the world.

From the podium the conference organizers provide an update. The remainder of the conference is cancelled. All flights out of Saint Louis are grounded. In lieu of the evening's planned social event, attendees unable to travel are invited to gather for dinner together.

Then they ask for a moment of silence. Soft sobs break over the hush.

George and I are especially conscious of Bill Conway and concerned about the welfare of our many friends in New York City at the Wildlife Conservation Society. Bill had returned to his hotel room to monitor events and to try to contact his staff. He also has forty of his colleagues with him in Saint Louis, and they have to find a way home to New York.

We all face the same predicament—fifteen hundred people gathered in Saint Louis from all around the country, with no air travel for the foreseeable future. As the aftershocks of the attacks rumble, the hotel lobby becomes an improvised coordination and dispatch center. People move from group to group trying to make connections to distant destinations. I myself have to find some way back to Wisconsin. I am supposed to attend another meeting the following day in LaCrosse, four hundred miles upstream on the Mississippi. Not likely.

The atmosphere in the lobby is one of subdued confusion. I find no Wisconsin connections. I throw in my lot with George and accept his offer of a ride to Chicago. George, I learn at that moment, has not stopped working. Calling home, he has instructed his staff to keep the Brookfield Zoo open, thinking that people will appreciate a place of calm and contrast today.

I go to my room, quickly pack my bags, and return to the lobby, now aswarm with activity: guests making and canceling reservations, travel plans being invented and changed from moment to moment, cell phones passing from ear to ear. As I work my way through the lobby, I spy Bill Conway at the entrance to the hotel restaurant. Bill and I had made plans to have lunch together that day. In my limited interactions with Bill, he has always struck me as an unusually steady fellow. Now my impressions are confirmed: having succeeded in reaching his colleagues back in New York, he is intent, even amid the circumstances, of keeping our lunch date. Hiding my astonishment, I tell him that I had better skip it and grab the ride to Chicago while I can.

It is up to Bill, as we part, to say the words that are being uttered all around the planet under myriad circumstances. With the soberest restraint he says, "The world won't be the same. This will change everything." We are all crossing another boundary.

✦ ✦

We pack the car for Chicago: me; George; Tim Sullivan, a conservation biologist with the Brookfield Zoo; and Lester and Wendy Fisher. Lester I knew by name and face. He is the former director of the Lincoln Park Zoo in Chicago, and a past president of the AZA. When I was growing up in Chicago, Lester appeared regularly on television as an envoy from the animal world. Wendy is also very active in AZA's work and helped George organize our panel.

We pull away from the hotel. Something is different. . . . The Gateway Arch has been cordoned off and is surrounded by security vehicles and armed personnel. Oh, no!? . . . Of course! *Of course*. It is the tallest monument in the western hemisphere. Earlier that morning, when it blinded me, it seemed to leap soaring from the earth and the river. Now it seems to tie down the sky.

We cross over the Mississippi River into East Saint Louis, bound for Chicago on Interstate 55—roughly, the old Route 66 corridor—listening for news on the radio, finally finding some moments to breathe the air and ponder what was happening. Over endless fields of tawny corn and soybeans the blue sky stretches on and on, devoid of contrails.

The surreal juxtaposition—of world-shattering events in the East and the fullness of late summer in the Midwest—hypnotizes. How stark! An unprecedented pain throbs at the edge of the nation. Here in Illinois, one feels only the deep consolation of the broad and solid middle, the well-buffered interior, the durable land. Over-corned and over-soybeaned, wiped clean of its native diversity, its soils too much eroded, its waters too deadened, stained by historic injustice, vulnerable to all manner of fleeting development, too proud of its manifest destiny and its manifest power, yet still offering an irrepressible comfort.

I have not been down I-55 in years. I notice, as one can especially notice in September in the Midwest, some prairie plants along the highway. For several years in the 1980s and early 1990s the state of Illinois planted native grasses along the right-of-way between the interstate highways and crop fields.[25] The high heads of big bluestem, switch grass, and Indian grass grow only, to be sure, as tokens of the vanquished prairies' rich diversity. They do testify, however, to the capacity for change. For a century and a half, prosperity has come *from*, yet at the expense *of*, the prairies of Illinois, of the whole Midwest. Disdained and deprived of their place, prairie plants and animals had no standing, as it were, in their native land. Only in the last few decades have human notions of progress given them a small stake in the land again. A few species, at least, in a few places, are now repatriated.

Once, crossing Illinois by bus in the summer of 1946, between Wisconsin and his hometown of Burlington, Iowa, Aldo Leopold was moved to comment on our indifference to land:

> The highway stretches like a taut tape across the corn, oats, and clover fields [gone the diversified farms of 1946!]; the bus ticks off the opulent miles; the passengers talk and talk and talk. About what? About baseball, taxes, sons-in-law, movies, motors, and funerals, but never about the heaving groundswell of Illinois that washes the windows of the speeding bus. Illinois has no genesis, no history, no shoals or deeps, no tides of life and death. To them, Illinois is only the sea on which they sail to ports unknown.[26]

In the "narrow thread of sod" along the roadside, Leopold noted "relics of what once was Illinois: the prairie." Observing prosperity and depletion in such immediate proximity on the farmlands of Illinois, Leopold asked two questions for the ages: "Just who is solvent? For how long?" Conservationists, against the tenor of our times, ask them still.

We come into Springfield and stop for lunch. The restaurant is within view of Illinois' historic Old State Capitol, where Abraham Lincoln, crossing the street from his law office, researched briefs, argued cases, and bantered with the court clerks. Where Lincoln served in the state house and delivered his "House Divided" speech: "I do not expect the Union to be dissolved—I do not expect the house to fall—but I do expect it will cease to be divided."[27] Where Lincoln organized his presidential campaign and prepared for the presidency. Where on the brink of the Civil War, just weeks before his death, Stephen Douglas made a final appeal to his fellow citizens to put their differences aside for the sake of the Union. Where in April 1865 Lincoln's body lay in state and tens of thousands of citizens came to pay their respects. Where, on the steps, a choir sang as Lincoln made his last ride to Oak Ridge Cemetery.

Today, all along this roadway, all of Illinois seems to say, we will endure . . . we have overcome worse than this . . . the saga of American nationhood continues . . . *the better angels of our nature.* . . . Look beyond, for now, the changes in the land, the relentless monoculture, the sudden sprawl, the cheap speculation, the cheaper politics, of recent years. Hope against hope. We will hold our place, as big bluestem somehow held a bit of ground, even while losing its native prairie empire. As Dred and Harriet Scott and Virginia Louisa Minor held their rights, even while losing their cases. As Lincoln held the nation, even while losing his life. *An irrepressible comfort.*

We roll on, my zoo friends and I, toward Chicago.

We roll, like the *City of New Orleans,* "past houses, farms, and fields."

We roll, like the blues rolled upstream from the delta to the city. Sweet home, Chicago . . . *baby, don't you wanna go?*

We come into the city as the afternoon wanes. The sun that illuminated the Gateway Arch at dawn reflects golden orange from Chicago's skyscrapers at sundown.

That night I stay with my mother on the north side. She remarks that at her office that day, all the kids—the "kids" in their twenties and thirties—were utterly disoriented. She told them about living through Pearl Harbor. Unlike those of her generation, they had no psychic reference point for the events of this day.

Early on the morning of September 12, determined at least to try to make my afternoon meeting in LaCrosse, I set out for O'Hare Airport, where I might catch a bus to Madison. The taxi, inexplicably, is allowed into the closed airport and drops me off, but the busses are not running. I walk alone through the stunningly vacant terminals of O'Hare.

Another option is to take a train out of the city. I ride the "L" into the Loop, emerging from the station just as the sun rises on the new day and casts its long rays over Lake Michigan waters, through the slot canyons of downtown Chicago. I walk across the Loop, past the foot of the Sears Tower, through a city that has never before seemed so triumphant, or so vulnerable.

A train to the Wisconsin border . . . a ride to Madison with my brother and a friend . . . a lift to LaCrosse with another friend . . . and once again I am on the banks of the Mississippi. The river, rolling on from Lake Itasca, its "true source" in the North, down toward its meeting place just above Saint Louis with the waters of the West.

III

The events of September 11 and its aftermath have altered the context of conservation and environmental concern, as they have other dimensions of life in the new century. Those who care about the living things of the earth, the vitality of landscapes and ecosystems, and the viability of human communities and economies as part of the land, face a bitter irony. As consumerism has come to define American society, not least in the 1980s and 1990s, the land has lost its claim on our attentions. In the boom times, conservationists struggled to be heard above the din of breakneck technological change, globalization fever, investment mania, dot-com hype, political struttings, and perpetual media blitz. Now, in more sober times, conservation's call is muted by fear of external threats, unilateralism at the international level, security concerns at home, and accelerated economic dislocation and uncertainty. Conservation was not, and is not now, a priority concern for most Americans.

With nothing to lose except further ground, conservation-minded citizens may now at least be more honest in our hopes and concerns. We might as well stand up and state directly: this society must at some point begin to think and act for the long term; foresight, self-restraint, and modesty are qualities of the strong, not the fearful; conservation, in its essence, represents an assumption of responsibility; it is illegitimate to exercise rights without assuming such responsibility; we reject the coarsening of civic life and the cynicism that feeds it; we regard the health of the American land as an ultimate measure and expression of our national progress; we hold, with Theodore Roosevelt, that "we are not building this nation for a day. It is to last through the ages."[28]

And we might as well be forceful in stating that no nation—the United States least of all—can go it alone, and none can remain blind to the environmental dimensions of national security. Any notion of security built on a narrow base of military might is untenable. Security is a function of dependable and respectful relationships, complex and multifaceted, varied and connected: political, economic, and environmental, legal, social, and cultural.

For a century, conservationists have argued and worked for a broader and longer-term definition of human progress and well-being, based on a view of the world that honors relationships and responsibilities. It has this realization to offer under these new conditions: security is an expression of the strength that comes from working for healthy landscapes and robust communities. Instead of an empty and abstract concept of the "homeland," conservation demands a hardheaded and forthright definition: take the land seriously if you care for it as your home.

For the moment, the phrase "homeland security" verges on the purely propagandistic: who speaks with heartfelt conviction for the health, security, and durability of the American land itself—the soils, waters, plants, animals, and people together? In the wake of another time of national crisis, World War II, Aldo Leopold refused to indulge in symbolic or sentimental odes to the American land. Instead, he asked tough questions: "Do we not already sing our love for and obligation to the land of the free and the home of the brave? Yes, but just what and whom do we love? Certainly not the soil, which we are sending helter-skelter downriver. Certainly not the waters, which we assume have no function except to turn turbines, float barges, and carry off sewage. Certainly not the plants, of which we exterminate whole communities without batting an eye. Certainly not the animals, of which we have already extirpated many of the largest and most beautiful species."[29]

In the political arena, conservation has too few champions working from a gut understanding of such realities. Rather, national officials can with impunity deride energy conservation (to cite just one example) as a mere "sign of personal virtue, but . . . not a sufficient basis for a sound, comprehensive energy policy."[30] For those with such a view, conservation is not connected to any notion of responsible citizenship, or leadership. And land, far from being appreciated as the fundamental source of life, health, wealth, stories, poetry, identity, belief, and, yes, patriotism, is just a raw resource and backdrop for busy modern lives.

Perhaps, by contrast, it took the trials of economic depression, land degradation, and world war to prompt Aldo Leopold to propose a land ethic. For those voices, known and unknown, who have contributed to its continuing evolution, conservation is not just a "sign of personal virtue." It is the basis of self-preservation and community renewal. It is an expression of commitment to democracy, justice, and stewardship, to future generations, and to the land itself.

In the days after September 11, George Rabb was asked by his colleagues in the World Conservation Union to prepare a statement in response to the acts of terror. His statement read, in part: "People everywhere are part of the natural world. Only if we respect and care for all fellow human beings can we be successful in conservation of the earth's living natural wealth and diversity, upon which we all depend. Caring for other creatures, for environments worldwide, and for one another should be societal goals of all people. Caring is the essence of conservation, justice, and peace globally."[31]

Conservation, in this changed world, is in crisis, and it is not something different from the security crisis (or the other crises) we face. The acute acts of terror we have suffered are not separate from, or an excuse to ignore, the chronic acts of deprivation, injustice, impoverishment, and environmental degradation that conservation must also seek to address. It is a single crisis of caring. The crisis was building long before terrorists seized the world's attention, foreshortened our view, and enthroned fear. If we are yet to "make the continent indissoluble," conservation must help to reclaim the future. It may do so by offering the lesson that it alone can offer so clearly: by taking care of the home land, the home land will continue to take care of us.

Introduction: Turning the Corner

1. M. Martone, *The Flatness and Other Landscapes* (Athens, Ga.: University of Georgia Press, 2000), p. 169. See chap. 9, n. 21.

2. Sources related to these trends are provided throughout this volume. See especially chap. 2, n. 16; chap. 5, n. 42; chap. 9, n. 3; chap. 9, n. 4; chap. 10, n. 5; and chap. 10, n. 26.

3. Sources for the history of conservation, environmentalism, environmental policy, and environmental thought are provided throughout this volume. For overviews of American conservation and environmentalism, see P. Matthiessen, *Wildlife in America*, rev. ed. (originally published 1959; New York: Viking Penguin, 1987); R. F. Nash, *Wilderness and the American Mind*, 4th ed. (1967; New Haven, Conn.: Yale University Press, 2001); J. B. Trefethen, *An American Crusade for Wildlife* (New York: Winchester Press, and the Boone and Crockett Club, 1975); D. Worster, *Nature's Economy: A History of Ecological Ideas* (1977; reprint, Cambridge: Cambridge University Press, 1985); S. Fox, *John Muir and His Legacy: The American Conservation Movement* (Boston: Little, Brown, 1981); L. Buell, *The Environmental Imagination: Thoreau, Nature Writing, and the Formation of American Culture* (Cambridge, Mass.: Harvard University Press, 1995); B. Kline, *First Along the River: A Brief History of the U.S. Environmental Movement* (San Francisco: Acada Books, 1997); J. Opie, *Nature's Nation: An Environmental History of the United States* (Forthworth, Texas: Harcourt Brace, 1998); H. Rothman, *The Greening of a Nation?: Environmentalism in the U. S. Since 1945* (Fort Worth, Texas: Harcourt Brace College Publishers 1998); R. N. Andrews, *Managing the Environment, Managing Ourselves: A History of Environmental Policy* (New Haven, Conn.: Yale University Press, 1999); T. Steinberg, *Down to Earth: Nature's Role in American History* (New York: Oxford University Press, 2002); C. Merchant, *The Columbia Guide to American Environmental History* (Irvington, New York: Columbia University Press, 2002); P. Shabecoff, *A Fierce Green Fire: The American Environmental Movement*, rev. ed. (Washington, D.C.: Island Press, 2003).

4. The original publication is C. Meine, "The Oldest Task in Human History," in *A New Century for Natural Resources Management*, edited by R. L. Knight and S. F. Bates (Washington, D.C.: Island Press, 1995), pp. 7–35.

5. The original publication is C. Meine, "Conservation and the Progressive Movement: Growing from the Radical Center,"in *Reconstructing Conservation: Finding Common Ground*, edited by B. A. Minteer and R. E. Manning (Washington, D.C.: Island Press, 2003), pp. 165–184. An abridged version of this essay also appeared in *Wild Earth* 13, nos. 2/3 (2003): 59–65.

6. The original publication is C. Meine, "Conservation Biology and Sustainable Societies: A Historical Perspective," in *After Earth Day: Continuing the Conservation Effort*, edited by M. Oelschlaeger (Denton, Texas: University of North Texas Press, 1992), pp. 37–65.

7. C. Meine, *Aldo Leopold: His Life and Work* (Madison: University of Wisconsin Press, 1988).

8. Works by and about Aldo Leopold include J. B. Callicott, ed., *Companion to* A Sand County Almanac: *Interpretive and Critical Essays* (Madison: University of Wisconsin Press, 1987); R. McCabe, *Aldo Leopold: The Professor* (Madison, Wisc.: Rusty Rock Press, 1987); T. Tanner, ed., *Aldo Leopold: The Man and His Legacy* (1987; reprint, Ankeny, Iowa: Soil and Water Conservation Society of America, 1995); S. L. Flader and J. B. Callicott, eds., *The River of the Mother of God and Other Essays by Aldo Leopold* (Madison: University of Wisconsin Press, 1991); S. Flader, *Thinking Like a Mountain: Aldo Leopold and the Evolution of an Ecological Attitude Toward Deer, Wolves, and Forests* (1974; reprint, Madison: University of Wisconsin Press, 1994); D. E. Brown and N. B. Carmony, eds., *Aldo Leopold's Southwest* (1990; reprint, Albuquerque: University of New Mexico Press, 1995); M. Lorbiecki, *Aldo Leopold: A Fierce Green Fire* (Helena, Mont.: Falcon Press, 1996); A. Leopold, *For the Health of the Land: Previously Unpublished Essays and Other Writings*, edited by J. B. Callicott and E. T. Freyfogle (Washington, D.C.: Island Press, 1999); C. Meine and R. L. Knight, eds., *The Essential Aldo Leopold: Quotations and Commentaries* (Madison: University of Wisconsin Press, 1999); R. L. Knight and S. Reidel, eds., *Aldo Leopold and the Ecological Conscience* (New York: Oxford University Press, 2002).

9. S. Schrepfer, "Wildlife Ecologist," review of C. Meine, *Aldo Leopold: His Life and Work, Science* 241, no. 4870 (1988): 1237.

10. The original publication is "The Utility of Preservation and the Preservation of Utility: Leopold's Fine Line," in *The Wilderness Condition: Essays on Environment and Civilization*, edited by M. Oelschlaeger (San Francisco: Sierra Club Books, 1992), pp. 131–172.

11. See chap. 9, n. 3.

12. The original publication is C. Meine, "Keeper of the Cogs," *Defenders* 67, no. 6 (1992): 9–17. This article, in turn, was based on a lecture that I have given regularly since 1990, "Emergence of an Idea: Aldo Leopold and the Conservation of Biological Diversity."

13. The original publication is C. Meine, "Giving Voice to Concern: Aldo Leopold's 'Marshland Elegy,'" in *Marshland Elegy*, edited by F. B. Miracle (Madison: Wisconsin Center for the Book at the Wisconsin Academy of Sciences, Arts and Letters, 1999), pp. 12–24.

14. A. Leopold, *A Sand County Almanac and Sketches Here and There* (New York: Oxford University Press, 1949), pp. 95–101.

15. The original publication is C. Meine, "Moving Mountains: Aldo Leopold and *A Sand County Almanac*," *Wildlife Society Bulletin* 26, no. 4 (1998): 697–706; reprinted in Knight and Reidel, *Aldo Leopold and the Ecological Conscience*, pp. 14–31.

16. The original publication is C. Meine, "The *Secret* Leopold; or, Who Really Wrote *A Sand County Almanac*," *Transactions of the Wisconsin Academy of Sciences, Arts and Letters* 88 (2000): 1–21.

17. The original publication is C. Meine, "Inherit the Grid," in *Placing Nature: Culture and Landscape Ecology*, edited by J. I. Nassauer (Washington, D.C.: Island Press, 1997), pp. 45–62. Joan Nassauer and Deborah Karasov coordinated the seminar, at the University of Minnesota.

18. The original publication is C. Meine and N. L. Bradley, "The Once and Future Land Ethic," in *From Conquest to Conservation: Our Public Lands Legacy*, edited by M. P. Dombeck, C. A. Wood, and J. E. Williams (Washington, D.C.: Island Press, 2003), pp. 118–120. Shorter versions of this essay also appeared in the newsletter of the Aldo Leopold Foundation, *The Leopold Outlook* 3, no. 2 (2001): 2, 6; and the newsletter of the Pheasants Forever / Leopold Education Project, *Strides* 8, no. 4 (2003): 1–2.

19. Originally published as C. Meine, "The Continent Indissoluble," in *Stewardship Across Boundaries*, edited by R. L. Knight and P. B. Landres (Washington, D.C.: Island Press, 1998), pp. 325–336.

20. Portions of this part of this essay are adopted from C. Meine, "Leave No Acre Behind: Renewing the Conservation Consensus," *Wingspread Journal* (2004), pp. 3–7.

1. The Oldest Task in Human History

The Ghost Dance verse is from V. I. Armstrong, ed., *I Have Spoken: American History Through the Voices of the Indians* (Athens, Ohio: Swallow Press / Ohio University Press, 1971), p. 129. The original source is J. Mooney, "The Ghost Dance Religion and the Sioux Outbreak of 1890," *14th Annual Report, 1892–1893*, part 2 (Washington, D.C.: U.S. Bureau of American Ethnology, 1893), p. 1072. Aldo Leopold's statement is from a lecture, "Engineering and Conservation," that he delivered on April 11, 1938, at the University of Wisconsin College of Engineering. See S. L. Flader and J. B. Callicott, eds., *The River of the Mother of God and Other Essays by Aldo Leopold* (Madison: University of Wisconsin Press, 1991), p. 254.

1. Filibert Roth, quoted in J. T. Curtis, *The Vegetation of Wisconsin* (Madison: University of Wisconsin Press, 1959), p. 469. The original source is F. Roth, *On the Forestry Conditions of Northern Wisconsin* (Madison: Wisconsin Geological and Natural History Survey Bulletin No. 1, 1898).

2. Among more recent accounts of the history of white pine exploitation and its impact on the development of forestry in the United States see especially M. Williams, *Americans and Their Forests: A Historical Geography* (Cambridge: Cambridge University Press, 1989), pp. 160–237; W. Cronon, *Nature's Metropolis: Chicago and the Great West* (New York: W. W. Norton, 1991), pp. 148–206; and *White Pine Symposium Proceedings: History, Ecology, Policy, and Management*, edited by R. B. Stine and M. J. Baughman (St. Paul, Minn.: Minnesota Extension Service, 1992).

3. A basic account of the Ghost Dance and the events at Wounded Knee can be found in R. K. Andrist, *The Long Death: The Last Days of the Plains Indian* (1964; reprint, New York: Macmillan, 1993), pp. 330–354.

4. F. J. Turner, *The Frontier in American History* (1920; reprint, New York: Holt, Rinehart and Winston, 1962), pp. 1–38. Turner's essay has been widely reprinted and debated. See M. Ridge, ed., *Frederick Jackson Turner: Wisconsin's Historian of the Frontier* (Madison: State Historical Society of Wisconsin, 1986); W. Cronon, "Revisiting the Vanishing Frontier: The Legacy of Frederick Jackson Turner," *Western Historical Quarterly* 18 (1987): 157–176; P. N. Limerick, "The Forest Reserves and the Argument for a Closing Frontier," in *Origins of the National Forests: A Centennial Symposium*, edited by H. K. Steen (Durham, N.C.: Forest History Society, 1992), pp. 10–18; P. N. Limerick, "Turnerians All: The Dream of a Helpful History in an Intelligible World," in *Something in the Soil: Legacies and Reckonings in the New West* (New York: W. W. Norton, 2000), pp. 141–165. See also P. N. Limerick, *The Legacy of Conquest: The Unbroken Past of the American West* (New York: W. W. Norton, 1987); R. White, *"It's Your Misfortune and None of My Own": A New History of the American West* (Norman: University of Oklahoma Press, 1991); S. T. Udall, *The Forgotten Founders: Rethinking the History of the Old West* (Washington, D.C.: Island Press, 2002).

5. S. Fox, *John Muir and His Legacy: The American Conservation Movement* (Boston: Little, Brown, 1981), pp. 103–107. See also M. Cohen, *The History of the Sierra Club, 1892–1970* (San Francisco: Sierra Club Books, 1988).

6. M. Frome, *Whose Woods Are These: The Story of the National Forests* (Garden City, N.Y.: Doubleday, 1962), pp. 48, 317; G. Pinchot, *Breaking New Ground* (1947; reprint, Washington, D.C.: Island Press, 1987), p. 85; M. P. Dombeck, C. A. Wood, and J. E. Williams, *From Conquest to Conservation: Our Public Lands Legacy* (Washington, D.C.: Island Press, 2003), pp. 19–20.

7. See Introduction, n. 3 above. For early developments in conservation, see L. Mumford, *The Brown Decades: A Study of the Arts in America, 1865–1895* (1931; reprint, New York: Dover Publications, 1955), pp. 57–106; H. Clepper, "The Conservation Movement: Birth and Infancy," in *Origins of Modern Conservation*, edited by H. Clepper (New York: Ronald Press, 1966), pp. 3–15; W. Stegner, "A Capsule History of Conservation," in *Where the Bluebird Sings to the Lemonade Springs: Living and Writing in the West* (New York: Random House, 1991), pp.

117–132; 57–106; A. Runte, *Public Lands, Public Heritage: The National Forest Idea* (Niwot, Colo.: Buffalo Bill Historical Center and Roberts Rinehart Publishers, 1991); R. Judd, *Common Lands, Common People: The Origins of Conservation in Northern New England* (Cambridge, Mass.: Harvard University Press, 1997); J. F. Reiger, *American Sportsmen and the Origins of Conservation*, 3rd ed. (Corvallis: Oregon State University Press, 2001).

8. J. Muir, *Our National Parks* (1901; reprint, Madison: University of Wisconsin Press, 1981), p. 2; *A Thousand Mile Walk to the Gulf* (Boston: Houghton Mifflin, 1916), p. 139.

9. J. B. Callicott, "Whither Conservation Ethics?" *Conservation Biology* 4, no. 1 (1991): 15–20.

10. Pinchot, *Breaking New Ground*, p. 23.

11. Pinchot, *Breaking New Ground*, p. 32.

12. Pinchot, *Breaking New Ground*, p. 32.

13. Pinchot, *Breaking New Ground*, p. 325.

14. Pinchot, *Breaking New Ground*, p. 31. Char Miller, in his biography *Gifford Pinchot and the Making of Modern Environmentalism* (Washington, D.C.: Island Press, 2001), argues that Pinchot's approach to forestry did, by his life's end, evolve beyond simple utilitarianism and the "tree farm" model, and toward a more ecological worldview. Long-term trends, as well as changes in the science and politics of forestry, "impelled Pinchot to articulate a more holistic vision of forests and their place in American culture" (p. 339).

15. E. Morris, *Theodore Rex* (New York: Random House, 2001), pp. 114–115, 218–232, 485–487, 514–519. In *Theodore Roosevelt: An Autobiography* (1913; reprint, New York: De Capo Press, 1985), Roosevelt lauded Pinchot for leading "the fight for preservation through use of our forests" (p. 409). See also C. Meine "Bio(graphical) Diversity," *Conservation Biology* 17, no. 4 (2003): 1179–1186.

16. See Fox, *John Muir and His Legacy*, pp. 139–147; Miller, *Gifford Pinchot*, pp. 136–141, 169–174; and L. Hott and D. Garey's documentary film *The Wilderness Idea: John Muir, Gifford Pinchot, and the First Great Battle for Wilderness* (Haydenville, Mass.: Florentine Films, 1989).

17. For insights on the "comparative analysis" of resource management fields in this section, I am especially indebted to Baird Callicott, Allen Cooperrider, Susan Flader, Rick Knight, Luna Leopold, Gary Meffe, Reed Noss, and Phil Pister. Further discussions of the themes here can be found in R. F. Noss and A. T. Cooperrider, *Saving Nature's Legacy: Protecting and Restoring Biodiversity* (Washington, D.C.: Island Press, 1994); R. L. Knight and S. F. Bates, eds., *A New Century for Natural Resources Management* (Washington, D.C.: Island Press, 1995); and C. S. Holling and G. K. Meffe, "Command and Control and the Pathology of Natural Resource Management," *Conservation Biology* 10, no. 2 (1996): 328–337.

18. Quoted in Pinchot, *Breaking New Ground*, p. 266.

19. See A. B. Meyer, "Forests and Forestry," in Clepper, *Origins of Modern Conservation*, pp. 38–56; Williams, *Americans and Their Forest*, pp. 425–465; R. H. Nelson, "The Federal Land Management Agencies," in Knight and Bates, *New Century*, pp. 37–59; N. Langston, *Forest Dreams, Forest Nightmares: The Paradox of Old Growth in the Inland West* (Seattle: University of Washington Press, 1995), pp. 157–200.

20. Pinchot, *Breaking New Ground*, pp. 20–21. The key expression of the call for an enhanced federal role in forestry was the 1933 report *A National Plan for American Forestry* (the "Copeland Report"). See Williams, *Americans and Their Forests*, pp. 323–330, 463; Miller, *Gifford Pinchot*, pp. 286–293.

21. See H. W. Pritchard, "Soil Conservation," in Clepper, *Origins of Modern Conservation*, pp. 38–56; C. Little, *Green Fields Forever* (Washington, D.C.: Island Press 1987); C. Merchant, ed., *Major Problems in Environmental History* (Lexington, Mass.: D.C. Heath, 1993), 94–169; Judd, *Common Lands, Common People*; S. Stoll, *Larding the Lean Earth: Soil and Society in Nineteenth-Century America* (New York: Hill and Wang, 2002). Little, in *Green Fields Forever*, notes that Jef-

ferson's innovative spirit could embrace both the moldboard plow ("It does beautiful work and is approved by everyone") as well as the early soil conservation measures needed to counter the plow's destructive impacts.

22. Quoted in N. P. Pittman, ed., *From the Land* (Washington, D.C.: Island Press, 1988), p. 4.

23. D. Worster, *Dust Bowl: The Southern Plains in the 1930s* (New York: Oxford University Press, 1979); R. D. Hurt, *American Agriculture: A Brief History* (Ames: Iowa State University Press, 1994); H. Prince, *Wetlands of the American Midwest: A Historical Geography of Changing Attitudes* (Chicago: University of Chicago Press, 1997); A. Vileisis, *Discovering the Unknown Landscape: A History of America's Wetlands* (Washington, D.C.: Island Press, 1997).

24. R. Harwood, "A History of Sustainable Agriculture," in C. A. Edwards, R. Lal, P. Madden, R. H. Miller, and G. House, eds., *Sustainable Agricultural Systems* (Ankeny, Iowa: Soil and Water Conservation Society, 1990), pp. 3–19.

25. Pritchard, "Soil Conservation"; R. S. Beeman and J. A. Pritchard, *A Green and Permanent Land: Ecology and Agriculture in the Twentieth Century* (Lawrence: University Press of Kansas, 2001), pp. 1–85. See also R. Anderson, "Coon Valley Days," *Wisconsin Academy Review* 48, no. 2 (2002): 42–48.

26. D. G. Wilson, "Range and Forage Resources," in Clepper, *Origins of Modern Conservation*, pp. 132–145; A. Johnston, "A History of the Rangelands of Western Canada," *Journal of Range Management* 23, no. 1 (1970): 3–8; M. A. Polling, "Legal Milestones in Range Management," *Renewable Resources Journal* 9, no. 2 (1991): 7–10.

27. L. A. Stoddart, A. D. Smith, and T. W. Box, *Range Management*, 3rd ed. (New York: McGraw-Hill, 1975), pp. 76–103. The first text in the field was A. W. Sampson, *Range and Pasture Management* (New York: John Wiley, 1923).

28. C. Meine, *Aldo Leopold: His Life and Work* (Madison: University of Wisconsin Press, 1988), pp. 187–193; E. A. Tucker, ed., *The Early Days: A Sourcebook of Southwestern Region History, Book 2*, Cultural Resources Management Report no. 11 (Albuquerque, N.Mex.: USDA Forest Service, Southwestern Region, 1991).

29. Polling, "Legal Milestones in Range Management."

30. For overviews of the history of American game and wildlife conservation, see P. Matthiessen, *Wildlife in America*, rev. ed. (New York: Viking Penguin, 1987); Reiger, *American Sportsmen and the Origins of Conservation* (Tucson: University of Arizona Press, 2000); J. B. Trefethen, *An American Crusade for Wildlife* (New York: Winchester Press, and the Boone and Crockett Club, 1975); T. R. Dunlap, *Saving America's Wildlife* (Princeton, N.J.: Princeton University Press, 1988); D. O. Belanger, *Managing American Wildlife: A History of the International Association of Fish and Wildlife Agencies* (Amherst: University of Massachusetts Press, 1988); L. S. Warren, *The Hunter's Game: Poachers and Conservationists in Twentieth-Century America* (New Haven, Conn.: Yale University Press, 1997); D. Wilcove, *The Condor's Shadow: The Loss and Recovery of Wildlife in America* (New York: W. H. Freeman, 1999).

31. The history of the Migratory Bird Treaty is told in K. Dorsey, *The Dawn of Conservation Diplomacy: U.S.-Canadian Wildlife Protection Treaties in the Progressive Era* (Seattle: University of Washington Press, 1998).

32. Aldo Leopold provided a succinct summary of the state of the field in "Ten New Developments in Game Management," published in *American Game* 14, no. 3 (1925): 7–8, 20. First on Leopold's list was the idea of "game as a crop": "The most important single development which the last ten years have brought forth is implied in the word 'management.' We have learned that game, to be successfully conserved, must be positively produced, rather than merely negatively protected." Another key document of the period is the "Report to the American Game Conference on an American Game Policy," published in *Transactions of the 17th Annual American Game Conference* (1930), pp. 284–309; Flader and Callicott, *River*, pp. 150–155.

33. A. Leopold, *Game Management* (New York: Charles Scribner's Sons, 1933).

34. C. Meine, "Conservation Biology and Wildlife Management in America: An Historical Perspective," in G. K. Meffe and R. C. Carroll and contributors, *Principles of Conservation Biology*, 1st ed. (Sunderland, Mass.: Sinauer Associates, 1994), pp. 310–312. See also Trefethen, *An American Crusade for Wildlife*, pp. 173–236; and chap. 5 in this volume.

35. J. J. Hickey, "Some Historical Phases in Wildlife Conservation," *Wildlife Society Bulletin 2*, no. 4 (1974): 164–170; Meine, *Aldo Leopold*, pp. 362–364.

36. R. Stroud, "Fisheries and Aquatic Resources: Lakes, Streams, and Other Inland Waters," in Clepper, *Origins of Modern Conservation*, pp. 57–73; Noss and Cooperrider, *Saving Nature's Legacy*, pp. 264–297; A. F. McEvoy, *The Fisherman's Problem: Ecology and Law in the California Fisheries, 1850–1980* (Cambridge: Cambridge University Press, 1986); W. F. Royce, "The Historical Development of Fisheries Science and Management," from a lecture given at the 1985 Fisheries Centennial Celebration, available at http://www.nefsc.noaa.gov/history/stories/fish_sci_history1.html; C. E. Atkinson, "Fisheries Management: An Historical Overview," *Marine Fisheries Review 50*, no. 4 (1988): 111–123; N. C. Parker, "History, Status, and Future of Aquaculture in the United States," *Critical Reviews in Aquatic Sciences 1*, no. 1 (1989): 97–109; G. K. Meffe, "Techno-Arrogance and Halfway Technologies: Salmon Hatcheries on the Pacific Coast of North America," *Conservation Biology 6*, no. 3 (1992): 350–354; M. Black, "Recounting a Century of Failed Fishery Policy Toward California's Sacramento River Salmon and Steelhead," *Conservation Biology 8*, no. 3 (1994): 892–894; J. E. Taylor III, *Making Salmon: An Environmental History of the Northwest Fisheries Crisis* (Seattle: University of Washington Press, 1999); M. B. Bogue, *Fishing the Great Lakes: An Environmental History, 1783–1933* (Madison: University of Wisconsin Press, 2000).

37. C. P. Idyll, "Coastal and Marine Waters," in Clepper, *Origins of Modern Conservation*, pp. 74–89. A starting point for many modern histories of marine fisheries is Thomas Henry Huxley's 1883 address at the opening of the Fisheries Exhibition in London. Despite understanding the varied nature of the resource ("there are fisheries and fisheries"), Huxley came down against "legislative restriction" and dismissed the notion that human action could have a substantial impact on major fisheries: "I believe . . . that the cod fishery, the herring fishery, the pilchard fishery, the mackerel fishery, and probably all the great sea fisheries, are inexhaustible; that is to say, that nothing we do seriously affects the number of fish. And any attempt to regulate these fisheries seems consequently . . . to be useless." Huxley's address is available at http://aleph0.clarku.edu/huxley/SM5/fish.html.

38. P. A. Larkin, "An Epitaph for the Concept of Maximum Sustained Yield," *Transactions of the American Fisheries Society 106* (1977): 1–11; D. Ludwig, R. Hilborn, and C. Walters, "Uncertainty, Resource Exploitation, and Conservation: Lessons from History," *Science 260*, no. 5104 (1993): 17, 36; L. W. Botsford, J. C. Castilla, and C. H. Peterson, "The Management of Fisheries and Marine Ecosystems," *Science 277*, no. 5325 (1997): 509–515.

39. D. G. Frey, ed., *Limnology in North America* (Madison: University of Wisconsin Press, 1963); A. L. Beckel, "Breaking New Waters: A Century of Limnology at the University of Wisconsin," and F. Egerton, "Wisconsin Limnology Community," in *Transactions of the Wisconsin Academy of Sciences, Arts and Letters*, special issue, edited by A. L. Beckel (Madison: Wisconsin Academy of Sciences, Arts and Letters, 1987); D. W. Schneider, "Local Knowledge, Environmental Politics, and the Founding of Ecology in the United States: Stephen Forbes and 'The Lake as a Microcosm' (1887)," *Isis 91*, no. 3 (2000): 681–705.

40. Stroud, "Fisheries and Aquatic Resources."

41. J. T. Bowen, "A History of Fish Culture as Related to the Development of Fishery Programs," in *A Century of Fisheries in North America*, edited by G. Benson (Washington, D.C.: American Fisheries Society, 1970), pp. 71–93. See also R. J. White, "Why Wild Fish Matter: A Biologist's

View," *Trout* 33, no. 3 (1992): 24–34, 44–49; R. J. White, "Why Wild Fish Matter: Balancing Ecological and Aquacultural Fishery Management," *Trout* 33, no. 4 (1992): 16–33, 44–48

42. Robert Grese explores this period through the work of Jens Jensen in *Jens Jensen: Maker of Natural Parks and Gardens* (Baltimore, Md.: Johns Hopkins University Press, 1992).

43. G. M. Wright, J. S. Dixon, and B. H. Thompson, *Fauna of the National Parks of the United States: A Preliminary Survey of Faunal Relations in National Parks*, Fauna Series 1 (Washington, D.C.: Government Printing Office, 1933). See C. L. Shafer, "Conservation Biology Trailblazers: George Wright, Ben Thompson, and Joseph Dixon," *Conservation Biology* 15, no. 2 (2001): 332–344. See also R. W. Sellars, *Preserving Nature in the Natural Parks: A History* (New Haven, Conn.: Yale University Press, 1997).

44. P. Sutter, *Driven Wild: How the Fight Against Automobiles Launched the Modern Wilderness Movement* (Seattle: University of Washington Press, 2002); D. G. Havlick, *No Place Distant: Roads and Motorized Recreation on America's Public Lands* (Washington, D.C.: Island Press, 2002).

45. A. Leopold, "Conserving the Covered Wagon," *Sunset Magazine* 54, no. 3 (1925): 21, 56; Flader and Callicott, *River*, p. 131. For a discussion of Leopold's wilderness protection activities during this period, see Flader and Callicott, *River*, pp. 24–27.

46. R. F. Nash, *Wilderness and the American Mind*, 4th ed. (1967; New Haven, Conn.: Yale University Press, 2001), p. 191.

47. See V. Shelford, "The Preservation of Natural Conditions," *Science* 51, no. 1317 (1920): 316–317; L. Sumner, "The Need for a More Serious Effort to Rescue a Few Fragments of Vanishing Nature," *Scientific Monthly* 10 (1920): 236–248; G. A. Pearson, "Preservation of Natural Areas in the National Forests," *Ecology* 3, no. 4 (1922): 284–287; V. Shelford, *A Naturalist's Guide to the Americas* (Baltimore, Md.: Williams and Wilkins, 1926); V. Shelford, "The Preservation of Natural Biotic Communities," *Ecology* 14, no. 2 (1933): 240–245; V. Shelford, "Nature Sanctuaries—A Means of Saving Natural Biotic Communities," *Science* 77, no. 1994 (1933): 281–282; see also R. A. Croker, *Pioneer Ecologist: The Life and Work of Victor Ernest Shelford, 1877–1968* (Washington, D.C.: Smithsonian Institution Press, 1991), pp. 120–146. See also chaps. 4 and 5 in this volume.

48. Pinchot, *Breaking New Ground*, p. 509. Emphasis added.

49. See n. 14 above.

50. J. B. Callicott, "Conservation Ethics and Fishery Management," *Fisheries* 16, no. 2 (1991): 24. Emphases in original.

51. A. Leopold, "The Conservation Ethic," *Journal of Forestry* 31, no. 6 (1933): 635; Flader and Callicott, *River*, p. 183. Emphases in original.

52. A. Leopold, "Wilderness as a Land Laboratory," *Living Wilderness* 6 (1941): 3; Flader and Callicott, *River*, p. 288. See also chap. 4 in this volume.

53. A. Leopold, *A Sand County Almanac and Sketches Here and There* (New York: Oxford University Press, 1949), p. 204.

54. Leopold, *Sand County Almanac*, p. ix.

55. A. Leopold, "A Biotic View of Land," *Journal of Forestry* 37, no. 9 (1939): 729; Flader and Callicott, *River*, p. 271. See R. L. Knight, "Aldo Leopold, the Land Ethic, and Ecosystem Management," *Journal of Wildlife Management* 60, no. 3 (1996): 471–474.

56. P. B. Sears, "The Fourth R: Resources," in Pittman, *From The Land*, p. 436.

57. Noss and Cooperrider, *Saving Nature's Legacy*, p. 80.

58. S. Hays, *Beauty, Health, and Permanence: Environmental Politics in the United States, 1955–1985* (Cambridge: Cambridge University Press, 1987), p. 396. The point is a fundamental one. In *Breaking New Ground*, for example, Gifford Pinchot granted that the scientific study of plants was valuable ("trees," he allowed, "are unquestionably vegetable"), but nonetheless insisted

that "forestry is not botany, but something vastly different." He distinguished between "forester's facts" and "mere botanical observations" (pp. 3, 88, 97). But see Miller, *Gifford Pinchot*, pp. 326–341, 357–380.

59. Hays, *Beauty, Health, and Permanence*, p. 395. For detailed examinations of postwar changes in forestry, see D. A. Clary, *Timber and the Forest Service* (Lawrence, Kans.: University Press of Kansas, 1986); P. Hirt, *A Conspiracy of Optimism: Management of the National Forests Since World War II* (Lincoln: University of Nebraska Press, 1994) and Langston, *Forest Dreams, Forest Nightmares*.

60. See M. W. Brunson and J. J. Kennedy, "Redefining 'Multiple Use': Agency Responses to Changing Social Values," in Knight and Bates, *New Century*, pp. 143–158.

61. See L. B. Leopold, "Ethos, Equity, and the Water Resource," *Environment* 32, no. 2 (1990): 16–20, 37–42; Noss and Cooperrider, *Saving Nature's Legacy*, pp. 72–80; S. H. Anderson, "Traditional Approaches and Tools in Natural Resources Management," in Knight and Bates, *New Century*, pp. 61–74.

62. For recent attempts to assess these changes in conservation, see Knight and Bates, *New Century*; and B. A. Minteer and R. E. Manning, eds., *Reconstructing Conservation: Finding Common Ground* (Washington, D.C.: Island Press, 2003).

63. A. Leopold, *Round River: From the Journals of Aldo Leopold*, edited by L. B. Leopold (New York: Oxford University Press, 1953), p. 155.

64. W. Stegner, "The Legacy of Aldo Leopold," in *Companion to* A Sand County Almanac: *Interpretive and Critical Essays*, edited by J. B. Callicott (Madison: University of Wisconsin Press, 1987), p. 245.

2. Conservation and the Progressive Movement

The Constitution of the Iroquois Confederacy is also called *Ne Gayaneshagowa*, the Great Binding Law, and the Great Law of Peace. The Great Law existed in oral tradition from at least the late fifteenth century before ethnographers recorded it beginning in the late 1800s. Several written versions of the Great Law exist. This version is from A. C. Parker, *The Constitution of the Five Nations*, New York State Bulletin No. 184 (Albany: University of the State of New York, 1916), pp. 38–39. See S. O'Brien, *American Indian Tribal Governments* (Norman: University of Oklahoma Press, 1989), pp. 17–20; D. Snow, *The Iroquois* (Cambridge, Mass.: Blackwell Publishers, 1994), pp. 57–60; and W. N. Fenton, *The Great Law and the Longhouse: A Political Theory of the Iroquois* (Norman: University of Oklahoma Press, 1998). Goethe's statement in the original German is: "Welche regierung die beste sei? Diejenige, die uns lehrt, uns selbst zu regieren." See B. Saunders, *The Maxims and Reflections of Goethe* (1893), p. 107. See n. 25 in this chapter.

1. S. Stromquist, "Prairie Politics and the Landscape of Reform," in *Recovering the Prairie*, edited by R. Sayre (Madison: University of Wisconsin Press, 1999), pp. 107–123. For biographical and topical coverage of these times, see D. Lowenthal, *George Perkins Marsh: Prophet of Conservation* (Seattle: University of Washington Press, 2000); C. Miller, *Gifford Pinchot and the Making of Modern Environmentalism* (Washington, D.C.: Island Press, 2001); E. Morris, *Theodore Rex* (New York: Random House, 2001); and M. McGerr, *A Fierce Discontent: The Rise and Fall of the Progressive Movement in America, 1870–1920* (New York: Free Press, 2003).

2. T. Roosevelt, *Theodore Roosevelt: An Autobiography* (1913; reprint, New York: De Capo Press, 1985), pp. 434, 420. See C. Meine, "Roosevelt, Conservation, and the Revival of Democracy," *Conservation Biology* 15, no. 4 (2001): 829–831.

3. See chap. 1, n. 2. Recent biographies include B. A. Weisberger, *The La Follettes of Wisconsin: Love and Politics in Progressive America* (Madison: University of Wisconsin Press, 1994); and N.

C. Unger, *Fighting Bob La Follette: The Righteous Reformer* (Chapel Hill: University of North Carolina Press, 2000).

4. T. Roosevelt, introduction to C. McCarthy, *The Wisconsin Idea* (New York: Macmillan, 1912), p. vii.

5. Quoted in Roosevelt, *Autobiography*, pp. 406–407.

6. W. Berry, "A Few Words in Praise of Edward Abbey," in *Resist Much, Obey Little: Remembering Ed Abbey*, edited by J. R. Hepworth and G. McNamee (San Francisco: Sierra Club Books, 1996), p. 3.

7. Roosevelt, *Autobiography*, p. 437.

8. T. Roosevelt, introduction to *The Wisconsin Idea*, p. ix.

9. G. Pinchot, *The Fight for Conservation* (1910; reprint, Seattle: University of Washington Press, 1967), p. 88.

10. C. Van Hise, *The Conservation of Natural Resources in the United States* (New York: Macmillan, 1910), p. 379.

11. See J. Nichols, "Wisconsin: A State of Continual and Fearless Sifting and Winnowing," in *These United States: Original Essays by Leading American Writers on Their State within the Union*, edited by J. Leonard (New York: Thunder's Mouth Press / Nation Books, 2003), pp. 485–494.

12. P. Sauer, "Reinhabiting Environmentalism: Picking Up Where Leopold and Carson Left Off," *Orion* 18, no. 3 (Summer 1999): 31.

13. J. B. Callicott and M. P. Nelson, eds., *The Great New Wilderness Debate* (Athens, Ga.: University of Georgia Press, 1998). See chap. 9, n. 3.

14. K. DeLuca, "Environmental Justice," *New York Times*, 18 July 2002, p. A22.

15. For a helpful discussion of the need to clarify the "linguistic muddle" in environmental history, see J. M. Taylor, "Charting American Environmentalism's Early (Intellectual) Geography, 1890–1920," *Wild Earth* 10, no. 2 (2000): 18–25.

16. O. Murie, "Ethics in Wildlife Management," *Journal of Wildlife Management* 18, no. 3 (1954): 292, 293; reprinted in *The Muries: Voices for Wilderness and Wildlife*, edited by N. Shea, S. Chase, M. Madison, and M. Daly (Sheperdstown, W.Va.: U.S. Fish and Wildlife Service, National Conservation Training Center, 2001), pp. 53–56. See C. Meine, "Murie's Choice: An Introduction to the Essay 'Ethics in Wildlife Management,'" in *The Muries*, pp. 51–52. For discussions at the confluence of social justice, cultural diversity, and conservation, see C. Merchant, *Ecological Revolutions: Nature, Gender, and Science in New England* (Chapel Hill: University of North Carolina Press, 1989); W. Berry, *The Hidden Wound* (New York: North Point Press, 1989); R. Nash, *The Rights of Nature: A History of Environmental Ethics* (Madison: University of Wisconsin Press, 1989); R. Bullard, ed., *Confronting Environmental Racism: Voices from the Grassroots* (Boston: South End Press, 1993); M. V. Melosi, "Equity, Eco-Racism, and Environmental History," *Environmental History Review* 19, no. 3 (1995): 1–16; G. P. Nabhan, *Cultures of Habitat: On Nature, Culture, and Story* (New York: Counterpoint Press, 1997); A. L. Herman, *Community, Violence, and Peace: Aldo Leopold, Mohandas K. Gandhi, Martin Luther King Jr., and Gautama the Buddha in the Twenty-First Century* (Albany: State University of New York Press, 1999); M. D. Spence, *Dispossessing the Wilderness: Indian Removal and the Making of the National Parks* (New York: Oxford University Press, 1999); P. Burnham, *Indian Country, God's Country: Native Americans and the National Parks* (Washington, D.C.: Island Press, 2000); T. Davis, *Sustaining the Forest, the People, and the Spirit* (Albany: State University of New York Press, 2000); K. M. Mutz, G. C. Bryner, and D. S. Kenney, *Justice and Natural Resources: Concepts, Strategies, and Applications* (Washington, D.C.: Island Press, 2001); A. H. Deming and L. E. Savoy, eds., *The Colors of Nature: Culture, Identity, and the Natural World* (Minneapolis, Minn.: Milkweed Editions, 2002); C. Merchant, "Shades of Darkness: Race and Environmental History," *Environmental History* 8, no. 3 (2003): 380–394. David Ehrenfeld explores the cultural

dimension of conservation in his volumes *Beginning Again: People and Nature in the New Millennium* (New York: Oxford University Press, 1993) and *Swimming Lessons: Keeping Afloat in the Age of Technology* (New York: Oxford University Press, 2002).

17. C. Meine, "Conservation Movement, Historical," in *Encyclopedia of Biodiversity*, edited by S. Levin (San Diego: Academic Press, 2001), 1: 883–896.

18. Pinchot, *Fight for Conservation*, p. 43.

19. Pinchot, *Fight for Conservation*, p. 46.

20. Miller, *Gifford Pinchot*, p. 11. The classic commentary is S. P. Hays, *Conservation and the Gospel of Efficiency: The Progressive Conservation Movement, 1890–1920* (Cambridge, Mass.: Harvard University Press, 1959).

21. See chap. 4 in this volume. Miller, *Gifford Pinchot*, pp. 1–12. J. M. Turner writes in "Charting American Environmentalism's Early (Intellectual) Geography," p. 23: "Little evidence exists that in the 1890s [the] 'preservationists' considered themselves the foes of any emerging group of 'conservationists.' Ambiguities in the 1890s language have made it easy for historians and environmentalists alike to overemphasize the early divisions underlying the nation's environmental movement."

22. T. Roosevelt, Eighth Annual Message to the United States Senate and House of Representatives, 8 December 1908. See E. Morris, *Theodore Rex*, pp. 506–508.

23. See A. Schlesinger Jr., "A Question of Power," *The American Prospect* 12, no. 7 (23 April 2001), p. 27.

24. D. Kemmis, *This Sovereign Land: A New Vision for Governing the West* (Washington, D.C.: Island Press, 2001), p. 38.

25. The origins of the dictum are obscure. Usually attributed to Thomas Paine or Thomas Jefferson, the author and original citation have never been definitively identified. On the general point, Jefferson is all over the map. In *Notes on Virginia*, he averred that "great societies cannot exist without government"; in a 1788 letter he observed that "We are now vibrating between too much and too little government, and the pendulum will rest finally in the middle"; in an 1824 letter, he expressed his view that "we have more machinery of government than is necessary, too many parasites on the labor of the industrious." See www.geocities.com/CapitolHill/7970/jefpc009.htm for a fuller discussion of this "best known of the doubtful Jefferson quotes." The most familiar use of the statement comes in the opening lines of Thoreau's 1849 essay "Civil Disobedience": "I heartily accept the motto,—'That government is best which governs least;' and I should like to see it acted up to more rapidly and systematically. Carried out, it amounts to this, which I also believe,—'That government is best which governs not at all;' and when men are prepared for it, that will be the kind of government which they will have." Thoreau himself provided no source. Perhaps he was drawing upon journalist John Lewis O'Sullivan's 1837 introduction to the new monthly *United States Magazine and Democratic Review*: "The best government is that which governs least." Perhaps he was drawing upon his friend Ralph Waldo Emerson's statement in the essay "Politics" (1844): "The less government we have the better—the fewer laws, and the less confided power." The statement now sometimes appears in an extended form—"That government is best which governs least, because its people discipline themselves"—again, without definitive attribution.

26. Kemmis, *This Sovereign Land*, p. 25. For an examination of the history of this "channel," see G. Wills, *A Necessary Evil: A History of American Distrust of Government* (New York: Simon and Schuster, 1999).

27. Pinchot, *Fight for Conservation*, p. 60.

28. Miller, *Gifford Pinchot*, p. 155.

29. R. S. Beeman and J. A. Pritchard, *A Green and Permanent Land: Ecology and Agriculture in the Twentieth Century* (Lawrence: University Press of Kansas, 2001), p. 82.

30. The quote is from an untitled manuscript, c. 1935; see C. Meine and R. L. Knight, eds., *The Essential Aldo Leopold: Quotations and Commentaries* (Madison: University of Wisconsin Press, 1999), pp. 161–162. Emphasis in original.

31. A. Leopold, "The Conservation Ethic," *Journal of Forestry* 31, no. 6 (1933): 638; S. L. Flader and J. B. Callicott, eds., *The River of the Mother of God and Other Essays by Aldo Leopold* (Madison: University of Wisconsin Press, 1991), p. 187. Leopold's most extensive critique of the New Deal approach to conservation at the time was his article "Conservation Economics," *Journal of Forestry* 32, no. 5: 537–544; Flader and Callicott, *River*, pp. 193–202. On the particular theme of soil erosion, Leopold held that the only solution lay in "the *conservative use of every acre on every watershed in America*, whether it be farm or forest, public or private. . . . This disease of erosion is a leprosy of the land, hardly to be cured by slapping a mustard plaster on the first sore. The only cure is the universal reformation of land-use, and the longer we dabble with palliatives, the more gigantic grows the job of restoration" (p. 539; emphasis in original). For a compilation of Leopold's writings on private land stewardship, see A. Leopold, *For the Health of the Land: Previously Unpublished Essays and Other Writings*, edited by J. B. Callicott and E. T. Freyfogle (Washington, D.C.: Island Press, 1999); see also Meine and Knight, *Essential Aldo Leopold*, pp. 155–167.

32. Meine and Knight, *Essential Aldo Leopold*, p. 162. See S. Flader, "Building Conservation on the Land: Aldo Leopold and the Tensions of Professionalism and Citizenship," in B. A. Minteer and R. E. Manning, eds., *Reconstructing Conservation: Finding Common Ground* (Washington, D. C.; Island Press, 2003) , pp. 115–132.

33. A. Leopold, *A Sand County Almanac and Sketches Here and There* (New York: Oxford University Press, 1949), p. 213.

34. Kemmis, *This Sovereign Land*, p. 51.

35. Quoted in J. L. Thomas, *A Country in the Mind: Wallace Stegner, Bernard De Voto, History, and the American Land* (New York: Routledge, 2000), p. 137.

36. M. W. T. Harvey, *A Symbol of Wilderness: Echo Park and the American Conservation Movement* (Seattle: University of Washington Press, 2000).

37. R. H. Nelson, "The Public Land Management Agencies," in *A New Century for Natural Resources Management*, edited by R. L. Knight and S. F. Bates (Washington, D.C: Island Press, 1995), p. 54.

38. Leopold, *A Sand County Almanac*, p. 210.

39. Meine, "Roosevelt, Conservation, and the Revival of Democracy," p. 830. For two recent and personal accounts of this transitional period, see: M. Frome, *Greenspeak: Fifty Years of Environmental Muckraking and Advocacy* (Knoxville: University of Tennessee Press, 2002); and R. Train, *Politics, Pollution, and Pandas: An Environmental Memoir* (Washington, D.C: Island Press, 2003). For a useful study of this period in Wisconsin, see T. R. Huffman, *Protectors of the Land and Water: Environmentalism in Wisconsin, 1961–1968* (Chapel Hill: University of North Carolina Press, 1994).

40. See n. 16 above; chap. 10, n. 26.

41. K. Brower, introduction to A. Leopold, *A Sand County Almanac with Essays on Conservation* (New York: Oxford University Press, 2001), p. 9.

42. R. L. Knight, "The Ecology of Ranching," in *Ranching West of the Hundredth Meridian: Culture, Ecology, and Economics*, edited by R. L. Knight, W. C. Gilgert, and E. Marston (Washington, D.C.: Island Press, 2002), pp. 123–144; J. Christensen, "Environmentalists Hail the Ranchers: Howdy, Pardners!" *New York Times*, 10 September 2002, p. F3; C. Meine, "Homegrown Conservation: The Revolution Is Here," *Wisconsin Academy Review* 48, no. 2 (2002), pp. 49–50; R. B. Keiter, *Keeping Faith with Nature: Ecosystems, Democracy, and America's Public Lands* (New Haven, Conn.: Yale University Press, 2003).

43. D. Worster, "Leopold and the Changing Landscape of History," in Meine and Knight, *Essential Aldo Leopold*, p. 239.

3. Conservation Biology and Sustainable Societies

Ray Dasmann's statement is from "The Land Ethic and the World Scene," a lecture he delivered in 1987 at Iowa State University in Ames, as part of a conference commemorating the hundredth anniversary of Aldo Leopold's birth. The lecture appears in *Aldo Leopold: The Man and His Legacy*, edited by T. Tanner (1987; reprint Ankeny, Iowa: Soil and Water Conservation Society of America, 1995), pp. 107–114.

1. The incident occurred at San Jose State University. Several other car-bashing (literally) events took place elsewhere in the country on Earth Day 1970. For a contrasting commentary, see D. Hayes, "Reclaiming the Vision of the First Earth Day," *The Seattle Times*, 22 April 2004.

2. E. Abbey, *Abbey's Road* (New York: E. P. Dutton, 1979), p. 127.

3. G. P. Marsh, *Man and Nature, or, Physical Geography as Modified by Human Action*, edited by David Lowenthal (1843; reprint, Cambridge, Mass.: Harvard University Press, 1965), p. 43.

4. Marsh, *Man and Nature*, pp. 42, 29. Emphasis added.

5. The undated manuscript, quoted here in full, is in the Aldo Leopold Papers (hereafter LP) 6B16, at the University of Wisconsin, Madison. For further context on Leopold's trip to Germany, see S. Flader, *Thinking Like a Mountain: Aldo Leopold and the Evolution of an Ecological Attitude toward Deer, Wolves, and Mountains* (1974; reprint, Madison: University of Wisconsin Press, 1994), pp. 139–144; C. Meine, *Aldo Leopold: His Life and Work* (Madison: University of Wisconsin Press, 1988), pp. 351–360. Emphasis added.

6. Leopold did try several times to develop his thoughts along these lines from his Germany trip. See especially his 1935 manuscript, also titled "Wilderness," in *The River of the Mother of God and Other Essays by Aldo Leopold*, edited by S. Flader and J. B. Callicott (Madison: University of Wisconsin Press, 1991), pp. 226–229.

7. A. Leopold, "The Outlook for Farm Wildlife," *Transactions of the Tenth North American Wildlife Conference* (Washington, D.C.: American Wildlife Institute, 1945), p. 168; Flader and Callicott, *River*, p. 326.

8. Quoted in R. Nash, *The Rights of Nature: A History of Environmental Ethics* (Madison: University of Wisconsin Press, 1989), p. 125; and S. Fox, *John Muir and His Legacy: The American Conservation Movement* (Boston: Little, Brown, 1981), p. 326.

9. M. Soulé, "History of the Society for Conservation Biology: How and Why We Got Here," *Conservation Biology* 1, no. 1 (1987): 4.

10. E. O. Wilson, "The Current State of Biological Diversity," in *Biodiversity*, edited by E. O. Wilson and F. M. Peter (Washington, D.C.: National Academy Press, 1988), p. 5. Wilson provided an autobiographical account of the island biogeography studies he undertook in partnership with Robert MacArthur in *Naturalist* (Washington, D.C.: Island Press, 1994), pp. 238–291. See also D. Quammen, *The Song of the Dodo: Island Biogeography in an Age of Extinctions* (New York: Simon and Schuster, 1996), pp. 409–447.

11. Of the texts that began to reorient biologists and resource managers toward biodiversity conservation, see: R. F. Dasmann, *Environmental Conservation*, 1st ed. (London: John Wiley and Sons, 1959; but see subsequent editions as well); R. F. Dasmann, *A Different Kind of Country* (New York: Macmillan, 1968); D. Ehrenfeld, *Biological Conservation* (New York: Holt, Rinehart and Winston, 1970); D. Ehrenfeld, *Conserving Life on Earth* (New York: Oxford University Press, 1972); D. Ehrenfeld, *The Arrogance of Humanism* (New York: Oxford University Press, 1978).

12. Key publications from this period include N. Myers, *The Sinking Ark: A New Look at the Problem of Disappearing Species* (Oxford, U.K.: Pergamon Press, 1979); P. R. Ehrlich and A. H. Ehrlich, *Extinction: The Causes and Consequences of the Disappearance of Species* (New York: Random House, 1981); and the U.S. National Research Council reports *Conversion of Tropical*

Moist Forests (1980), *Research Priorities in Tropical Biology* (1980), and *Ecological Aspects of Development in the Humid Tropics* (1982) (Washington, D.C.: National Academy Press).

13. I am grateful (still!) to Sherri Boykin Kuhl for compiling a chronology of these events in her presentation "Brief History of the Rise of Conservation Biology," prepared for the Conservation Ecology Seminar at the University of Wisconsin, Madison, 3 February 1987.

14. As early as 1934, Leopold in his article "Conservation Economics" (*Journal of Forestry* 32, no. 5: 543) used the term "conservation ecologist." In 1936, agency and academic researchers (including Leopold, Ralph T. King, Herb Stoddard, Ernest Holt, and W. L. McAtee) debated the term they would adopt in establishing a new professional organization for wildlife biologists. In a 14 August 1936 letter to McAtee, Holt wrote: "'Conservation Biologists' is all right with me, but I do feel that we should designate the Society as the 'Society of Conservation Biologists.' 'The Conservation Biologist' would be, I believe, a very snappy title for the magazine. I must admit, however, that I am a little superstitious about Conservation Biologist. That was my title when I was fired by Mr. Ickes!" (Leopold Papers 2B9). Ultimately, they reached consensus and named the new organization "The Wildlife Society." Paul Errington and Frederick Hamerstrom, in the first lines of the first article of the inaugural issue of the society's publication, the *Journal of Wildlife Management*, referred to "the new and growing field of conservation biology" ("The Evaluation of Nesting Losses and Juvenile Mortality of the Ring-necked Pheasant," *Journal of Wildlife Management* 1, nos. 1–2 [1937]: 3). In the same issue, leaders of the new organization published a "Statement of Policy," declaring that "wildlife management along sound biological lines is . . . part of the greater movement for conservation of our entire native flora and fauna."

15. Out of this initial conference emerged the volume *Conservation Biology: An Evolutionary-Ecological Perspective*, edited by M. E. Soulé and B. A. Wilcox (Sunderland, Mass.: Sinauer Associates, 1980). The emergence of conservation biology as a self-conscious field during this period can be traced through this and other volumes: R. H. MacArthur and E. O. Wilson, *The Theory of Island Biogeography* (Princeton, N.J.: Princeton University Press, 1967); R. H. MacArthur, *Geographical Ecology: Patterns in the Distribution of Species* (Princeton, N.J.: Princeton University Press, 1972); O. H. Frankel and M. E. Soulé, *Conservation and Evolution* (Cambridge: Cambridge University Press, 1981); C. M. Schonewald-Cox, S. M. Chambers, B. MacBryde, and W. L. Thomas, eds., *Genetics and Conservation: A Reference for Managing Wild Animal and Plant Populations* (Menlo Park, Calif.: Benjamin / Cummings, 1983); L. D. Harris, *The Fragmented Forest: Island Biogeographical Theory and the Preservation of Forests* (Chicago: University of Chicago Press, 1984); M. E. Soulé, ed., *Conservation Biology: The Science of Scarcity and Diversity* (Sunderland, Mass.: Sinauer Associates, 1986); M. E. Soulé, *Viable Populations for Conservation* (Cambridge: Cambridge University Press, 1987). For additional historical background, see Soulé, "History of the Society for Conservation Biology"; R. P. McIntosh, *The Background of Ecology: Concept and Theory* (Cambridge: Cambridge University Press, 1985); F. B. Golley, *A History of the Ecosystem Concept in Ecology: More Than the Sum of the Parts* (New Haven, Conn.: Yale University Press, 1993); C. Meine, "Conservation Biology and Wildlife Management in America: An Historical Perspective," in G. K. Meffe and R. C. Carroll and contributors, *Principles of Conservation Biology*, 1st ed. (Sunderland, Mass.: Sinauer Associates, 1994), pp. 310–312; D. Quammen, *The Song of the Dodo*; D. Takacs, *The Idea of Biodiversity: Philosophies of Paradise* (Baltimore, Md.: Johns Hopkins University Press, 1996); R. Noss, "Is There a Special Conservation Biology?" *Ecography* 22, no. 2 (1999): 113–122. See also chap. 5 in this volume.

16. Wilson, *Biodiversity*, p. vi. See also Takacs, *Idea of Biodiversity*, pp. 34–40. I am indebted to Walt Rosen for recounting the events surrounding the 1986 forum in a 1992 interview.

17. Wilson, *Biodiversity*, p. 3.

18. See, for example, the articles in the "In My Opinion . . . " section of the *Wildlife Society Bulletin* 17, no. 3 (1989), 335–365. For a postmodern critique, see Takacs, *Idea of Biodiversity*.

19. Wilson, *Biodiversity*, pp. v.

20. Dasmann, "Land Ethic and the World Scene," pp. 113, 114.

21. Marsh, *Man and Nature*, pp. 13, 44.

22. A. Leopold, "Land Pathology," 15 April 1935 lecture, LP 6B16; Flader and Callicott, *River*, p. 212.

23. A. Leopold, "A Biotic View of Land," *Journal of Forestry* 37, no. 9 (1939): 728; Flader and Callicott, *River*, pp. 267, 273.

24. R. Paehlke, *Environmentalism and the Future of Progressive Politics* (New Haven, Conn.: Yale University Press, 1989), p. 46.

25. F. Osborn, *Our Plundered Planet* (Boston: Little, Brown, 1948), p. 201.

26. W. Vogt, *Road to Survival* (New York: William Sloane Associates, 1948), p. 286. Emphasis added.

27. For fuller discussion of the emergence of the concept of "sustainability," see S. P. Hays, *Beauty, Health, and Permanence: Environmental Politics in the United States, 1955–1985* (Cambridge: Cambridge University Press, 1987); Paehlke, *Environmentalism and the Future of Progressive Politics*; N. Harrison, *Constructing Sustainable Development* (Albany: State University of New York Press, 2000); G. C. Bryner, *Gaia's Wager: Environmental Movements and the Challenge of Sustainability* (Lanham, Md.: Rowman & Littlefield, 2001). For a helpful summary of the literature of the 1970s and 1980s, see R. W. Merideth and L. S. Z. Greenberg, "Global Sustainability: A Selected, Annotated Bibliography," *Institute for Environmental Studies Report 137* (Madison: University of Wisconsin-Madison, Institute for Environmental Studies, 1990).

28. See W. Jackson, W. Berry, and B. Colman, eds., *Meeting the Expectations of the Land: Essays in Sustainable Agriculture and Stewardship* (San Francisco: North Point Press, 1984); C. E. Little, *Green Fields Forever: The Conservation Tillage Revolution in America* (Washington, D.C.: Island Press, 1987); R. Harwood, "A History of Sustainable Agriculture," in *Sustainable Agricultural Systems*, edited by C. A. Edwards, R. Lal, P. Madden, R. H. Miller, and G. House (Ankeny, Iowa: Soil and Water Conservation Society, 1990), pp. 3–19; and R. S. Beeman and J. A. Pritchard, *A Green and Permanent Land: Ecology and Agriculture in the Twentieth Century* (Lawrence: University Press of Kansas, 2001).

29. For a useful overview, see K. A. Dahlberg, "Sustainable Agriculture," in *Conservation and Environmentalism: An Encyclopedia*, edited by R. Paehlke (New York: Garland Publishing, 1995), pp. 613–615. For assessments over this period, see K. A. Dahlberg, *Beyond the Green Revolution: The Ecology and Politics of Global Agricultural Development* (New York, Plenum, 1979); G. K. Douglass, ed., *Agricultural Sustainability in a Changing World Order* (Boulder, Colo.: Westview Press, 1984); M. Altieri, *Agroecology: The Scientific Basis of Alternative Agriculture* (Boulder, Colo.: Westview Press, 1987); C. Benbrook, "The Den Bosch Declaration: Grappling with the Challenges of Sustainability," *Journal of Soil and Water Conservation* 46, no. 5 (1991): 349–352; R. B. Norgaard, "The Development of Tropical Forest Economics," and S. Gliessman and R. Grantham, "Agroecology," in *Lessons of the Rainforest*, edited by S. Head and R. Heinzman (San Francisco: Sierra Club Books, 1990); T. L. Grove and C. A. Edwards, "Do We Need a New Development Paradigm?" *Agriculture, Ecosystems and Environment* 46, nos. 1–4 (1993): 135–145; and the U.S. National Research Council reports *Alternative Agriculture* (1989), *Sustainable Agriculture: Research and Education in the Field* (1991), and *Sustainable Agriculture in the Humid Tropics* (1993) (Washington, D.C.: National Academy Press).

30. World Commission on Environment and Development (WCED), *Our Common Future* (New York: Oxford University Press, 1987), p. 43.

31. These titles are drawn from Merideth and Greenberg, "Global Sustainability." See also L. W. Milbrath, "Sustainability," in Paehlke, *Conservation and Environmentalism*, pp. 612–613; and R.

Paehlke, "Sustainable Development," in Paehlke, *Conservation and Environmentalism*, pp. 615–616.

32. See, for example, see N. C. Brady, "Making Agriculture a Sustainable Industry," in C. Edwards et al., *Sustainable Agricultural Systems*, pp. 20–32; K. Dahlberg, "Sustainable Agriculture—Fad or Harbinger?" *BioScience* 41, no. 5 (1991): 337–340; H. Salwasser, "Sustainability and Wilderness," *Conservation Biology* 5, no. 1 (1992): 120–122; D. Worster, "The Shaky Ground of Sustainable Development," in *The Wealth of Nature: Environmental History and the Ecological Imagination* (New York: Oxford University Press, 1993), pp. 142–155; Harrison, *Constructing Sustainable Development*.

33. J. Lubchenko, A. M. Olson, L. B. Brubaker, S. R. Carpenter, A. M. Holland, S. P. Hubbell, S. A. Levin, J. A. MacMahon, P. A. Matson, J. M. Melillo, H. A. Mooney, C. H. Peterson, H. R. Pulliam, L. A. Real, P. J. Regal, and P. G. Risser, "The Sustainable Biosphere Initiative: An Ecological Research Agenda," *Ecology* 72, no. 2 (1991): 373.

34. Royal Society of London and the U.S. National Academy of Sciences, "Population Growth, Resource Consumption, and a Sustainable World" (London and Washington, D.C., 1992).

35. IUCN (The World Conservation Union) / UNEP (United Nations Development Programme) / WWF (World Wide Fund for Nature), *Caring for the Earth: A Strategy for Sustainable Living* (Gland, Switzerland, IUCN / UNEP / WWF, 1991).

36. See Milbrath, "Sustainability," 612; D. Arnold, "U.S. vs. the World," *Boston Globe*, 20 August 2002.

37. Quoted in Arnold, "U.S. vs. the World."

4. Leopold's Fine Line

Theodore Roosevelt's statement is from an address on conservation at Stanford University on 12 May 1903. See E. Morris, *Theodore Rex* (New York: Random House, 2001), pp. 225–228. Aldo Leopold's is from his review of A. E. Parkins and J. R. Whitaker, *Our Natural Resources and Their Conservation*, *Bird-Lore* 39, no. 1 (1937): 75.

1. See chap. 9, n. 3.

2. A. Leopold, "Wherefore Wildlife Ecology," c. 1947 (Aldo Leopold Papers [hereafter LP] 6B16); S. L. Flader and J. B. Callicott, eds., *The River of the Mother of God and Other Essays by Aldo Leopold* (Madison: University of Wisconsin Press, 1991), p. 337.

3. C. Meine, *Aldo Leopold: His Life and Work* (Madison: University of Wisconsin Press, 1988), pp. 62–83.

4. A. Leopold, "To the Forest Officers of the Carson," *Carson Pine Cone*, 15 July 1913 (LP 11B1); Flader and Callicott, *River*, p. 43.

5. A. Leopold, "Address before the Albuquerque Rotary Club on Presentation of the Gold Medal of the Permanent Wild Life Protection Fund," c. July 1917 (LP 8B8).

6. A. Leopold, "Social Consequences of Conservation," unpublished manuscript, c. 1930 (LP 6B16).

7. A. Leopold, "Game and Wild Life Conservation," *The Condor* 34, no. 2 (1932): 104; Flader and Callicott, *River*, p. 166.

8. A. Leopold, "Game Cropping in Southern Wisconsin," *Our Native Landscape* (December 1933).

9. A. Leopold, *Game Management* (New York: Charles Scribner's Sons, 1933), p. 3.

10. Leopold, *Game Management*, p. 21.

11. See chap. 5 in this volume.

12. Leopold, *Game Management*, pp. 404, 405. Emphasis in original.

13. Leopold, *Game Management*, pp. 421–422.

14. A. Leopold, "A Biotic View of Land," *Journal of Forestry* 37, no. 9 (1939): 727; Flader and Callicott, *River*, pp. 266–267.

15. A. Leopold, "The Outlook for Farm Wildlife," *Transactions of the Tenth North American Wildlife Conference* (Washington, D.C.: American Wildlife Institute, 1945), p. 168; Flader and Callicott, *River*, p. 326.

16. See chaps. 6 and 7 in this volume.

17. A. Leopold, *A Sand County Almanac and Sketches Here and There* (New York: Oxford University Press, 1949), p. 18.

18. A. Leopold, "The Wilderness and Its Place in Forest Recreation Policy," *Journal of Forestry* 19, no. 7 (1921): 718–719; Flader and Callicott, *River*, p. 79.

19. Leopold, "The Wilderness and Its Place," p. 719; Flader and Callicott, *River*, p. 79.

20. Leopold, "The Wilderness and Its Place," p. 721; Flader and Callicott, *River*, p. 81.

21. Leopold, "The Wilderness and Its Place," p. 719; Flader and Callicott, *River*, p. 79. In his 1925 article "Conserving the Covered Wagon," *Sunset Magazine* 54, no. 3 (1925), Leopold wrote: "It is the opportunity, not the desire, on which the well-to-do are coming to have a monopoly. And the reason is the gradually increasing destruction of the nearby wilderness by good roads. The American of moderate means can not go to Alaska, or Africa, or British Columbia. He must seek his big adventure in the nearby wilderness, or go without it" (Flader and Callicott, *River*, p. 130).

22. See D. Baldwin, *The Quiet Revolution: The Grass Roots of Today's Wilderness Preservation Movement* (Boulder, Colo.: Pruett Publishing, 1972), pp. 11–30; R. Nash, *Wilderness and the American Mind*, 4th ed. (1967; New Haven, Conn.: Yale University Press, 2001), pp. 185–186; S. Flader, review of *The Quiet Revolution, Journal of Forest History* 18, no. 1–2 (1974): 36; L. Lakestraw, "News, Comments, and Letters," *Journal of Forest History* 19, no. 1 (1975): 41; R. Nash, "Arthur Carhart: Wildland Advocate," *Living Wilderness* 44, no. 151 (1980): 32–34.

23. A. Leopold, "The River of the Mother of God," c. December 1924 (LP 6B16); Flader and Callicott, *River*, p. 127.

24. Leopold, "Conserving the Covered Wagon," p. 56; Flader and Callicott, *River*, p. 132.

25. Leopold, "Conserving the Covered Wagon," p. 21; Flader and Callicott, *River*, p. 129.

26. A. Leopold, "The Pig in the Parlor," *USFS Service Bulletin* 9, no. 23 (1925): 1–2; Flader and Callicott, *River*, p. 133.

27. A. Leopold, "Wilderness as a Form of Land Use," *The Journal of Land and Public Utility Economics* 1, no. 4 (1925): 398, 399–400; Flader and Callicott, *River*, pp. 134, 136.

28. Leopold, "Wilderness as a Form of Land Use," p. 401; Flader and Callicott, *River*, p. 138.

29. Leopold, "Wilderness as a Form of Land Use," p. 400; Flader and Callicott, *River*, p. 137.

30. A. Leopold, "Why the Wilderness Society?," *Living Wilderness* 1, no. 1 (1935): 6. Emphasis in original.

31. A. Leopold, "Planning for Wildlife," 26 September 1941 (LP 6B16); A. Leopold, *For the Health of the Land: Previously Unpublished Essays and Other Writings*, edited by J. B. Callicott and E. T. Freyfogle (Washington, D.C.: Island Press, 1999), 197.

32. A. Leopold, "Wilderness as a Land Laboratory," *Living Wilderness* 6 (1941): 3; Flader and Callicott, *River*, p. 289.

33. Leopold, *Sand County Almanac*, p. 188.

34. Meine, *Aldo Leopold*, p. 79.

35. A. Leopold, "Some Fundamentals of Conservation in the Southwest," c. 1923 (LP 6B16); Flader and Callicott, *River*, p. 95.

36. Leopold, "Some Fundamentals"; Flader and Callicott, *River*, p. 94. Leopold was referencing one of his favorite illustrative biblical passages, Ezekiel 34:18: "Seemeth it a small thing unto you to have fed upon good pasture, but ye must tread down with your feet the residue

of your pasture? And to have drunk of the clear waters, but ye must foul the residue with your feet."

37. Leopold, "Some Fundamentals"; Flader and Callicott, *River*, p. 95.

38. A. Leopold, "The Conservation Ethic," *Journal of Forestry* 31, no. 6 (1933): 639; Flader and Callicott, *River*, p. 188. Emphasis in original.

39. Leopold, "The Conservation Ethic," pp. 641–642; Flader and Callicott, *River*, p. 191.

40. A. Leopold, "Land Pathology," 15 April 1935 (LP 6B16); Flader and Callicott, *River*, p. 213.

41. Leopold, "Land Pathology"; Flader and Callicott, *River*, p. 213.

42. Leopold, "Land Pathology"; Flader and Callicott, *River*, p. 214.

43. Leopold, "Land Pathology"; Flader and Callicott, *River*, p. 216.

44. Leopold, "Land Pathology"; Flader and Callicott, *River*, p. 217.

45. A. Leopold, *Round River: From the Journals of Aldo Leopold*, edited by L. B. Leopold (New York: Oxford University Press, 1953), p. 165.

46. A. Leopold, "The Farmer as a Conservationist," *American Forests* 45, no. 6 (1939), 298; Flader and Callicott, *River*, p. 259.

47. Leopold, *Round River*, p. 64.

48. See J. B. Callicott, "Leopold's Land Aesthetic," in *In Defense of the Land Ethic: Essays in Environmental Philosophy* (Albany: State University of New York Press, 1989), pp. 239–247.

49. A. Leopold, "Economics, Philosophy, and Land," unpublished manuscript, 23 November 1938 (LP 6B16).

50. A. Leopold, untitled manuscript, c. 1946 (LP 6B16).

51. Leopold, *Sand County Almanac*, p. viii.

52. A. Leopold, "The Meaning of Conservation," unpublished lecture notes, c. 1944 (LP 6B16).

5. Emergence of an Idea

Ernst Mayr's words are from *The Growth of Biological Thought: Diversity, Evolution, and Inheritance* (Cambridge, Mass.: Harvard University Press, 1982), p. 133.

1. A. Leopold, *A Sand County Almanac and Sketches Here and There* (New York: Oxford University Press, 1949), p. 210.

2. See chap. 3 in this volume.

3. D. Takacs, *The Idea of Biodiversity: Visions of Paradise* (Baltimore, Md.: Johns Hopkins University Press, 1996), pp. 1–2. "In the name of biodiversity," Takacs elaborates, "biologists hope to increase their say in policy decisions, to accrue resources for research, gain a pivotal position in shaping our view of nature, and, ultimately, stem the rampant destruction of the natural world. . . . By staking out new sources of power for themselves, they ultimately hope to gain control over nature—over how and where and even why wild organisms and natural processes are allowed to endure" (p. 2).

4. The history of the theme of diversity in the development of biological science is laid out in Ernst Mayr's *The Growth of Biological Thought*. Raymond Dasmann was ahead of his time in exploring the interwoven themes of cultural and biological diversity in *A Different Kind of Country* (New York: Macmillan, 1968). E. O. Wilson provided a primer with *The Diversity of Life* (New York: W. W. Norton, 1992). David Quammen surveyed the background of biodiversity science and conservation in *The Song of the Dodo: Island Biogeography in an Age of Extinction* (New York: Simon and Schuster, 1996). See also D. H. Pimlott, "The Value of Diversity," *Transactions of the North American Wildlife and Natural Resources Conference* 34 (1969): 265–280; and J. J. Hickey, "Some Historical Phases in Wildlife Conservation," *Wildlife Society Bulletin* 2, no. 4 (1974): 164–170.

5. C. Meine, "Conservation Movement, Historical" in *Encyclopedia of Biodiversity*, edited by S. Levin (San Diego: Academic Press, 2001), 1: 883–896. See also R. D. E. MacPhee, ed., *Extinctions in Near Time: Contexts, Causes, and Consequences* (New York: Plenum Press, 1999).

6. Jeffery Burley writes in "Forest Biological Diversity: An Overview," *Unasylva* 53, no. 209 (2002): 3–9: "Despite the impression given by recent international policy processes . . . biological diversity and its conservation are not new subjects. Herodotus in 450 BC was aware of the importance of intraspecific variation in tree species although he did not know the word 'genetic.' Charles Darwin in the middle of the nineteenth century was well aware of biological diversity and its importance for evolution and ecosystem stability. Foresters at the same time were preparing forest working plans in Europe and India that fully recognized the multiple values of forests, including species diversity, for sustainable use and ecosystem stability for the maintenance of human environments and life processes."

7. J. Muir, *The Story of My Boyhood and Youth* (1913; reprint, San Francisco: Sierra Club Books, 1988), p. 36.

8. Muir, *Boyhood and Youth*, p. 157. It is no understatement to say that this initial exposure to taxonomic methods was a spiritual experience for Muir. In the remainder of the passage, Muir demonstrated the same conflation of science and religious sentiment that Wallace and Marsh did (see text): "Like everyone else," Muir wrote, "I was always fond of flowers, attracted by their external beauty and purity. Now my eyes were opened to their inner beauty, all alike revealing glorious traces of the thoughts of God, and leading on and on into the infinite cosmos. I wandered away at every opportunity, making long excursions round the [Madison] lakes, gathering specimens and keeping them fresh in a bucket in my room to study at night after my regular class tasks were learned; for my eyes never closed on the plant glory I had seen."

9. Wallace's address "On the Physical Geography of the Malay Archipelago" appeared in the *Journal of the Royal Geographical Society* 33 (1863). I am grateful to Phil Pister for bringing this quotation to my attention (as, over the years, he has brought it to the attention of thousands of conservation biologists and resource managers).

10. G. P. Marsh, *Man and Nature: Or, Physical Geography as Modified by Human Action*, edited by D. Lowenthal (1864; reprint, Cambridge, Mass.: Harvard University Press, 1965), pp. 54, 96, 110, 112. See also M. Hall, "Restoring the Countryside: George Perkins Marsh and the Italian Land Ethic (1861–1882)," *Environment and History* 4, no. 1 (1998): 91–103; D. Lowenthal, *George Perkins Marsh: Prophet of Conservation* (Seattle: University of Washington Press, 2000); and S. Trombulak, ed., *So Great a Vision: The Conservation Writings of George Perkins Marsh* (Middlebury, Vt., and Lebanon, N. H.: Middlebury College Press and the University Press of New England, 2001).

11. A. Leopold, *Round River: From the Journals of Aldo Leopold*, edited by L. B. Leopold (New York: Oxford University Press, 1953), p. 146.

12. Leopold, *Round River*, pp. 146–147. This much-quoted passage derives from manuscripts that were unpublished at the time of Leopold's death in 1948. It first appeared in print in the essay "Conservation" in *Round River* (1953) and was later included in the expanded paperback edition *A Sand County Almanac with Essays on Conservation from Round River* (New York: Sierra Club / Ballantine Books, 1970) in the reedited essay "The Round River," p. 190.

13. See introduction to C. Meine and R. L. Knight, eds., *The Essential Aldo Leopold: Quotations and Commentaries* (Madison: University of Wisconsin Press, 1999), pp. xiv–xix. In the same volume, see G. K. Meffe, "Standing on Solid Shoulders," pp. 127–129; and quotations in chap. 9, "Biodiversity and Conservation Biology," pp. 130–151.

14. A. Leopold, *Game and Fish Handbook* (Albuquerque, N.Mex.: USDA Forest Service, 1915). In this same publication, the novice Leopold revealed the extent of his early naiveté concerning global biological diversity and evolutionary processes, and his willingness to cite foggy statistics in the cause of game protection: "North America, in its natural state, possessed the richest fauna

in the world. Its stock of game has been reduced 98%. Eleven species have been already exterminated, and twenty-five more are now candidates for oblivion. Nature was a million years, or more, in developing a species. . . . Man, with all his wisdom, has not evolved so much as a ground squirrel, a sparrow, or a clam." These statements reflected the influence of William Temple Hornaday at this key moment in Leopold's youthful conservation advocacy; see C. Meine, *Aldo Leopold: His Life and Work* (Madison: University of Wisconsin Press, 1988), pp. 144–147. Emphasis added.

15. A. Leopold, "Forestry and Game Conservation," *Journal of Forestry* 16, no. 4 (1918): 410; S. L. Flader and J. B. Callicott, eds., *The River of the Mother of God and Other Essays by Aldo Leopold* (Madison: University of Wisconsin Press, 1991), p. 59. Leopold compared this interest in "variety in game" with the forester's choice in prescribing "either a mixed stand or a pure one." Game management, he suggested, "should always prescribe a mixed stand" of native wild game species.

16. A. Leopold, "Wild Lifers vs. Game Farmers: A Plea for Democracy in Sport," *Bulletin of the American Game Protective Association* 8, no. 2 (1919): 6; Flader and Callicott, *River*, p. 64. Emphasis added.

17. Leopold, "Wild Lifers vs. Game Farmers," p. 6; Flader and Callicott, *River*, p. 65.

18. A. Leopold, "The Game Situation in the Southwest," *Bulletin of the American Game Protective Association* 9, no. 2 (1920): 5.

19. A. Leopold, untitled address, *Proceedings of the Second National Conference on Outdoor Recreation, January 20–21, 1926* (69th Cong., 1st sess., S. Doc. 117): 65.

20. A. Leopold, chair, "Report of the Committee on American Wild Life Policy," *Transactions of the Sixteenth North American Game Conference* (1929): 196, 197–198. Emphasis added.

21. A. Leopold, chair, *Report to the National Game Conference on an American Game Policy* (Washington, D.C.: American Game Association, 1930), p. 6; Flader and Callicott, *River*, pp. 153–154.

22. See T. R. Dunlap, *Saving America's Wildlife* (Princeton, N.J.: Princeton University Press, 1988), pp. 47–61.

23. The Kaibab story has long provided fodder for ecological debate. Dunlap provides an overview of the episode in *Saving America's Wildlife*, pp. 65–70. See also S. Flader, *Thinking Like a Mountain: Aldo Leopold and the Evolution of an Ecological Attitude Toward Deer, Wolves, and Forests* (1974; reprint, Madison: University of Wisconsin Press, 1994). The first book-length review is C. C. Young, *In the Absence of Predators: Conservation and Controversy on the Kaibab Plateau* (Lincoln: University of Nebraska Press, 2002). A recent study using aspen age structure data to test the "classic" story of the Kaibab is D. Binkley, M. M. Moore, W. H. Romme, and P. M. Brown, "Was Aldo Leopold Right about the Kaibab Deer Herd? The Aspen Story," (in prep).

24. Leopold, "American Game Policy, " p. 18.

25. C. Elton, *Animal Ecology* (1927; reprint, Chicago: University of Chicago Press, 2001). See Meine, *Aldo Leopold*, pp. 282–284; P. Crowcroft, *Elton's Ecologists: A History of the Bureau of Animal Populations* (Chicago: University of Chicago Press, 1991).

26. A. Leopold, *Game Management* (New York: Charles Scribner's Sons, 1933), p. 403. Emphasis in original.

27. A. Leopold, "The Conservation Ethic" *Journal of Forestry* 31, no. 6 (1933): 641; Flader and Callicott, *River*, pp. 190–191. Emphasis in original.

28. R. McCabe, *Aldo Leopold: The Professor* (Madison, Wisc.: Rusty Rock Press, 1987), pp. 36–46; B. Silbernagel and J. Silbernagel, "Tracking Aldo Leopold through Riley's Farmland," *Wisconsin Magazine of History* 86, no. 4 (2003): 34–45.

29. McCabe, *Aldo Leopold*, pp. 46–50; C. Meine, "Reimagining the Prairie: Aldo Leopold and the Origins of Prairie Restoration," in *Recovering the Prairie*, edited by R. Sayre (Madison: University of Wisconsin Press, 1999), pp. 144–160; W. L. Jordan III, *The Sunflower Forest:*

Ecological Restoration and the New Communion with Nature (Berkeley: University of California Press, 2003).

30. A. Leopold, "Land Pathology," 15 April 1935 lecture (Aldo Leopold Papers [hereafter LP] 6B16); Flader and Callicott, *River*, p. 217.

31. A. Leopold, "Wilderness," undated manuscript, c. 1935 (LP 6B16); Flader and Callicott, *River*, p. 229.

32. A. Leopold, "Threatened Species: A Proposal to the Wildlife Conference for an Inventory of the Needs of Near-Extinct Birds and Animals," *American Forests* 42, no. 3 (1936): 116; Flader and Callicott, *River*, p. 231. Emphasis in original.

33. Leopold, "Threatened Species," pp. 117, 118; Flader and Callicott, *River*, pp. 231, 233.

34. Leopold, "Threatened Species"; Flader and Callicott, *River*, pp. 231–232. For discussion of the use of the terms "wild life," "wild-life," and "wildlife" at this time, see Hickey, "Some Historical Phases in Wildlife Conservation."

35. A. Leopold, "Conservationist in Mexico," *American Forests* 43, no. 3 (1937): 118–120, 146; Flader and Callicott, *River*, p. 239. See Flader, *Thinking Like a Mountain*, pp. 153–156; Meine, *Aldo Leopold*, pp. 367–368, 379–380; W. Forbes and T. S. Haas, "Leopold's Legacy in the Rio Gavilan: Revisiting an Altered Mexican Wilderness," *Wild Earth* 10, no. 1 (2000): 61–67.

36. A. Leopold, "Foreword," 31 July 1947 (LP 6B16); Callicott, *Companion*, pp. 285–286.

37. Leopold, "Conservationist in Mexico," p. 120; Flader and Callicott, *River*, p. 241.

38. A. Leopold, "Planning for Wildlife," 26 September 1941 (LP 6B16); A. Leopold, *For the Health of the Land: Previously Unpublished Essays and Other Writings*, edited by J. B. Callicott and E. T. Freyfogle (Washington, D.C.: Island Press, 1999), p. 197.

39. A. Leopold, "A Biotic View of Land," *Journal of Forestry* 37, no. 9 (1939): 728; Flader and Callicott, *River*, p. 269.

40. Leopold, "A Biotic View of Land," p. 727; Flader and Callicott, *River*, p. 267.

41. A. Leopold, "Improving the Wildlife Program of the Soil Conservation Service," unpublished manuscript, 3 May 1940 (LP 6B16). Such statements were increasingly common in the last decade of Leopold's life. In 1945, for example, he wrote: "The aim in all wildlife conservation . . . should be reasonable levels for all members of the native wildlife community" ("Deer, Wolves, Foxes, and Pheasants," *Wisconsin Conservation Bulletin* 10, no. 4 [1945]: 5).

42. See J. B. Callicott, "Do Deconstructive Ecology and Sociobiology Undermine Leopold's Land Ethic," *Environmental Ethics* 18, no. 4 (1996): 353–372; and J. B. Callicott, "From the Balance of Nature to the Flux of Nature: The Land Ethic in a Time of Change," in *Aldo Leopold and the Ecological Conscience*, edited by R. L. Knight and S. Reidel (New York: Oxford University Press, 2002), pp. 90–105. Leopold understood early in his career that both natural disturbance and human agents were, historically and contemporarily, forces of landscape change. Careful reading reveals that Leopold slowly, steadily, and carefully reconsidered his understanding of equilibrium conditions throughout the 1920s and 1930s. In his unpublished 1927 manuscript "Southwestern Game Fields," for example, Leopold states: "Nature is not undisturbed; civilization has upset every factor of productivity for better or worse. Game management proposes to substitute a new and objective equilibrium for the natural one which civilization has destroyed" (LP 6B10). In 1933, in *Game Management*, he returns to the theme in the context of population biology: "The so-called 'balance of nature' is simply a name for the assumed tendency of the population curves of various species in an undisturbed plant and animal community to keep each other horizontal. The growth of biological knowledge tends strongly to show that while population curves may oscillate about a horizontal median, a single curve seldom or never stays horizontal from year to year even in virgin terrain. Fluctuation in numbers is nearly universal." He then carefully restated his earlier draft sentence: "Game management proposes to substitute a new and objective equilibrium for any natural one which civilization may have destroyed" (*Game Management*, p. 26).

In 1939, in "A Biotic View of Land," he stated his qualms explicitly: "The 'balance of nature' is a mental image for land and life which grew up before and during the transition to ecological thought. It is commonly employed in describing the biota to laymen, but ecologists among each other accept it only with reservations, and its acceptance by laymen seems to depend more on convenience than conviction. . . . To the ecological mind, balance of nature has merits and also defects. Its merits are that it conceives of a collective total, that it imputes some utility to all species, and that it implies oscillations when balance is disturbed. Its defects are that there is only one point at which balance occurs, and that balance is normally static" (Flader and Callicott, *River*, 267). In 1947, in his final version of "The Land Ethic," he is even more direct: "The image commonly employed in conservation education is 'the balance of nature.' For reasons too lengthy to detail here, this figure of speech fails to describe accurately what little we know about the land mechanism" (Leopold, *Sand County Almanac*, p. 214).

43. Leopold, "Land Pathology"; Flader and Callicott, *River*, p. 217.

44. A. Leopold, "Biotic Land-Use," manuscript c. 1940 (LP 6B16); Leopold, *Health of the Land*, p. 203.

45. A. Leopold, "The Land-Health Concept and Conservation," 21 December 1946 (LP 6B16); in Leopold, *Health of the Land*, pp. 218–226. See J. B. Callicott, "Aldo Leopold's Metaphor," in *Ecosystem Health: New Goals for Environmental Management*, edited by R. Costanza, B. G. Norton, and B. D. Haskell (Washington, D.C.: Island Press, 1992), pp. 42–56; D. Rapport, R. Costanza, P. R. Epstein, C. Gaudet, and R. Levins, eds., *Ecosystem Health* (Malden, Mass.: Blackwell Science, 1998); E. Freyfogle and J. Newton, "Putting Science in Its Place," *Conservation Biology* 16, no. 4 (2002): 863–873.

46. A. Leopold, "Conservation: In Whole or in Part?" 1 November 1944 (LP 6B16); Flader and Callicott, *River*, p. 310.

47. Leopold, "Conservation: In Whole or in Part?"; Flader and Callicott, *River*, p. 315.

48. Leopold, "Conservation: In Whole or in Part?"; Flader and Callicott, *River*, p. 315. In his manuscript, Leopold referenced Sauer's article "Theme of Plant and Animal Destruction in Economic History," *Journal of Farm Economics* 20, no. 4 (1938): 765–775.

49. Leopold, *Sand County Almanac*, p. ix.

50. A. Leopold, "The Ecological Conscience" *The Bulletin of the Garden Club of America* (1947); Flader and Callicott, *River*, p. 345.

51. Leopold, *Sand County Almanac*, p. 210. In 1997, the Aldo Leopold Chapter of the Society for Conservation Biology organized a special symposium on the state of knowledge of species diversity in the state of Wisconsin. Information provided at the symposium suggested, first, that Leopold's estimate of the number of species of "higher plants and animals" was in fact much too low; and, second, that the degree of uncertainty in estimates of species richness (even in a well-studied locale like Wisconsin) remains high. A more likely range for the total species diversity of fungi, plants, and animals in the state is 53,000–110,000. See R. Hoffman, *Wisconsin's Natural Communities: How to Recognize Them, Where to Find Them* (Madison: University of Wisconsin Press, 2002), pp. 4–5.

6. Giving Voice to Concern

The definition is from *Webster's New Collegiate Dictionary* (Springfield, Mass.: G. & C. Merriam, 1976), p. 367.

1. "Marshland Elegy" was first published in *American Forests* 43, no. 10 (1937): 472–474.

2. For a complete bibliography of Leopold's publications, see S. L. Flader and J. B. Callicott, eds., *The River of the Mother of God and Other Essays by Aldo Leopold* (Madison: University of Wis-

consin Press, 1991), pp. 349–370. For a thorough account of the development of the manuscript of *Sand County Almanac* see Dennis Ribbens, "The Making of *A Sand County Almanac*," in J. B. Callicott, ed., *Companion to* A Sand County Almanac: *Interpretive and Critical Essays* (Madison: University of Wisconsin Press, 1987), pp. 91–109.

3. All quotations of "Marshland Elegy" are from A. Leopold, *A Sand County Almanac and Sketches Here and There* (New York: Oxford University Press, 1949), pp. 95–101.

4. A. Leopold, "The Thick-Billed Parrot in Chihuahua," *The Condor* 39, no. 1 (1937): 10. Leopold included the essay in *Sand County Almanac* under the title "Guacamaja."

5. For historical overviews of the status of sandhill and whooping crane populations, see R. P. Allen's classic *The Whooping Crane*, Research Report No. 3 (New York: National Audubon Society, 1952); P. A. Johnsgard, *Cranes of the World* (Bloomington: Indiana University Press, 1983); R. Doughty, *Return of the Whooping Crane* (Austin: University of Texas Press, 1989); P. A. Johnsgard, *Crane Music: A Natural History of North American Cranes* (Washington, D.C.: Smithsonian Institution Press, 1991); C. Meine and G. Archibald, compilers, *The Cranes: Status Survey and Conservation Action Plan* (Gland, Switzerland: The World Conservation Union, 1996).

6. Leopold's early ornithological notes are in the Aldo Leopold Papers (hereafter LP) 7B1 in the University of Wisconsin, Madison, Archives.

7. A. Leopold, "New Mexico Journal" (LP 7B2).

8. A. Leopold, "Notes on New Mexico Birds," unpublished notes prepared for Florence Merriam Bailey, 17 January 1919 (LP 3B8).

9. Leopold, "New Mexico Journal." Leopold's journal entries from this trip were later published in *Round River: From the Journals of Aldo Leopold*, edited by L. B. Leopold (New York: Oxford University Press, 1953), pp. 10–30. Emphasis added.

10. Leopold, *Sand County Almanac*, 148. Aldo and Carl did confidently observe sandhill cranes several times over the course of their trip.

11. A. Leopold, "Report on a Game Survey of Mississippi," p. 40, 1 February 1929 (LP 6B11).

12. A. Leopold, "Report on a Game Survey of Wisconsin," p. 132, 1 October 1929 (LP 6B11).

13. See L. Walkinshaw to W. Scott, 15 September 1940, in the Ron Sauey Memorial Library for Bird Conservation, International Crane Foundation, Baraboo, Wisc.

14. A. Leopold, "The Wisconsin River Marshes," *National Waltonian* 2, no. 3 (1934): 5.

15. Schmidt's observations were related in later correspondence between Wallace Grange and Lawrence Walkinshaw (see n. 13 above).

16. A. Leopold, "Sandhill Cranes in the Endeavor Marsh," 20 July 1934 (LP 3B2); see C. Meine, "Aldo Leopold and the Endeavor Marsh," *The ICF Bugle* 21, no. 4 (1995): 2, 4.

17. Franklin S. Henika, "Sand-hill Cranes in Wisconsin and Other Lake States," *Proceedings of the North American Wildlife Conference* (Washington, D.C.: Government Printing Office, 1936), pp. 644–646. Henika's published report contained the first (and since oft-cited) estimate that "The total sand-hill crane population of Wisconsin is therefore estimated at about 25 breeding pairs." Henika concluded that "Sand-hill cranes in the Lake States are so rare that no effort should be spared to insure their preservation and increase."

18. Fred Hamerstrom, "Central Wisconsin Crane Study," *Wilson Bulletin* 50, no. 3 (1938): 175.

19. Leopold's sandhill crane file is in the Aldo Leopold Papers (LP 4B4).

20. The passage is from Book 7 of Milton's *Paradise Lost*.

21. A. Leopold, "Naturschutz in Germany," *Bird-Lore* 38, no. 2 (1936): 104. The common crane (*Grus grus*) is also known as the Eurasian crane.

22. A. Leopold, "Threatened Species: A Proposal to the Wildlife Conference for an Inventory of the Needs of Near-extinct Birds and Animals," *American Forests* 42, no. 3 (1936): 118. Oddly, Leopold did not list the whooping crane in the article—further indication perhaps that even among conservationists the species had been "written off." Publication of Leopold's landmark

article coincided with an important session on "The Problem of Vanishing Species" at the March 1936 North American Wildlife Conference (see n. 17 above). Henika's paper on the Lake States' sandhill cranes was delivered in this session.

23. See J. B. Callicott, "Leopold's Land Aesthetic," in *In Defense of the Land Ethic: Essays in Environmental Philosophy* (Albany: State University of New York Press, 1989), pp. 239–247.

24. Baird Callicott has observed that the second sentence of this quotation does not appear in the 1970 Ballantine paperback edition of *Sand County Almanac*.

25. A. Leopold, *Game Management* (New York: Charles Scribner's Sons, 1933), p. 7.

26. B. Berg, *To Africa with the Migratory Birds* (New York: G. P. Putnam's Sons, 1930), p. 134.

27. See W. Cronon, "Landscape and Home: Environmental Traditions in Wisconsin," *Wisconsin Magazine of History* 74, no. 2 (1990–1991): 83–105; D. Worster, "Leopold and the Changing Landscape of History," in C. Meine and R. L. Knight, eds., *The Essential Aldo Leopold: Quotations and Commentaries* (Madison: University of Wisconsin Press, 1999), pp. 237–239.

28. Leopold, "The Wisconsin River Marshes," p. 4.

29. O. Gromme to A. Leopold, 21 December 1937 (LP 4B4). Emphasis in original. Cranes and wetlands would later figure prominently in several of Gromme's paintings. One of his canvases, "Marshland Elegy," featured sandhill cranes dancing near the Leopold shack in Sauk County, Wisconsin. Gromme also contributed limited edition prints of "Salute to the Dawn," a depiction of nesting whooping cranes, to help establish the International Crane Foundation.

30. A. Leopold, "Wisconsin Journal" (LP 7B2).

31. F. S. Dayton, "Sandhill Cranes Breed at New London," *The Passenger Pigeon* 3, no. 10 (1941): 91.

32. These articles are collected in A. Leopold, *For the Health of the Land: Previously Unpublished Essays and Other Writings*, edited by J. B. Callicott and E. Freyfogle (Washington, D.C.: Island Press, 1999).

33. C. Meine, *Aldo Leopold: His Life and Work* (Madison: University of Wisconsin Press, 1988), p. 460. See Ribbens, "The Making of *A Sand County Almanac*" and chap. 7 in this volume.

34. H. Albert Hochbaum, untitled manuscript, 22 April 1948 (LP 8B3).

35. K. Rexroth, *One Hundred Poems from the Chinese* (New York: New Directions Books, 1959), p. 31.

36. See Meine and Archibald, *The Cranes: Status Survey and Conservation Action Plan*. Peter Matthiessen tells the global story of cranes and crane conservation in *The Birds of Heaven: Travels with Cranes* (New York: North Point Press, 2001).

7. Moving Mountains

Leopold's line is from his essay "On a Monument to the Pigeon" in *A Sand County Almanac and Sketches Here and There* (New York: Oxford University Press, 1949), p. 112.

1. S. L. Flader and J. B Callicott, eds., *The River of the Mother of God and Other Essays by Aldo Leopold* (Madison: University of Wisconsin Press, 1991), p. 19.

2. A. Leopold, "The State of the Profession," *Journal of Wildlife Management* 4, no. 3 (1940): 343; Flader and Callicott, *River*, p. 276.

3. Leopold, "State of the Profession," p. 343; Flader and Callicott, *River*, p. 276.

4. Leopold, "State of the Profession," p. 344; Flader and Callicott, *River*, p. 277.

5. C. Meine, *Aldo Leopold: His Life and Work* (Madison: University of Wisconsin Press, 1988), pp. 1–83.

6. Leopold, "State of the Profession," p. 346; Flader and Callicott, *River*, p. 280.

7. Leopold, "State of the Profession," p. 344; Flader and Callicott, *River*, p. 277.

8. Leopold, "State of the Profession," p. 344; Flader and Callicott, *River*, p. 277.

9. A. Leopold, "Conservation Esthetic," *Bird-Lore* 40, no. 2 (1938): 107; Leopold, *Sand County Almanac*, p. 174.

10. A. Leopold, "Teaching Wildlife Conservation in Public Schools," in *Transactions of the Wisconsin Academy of Sciences, Arts and Letters* 30 (1937): 80.

11. See D. Ribbens, "The Making of *A Sand County Almanac*," in *Companion to* A Sand County Almanac: *Interpretive and Critical Essays*, edited by J. B. Callicott (Madison: University of Wisconsin Press, 1987), pp. 91–109.

12. Ribbens, "Making of *A Sand County Almanac*"; Meine, *Aldo Leopold*, pp. 450–461.

13. A. Hochbaum to A. Leopold, 4 February 1944 (Aldo Leopold Papers [hereafter LP] 10B5); Meine, *Aldo Leopold*, p. 457.

14. Ribbens, "Making of *A Sand County Almanac*."

15. A. Leopold to A. Hochbaum, 20 November 1944 (LP 2B3); Ribbens, "Making of *A Sand County Almanac*," p. 101.

16. C. Simpson to A. Leopold, 29 April 1946 (LP 2B3); Ribbens, "Making of *A Sand County Almanac*," p. 101.

17. Leopold compiled "The Land Ethic" in July 1947. For a summary of the process Leopold followed, see C. Meine, "Building 'The Land Ethic'," in Callicott, *Companion*, pp. 172–185.

18. Leopold's original foreword was published in Callicott, *Companion*, pp. 277–288.

19. C. Simpson to A. Leopold, 5 November 1947 (LP 6B5); Meine, *Aldo Leopold*, p. 509.

20. W. Vogt, *Road to Survival* (New York: William Sloane Associates, 1948).

21. A. Leopold to P. Vaudrin, 2 December 1947 (LP 6B5); Meine, *Aldo Leopold*, p. 510.

22. A. Leopold, untitled memo, c. early 1948 (LP 6B5). The intended recipients of Leopold's memo included Robert McCabe, Frederick and Frances Hamerstrom, Joe and Peggy Hickey, Al Etter, William Vogt, Allen and Alice Harper Stokes, and several other students. Leopold's wife Estella was also reading her husband's manuscript at this time.

23. See Meine, *Aldo Leopold*, pp. 523–524.

24. Leopold, *Sand County Almanac*, p. 83.

25. Leopold, *Sand County Almanac*, p. 200.

26. Leopold, *Sand County Almanac*, p. 204.

27. A. Leopold, "On a Monument to the Passenger Pigeon," 25 August 1946 (LP 6B9). The address was delivered on 6 April 1946. See Meine, *Aldo Leopold*, p. 483. Versions of this address were later published in *Silent Wings: A Memorial to the Passenger Pigeon* (Madison: Wisconsin Society for Ornithology, 1947) and *Sand County Almanac* (pp. 108–112). These later versions omit Leopold's more strident criticisms of postwar science.

28. A. Leopold, "Wherefore Wildlife Ecology," c. 1947 (LP 6B16); Flader and Callicott, *River*, p. 337.

29. Leopold, "Wherefore Wildlife Ecology"; Flader and Callicott, *River*, p. 337.

8. The *Secret* Leopold

Twain's observation comes from the opening of the posthumously published *Mark Twain's Autobiography*, Vol. 1 (New York: Harper and Brothers, 1924), p. 2.

1. B. Zeide, "Another Look at Leopold's Land Ethic," *Journal of Forestry* 96, no. 1 (1998): 13.

2. J. B. Callicott, "A Critical Examination of 'Another Look at Leopold's Land Ethic'," *Journal of Forestry* 96, no. 1 (1998): 20–26. The April 1998 issue of the *Journal of Forestry* featured eight additional commentaries. These and other articles were reprinted by the Society for American Foresters (SAF) in a Forestry Forum publication, *The Land Ethic: Meeting Human Needs for the Land and Its Resources* (Bethesda, Md.: SAF, 1998).

3. See C. Meine and R. L. Knight, eds., *The Essential Aldo Leopold: Quotations and Commentaries* (Madison: University of Wisconsin Press, 1999).

4. A. Hawkins, interview with author, 4 December 1999.

5. F. Hamerstrom, quoted in C. Meine, *Aldo Leopold: His Life and Work* (Madison: University of Wisconsin Press, 1988), p. 378.

6. A. Hochbaum to A. Leopold, 4 February 1944 (Aldo Leopold Papers [hereafter LP] 10B5); Meine, *Aldo Leopold*, pp. 456–457.

7. A. Hochbaum to A. Leopold, 26 December 1947 (LP 2B3); Meine, *Aldo Leopold*, p. 511. Emphases in original.

8. A. Leopold, *A Sand County Almanac and Sketches Here and There* (New York: Oxford University Press, 1949), pp. 129–133.

9. A. Leopold, "Adventures of a Conservation Commissioner," 1 December 1946 (LP 6B16); S. L. Flader and J. B. Callicott, eds., *The River of the Mother of God and Other Essays by Aldo Leopold* (Madison: University of Wisconsin Press, 1991), p. 330.

10. A. Derleth, "Of Aldo Leopold," *Capital Times* (Madison, Wisc.), 5 November 1949. Emphasis added.

11. L. Gannett, "Books and Things," *New York Herald Tribune*, 27 October 1949.

12. Leopold, *Sand County Almanac*, p. 221.

13. Leopold, *Sand County Almanac*, p. 226. Leopold first used the phrase in "The Conservation Ethic," *Journal of Forestry* 31, no. 6 (1933): 637.

14. See chaps. 1 and 3 in this volume.

15. R. L. Knight, "Aldo Leopold, the Land Ethic, and Ecosystem Management," *Journal of Wildlife Management* 60, no. 3 (1996): 471–474. See chap. 10, n. 26.

16. Leopold, *Sand County Almanac*, 210.

17. See chap. 10, n. 26. For a broad discussion of these trends, see R. Putnam, *Bowling Alone: The Collapse and Revival of American Community* (New York: Simon and Schuster, 2000).

18. R. Mann, "Aldo Leopold: Priest and Prophet," *American Forests* 60, no. 8 (1954): 23, 42–43. See J. B. Callicott, *In Defense of the Land Ethic: Essays in Environmental Philosophy* (Albany: State University of New York Press, 1989), p. 279n.1.

19. E. Swift, "Aldo Leopold: Wisconsin's Conservation Prophet," *Wisconsin Tales and Trails* 2, no. 3 (1961): 2–5.

20. R. Nash, *Wilderness and the American Mind*, 4th ed. (1967; New Haven, Conn.: Yale University Press, 2001), pp. 182–199.

21. W. Stegner, "The Legacy of Aldo Leopold" in *Companion to* A Sand County Almanac: *Interpretive and Critical Essays*, edited by J. B. Callicott (Madison: University of Wisconsin Press, 1987), p. 233; originally published as "Living on Our Principal," *Wilderness* 48, no. 168 (1985): 5–21.

22. "Making Forestlands Serve America Better Through Good Management," *Saturday Evening Post* 228, no. 34 (18 February 1956): 89. Emphasis in original.

23. Leopold, *Sand County Almanac*, 200. Michael Nelson notes that, in the 1970 Ballantine paperback edition of *Sand County Almanac*, the ending of the sentence was changed: "and vigilantly available for action."

24. See B. Devall and G. Sessions, *Deep Ecology: Living as if Nature Mattered* (Layton, Utah: Peregrine Smith Books, 1985); D. Foreman, *Confessions of an Eco-Warrior* (New York: Harmony Books, 1991); M. Oelschlaeger, *The Idea of Wilderness: From Prehistory to the Age of Ecology* (New Haven, Conn.: Yale University Press, 1991). See also S. Zakin, *Coyotes and Town Dogs: Earth First! and the Environmental Movement* (New York: Viking Press, 1993).

25. Letters to the editor, *Journal of Forestry* 88, no. 2 (1990): 4; and 89, no. 9 (1991): 5.

26. See J. B. Callicott, "The Conceptual Foundations of the Land Ethic," in *In Defense of the Land Ethic*, pp. 75–99.

27. All quoted in Callicott, *In Defense of the Land Ethic*, pp. 75–76, 279n.4.

28. See discussions of Leopold in, for example, R. Paehlke, *Environmentalism and the Future of Progressive Politics* (New Haven, Conn.: Yale University Press, 1989); C. B. Short, *Ronald Reagan and the Public Lands: America's Conservation Debate, 1979–1984* (College Station: Texas A&M Press, 1989); B. G. Norton, *Toward Unity Among Environmentalists* (New York: Oxford University Press, 1991); H. L. Ulman, "'Thinking Like a Mountain': Persona, Ethos, and Judgment in American Nature Writing," in *Green Culture: Environmental Rhetoric in Contemporary America*, edited by C. G. Herndl and S. C. Brown (Madison: University of Wisconsin Press, 1996), pp. 46–81; E. Freyfogle, *The Land We Share: Private Property and the Common Good* (Washington, D.C.: Island Press, 2003).

29. N. Yates, "The Inadequate Politics of Aldo Leopold," in *Proceedings of the Fifth Midwest Prairie Conference* (Ames: Iowa State University, 1978), pp. 220, 221.

30. At the time I was a busy graduate student and had no time to seize the opportunity. My response (only half-joking) at the time was, "I'll write the article, and if you can get *The Progressive* to publish it at the same time, I'll do it." Nothing came of the suggestion.

31. See S. Flader, "Building Conservation on the Land: Aldo Leopold and the Tensions of Professionalism and Citizenship," in *Reconstructing Conservation: Finding Common Ground*, edited by B. A. Minteer and R. E. Manning (Washington, D.C.: Island Press, 2003), pp. 115–132.

32. A. Leopold, "Land Pathology," 15 April 1935 lecture, LP 6B16; Flader and Callicott, *River*, p. 215.

33. Meine, *Aldo Leopold*, p. 525.

34. Zeide, "Another Look at Leopold's Land Ethic," p. 17.

35. "Can You Eat Meat and Consider Yourself an Environmentalist?" *Sierra* 76, no. 6 (1991): 122.

36. See, for example, J. B. Callicott, "The Conceptual Foundations of the Land Ethic"; M. Nelson, "Holists and Fascists and Paper Tigers . . . Oh My!," *Ethics and the Environment* 1, no. 2 (1996): 103–117.

37. F. Lepine, "Shut Down Leopold," *Iowa State Daily*, 26 February 1993, p. 3.

38. A. G. Etter, "A Day with Aldo Leopold," in *From The Land*, edited by N. P. Pittman (Washington D.C.: Island Press, 1988), p. 385. Originally published in *The Land* 7, no. 3 (1948): 337–340.

39. P. Errington, "In Appreciation of Aldo Leopold," *Journal of Wildlife Management* 12, no. 4 (1948): 350, 349.

40. P. Nunnally, "A Mind at Work: Aldo Leopold's *Sand County Almanac*," *North Dakota Quarterly* 56, no. 3 (1988): 85.

9. Inherit the Grid

The opening quotations are from R. G. Stapledon, *The Land: Now and Tomorrow* (London: Faber and Faber, 1935), p. 1; and D. W. Orr, *Earth in Mind: On Education, Environment, and the Human Prospect* (Washington, D.C.: Island Press, 1994), pp. 104–105. See also D. W. Orr, *The Nature of Design: Ecology, Culture, and Human Intention* (New York: Oxford University Press, 2002).

1. V. Scully, *Architecture: The Natural and the Manmade* (New York: St. Martin's Press, 1991), p. xi.

2. Scully, *Architecture*, p. 1. Emphasis added.

3. For a collection of wilderness critiques, responses, and counterresponse, see J. B. Callicott and M. P. Nelson, eds., *The Great New Wilderness Debate* (Athens, Ga.: University of Georgia Press, 1998). See also W. Cronon, ed., *Uncommon Ground: Toward Reinventing Nature* (New York: W. W. Norton, 1995); M. Soulé and G. Lease, eds., *Reinventing Nature?: Responses to Postmodern*

Deconstruction (Washington, D.C.: Island Press, 1995); G. Snyder, "Nature as Seen from Kitkitdizze Is No 'Human Construction,'" *Wild Earth* 6, no 4. (1996): 8–9; D. Worster, "The Wilderness of History," *Wild Earth* 7, no. 3 (1997): 9–13; D. W. Orr, "The Not-So Great Wilderness Debate . . . Continued," *Wild Earth* 9, no. 2 (1999): 74–80; D. Foreman, "The Pristine Myths," *Wild Earth* 11, no. 1 (2001): 1–2; W. Cronon, "The Riddle of the Apostle Islands," *Orion* 22, no. 3 (2003): 36–42; B. A. Minteer and R. E. Manning, eds., *Reconstructing Conservation: Finding Common Ground* (Washington, D.C.: Island Press, 2003); T. Vale, ed., *Fire, Native Peoples, and the Natural Landscape* (Washington, D.C.: Island Press, 2003).

4. See F. N. Egerton, "Changing Concepts of the Balance of Nature," *Quarterly Review of Biology* 48, no. 2 (1973): 322–350; D. B. Botkin, *Discordant Harmonies: A New Ecology for the Twenty-First Century* (New York: Oxford University Press, 1990); S. L. Pimm, *The Balance of Nature? Ecological Issues in the Conservation of Species and Communities* (Chicago: University of Chicago Press, 1991); R. E. Grumbine, *Ghost Bears: Exploring the Biodiversity Crisis* (Washington, D.C.: Island Press, 1992); S. T. A. Pickett, V. T. Parker, and P. L. Fiedler, "The New Paradigm in Ecology: Implications for Conservation Biology above the Species Level," in *Conservation Biology: The Theory and Practice of Nature Conservation, Preservation, and Management*, edited by P. L. Fiedler and S. K. Jain (New York: Chapman and Hall, 1992), pp. 65–88; W. S. Alverson, W. Kuhlmann, and D. M. Waller, *Wild Forests: Conservation Biology and Public Policy* (Washington, D.C.: Island Press, 1994), pp. 39–63; S. T. A. Pickett and R. S. Ostfeld, "The Shifting Paradigm in Ecology," in *A New Century for Natural Resources Management*, edited by R. L. Knight and S. F. Bates (Washington, D.C.: Island Press, 1995), pp. 261–278; J. Wu and O. L. Loucks, "From Balance of Nature to Hierarchical Patch Dynamics: A Paradigm Shift in Ecology," *Quarterly Review of Biology* 70, no. 44 (1995): 439–466; G. K. Meffe, C. R. Carroll and contributors, *Principles of Conservation Biology*, 2nd ed. (Sunderland, Mass.: Sinauer Associates, 1997), pp. 16–20. See also chap. 5, note 42.

5. J. B. Jackson, *A Sense of Place, a Sense of Time* (New Haven, Conn.: Yale University Press, 1994), p. 153.

6. H. B. Johnson, *Order Upon the Land: The U.S. Rectangular Land Survey and the Upper Mississippi Country* (New York: Oxford University Press, 1976), p. i.

7. W. Jackson, *Becoming Native to This Place* (Lexington: University Press of Kentucky, 1994), pp. 17–18. For recent commentaries on the environmental, political, and cultural consequences of the land survey grid, see J. Hildebrand, *Mapping the Farm: The Chronicle of a Family* (New York: Alfred A. Knopf, 1995), pp. 15–19; D. Worster, "A Tapestry of Change: Nature and Culture on the Prairie," in T. Evans, *The Inhabited Prairie* (Lawrence: University Press of Kansas, 1998), pp. xi–xvii; J. C. Scott, *Seeing Like a State: How Certain Schemes to Improve the Human Condition Have Failed* (New Haven, Conn.: Yale University Press, 1998), pp. 11–52; R. Sayre, "Squaring Off," in *Prairie Roots: 2001 Harvest Symposium* (North Liberty, Iowa: Ice Cube Press, 2001), pp. 33–57; J. W. Simpson, *Yearning for the Land: A Search for Homeland in Scotland and America* (New York: Vintage Books, 2002), pp. 74–78; and A. Linklater, *Measuring America: How the United States Was Shaped by the Greatest Land Sale in History* (New York: Plume, 2002), especially pp. 160–175.

8. On the changing West, see W. H. Romme, "Creating Pseudo-rural Landscapes in the Mountain West," in *Placing Nature: Culture and Landscape Ecology*, edited by J. I. Nassauer (Washington, D.C.: Island Press, 1997), pp. 139–161; and R. L. Knight, "Field Report from the New American West," in *Wallace Stegner and the Continental Vision: Essays on Literature, History, and Landscape* (Washington, D.C.: Island Press, 1997), pp. 181–200; R. Keiter, *Reclaiming the Native Home of Hope: Community, Ecology, and the American West* (Salt Lake City: University of Utah Press, 1998).

9. Johnson, *Order Upon the Land*, p. 235.

10. G. Snyder, *The Practice of the Wild* (New York: North Point Press, 1990), p. 7.

11. A. Leopold, *A Sand County Almanac and Sketches Here and There* (New York: Oxford University Press, 1949), pp. 200–201.

12. Snyder, *Practice of the Wild*, p. 24.

13. See H. W. Ottoson, ed., *Land Use Policy and Problems in the U. S.* (Lincoln: University of Nebraska Press, 1963); V. Carstensen, ed., *The Public Lands: Studies in the History of the Public Domain* (Madison: University of Wisconsin Press, 1963); P. W. Gates, *History of Public Land Law Development* (Washington, D.C.: Public Land Law Commission, 1968); M. J. Rohrbough, *The Land Office Business: The Settlement and Administration of American Public Lands, 1789–1837* (New York: Oxford University Press, 1968); J. W. Ernst, *With Compass and Chain: Federal Land Surveyors in the Old Northwest, 1785–1816* (New York: Arno Press, 1979); Wallace Stegner, *Wolf Willow: A History, a Story, and a Memory of the Last Plains Frontier* (Lincoln: University of Nebraska Press, 1980), pp. 81–99; C. A. White, *A History of the Rectangular Survey System* (Washington, D.C.: U.S. Government Printing Office, 1983); W. D. Ellis, *The Ordinance of 1787: The Nation Begins* (Dayton, Ohio: Landfall Press, 1987). Western Canada's land survey system, initiated in the early 1870s, closely followed the United States' system. See R. B. McKercher and B. Wolfe, *Understanding Western Canada's Dominion Land Survey System* (Saskatoon: Division of Extension and Community Relations, University of Saskatchewan, 1986).

14. Johnson, *Order Upon the Land*, p. 30.

15. Quoted in Johnson, *Order Upon the Land*, p. 39. For discussions of Jefferson's views on land, nature, and democracy, see J. M. Brewster, "The Relevance of the Jeffersonian Dream Today," in Ottoson, *Land Use Policy and Problems in the U.S.*, pp. 86–136; C. Miller, *Jefferson and Nature: An Interpretation* (Baltimore, Md.: Johns Hopkins University Press, 1988); E. Hargrove, *Foundations of Environmental Ethics* (Englewood Cliffs, N.J.: Prentice Hall, 1989), pp. 48–75; P. W. Gates, *The Jeffersonian Dream: Studies in the History of American Land Policy and Development*, edited by A. G. Bogue and M. B. Bogue (Albuquerque: University of New Mexico Press, in cooperation with the Historical Society of New Mexico, 1995).

16. White, *Rectangular Survey System*, pp. 14–15.

17. W. Stegner, *Beyond the Hundredth Meridian: John Wesley Powell and the Second Opening of the West* (New York: Penguin Books, 1992), p. 213. For discussion of the "checkerboard" image in descriptions of the grid and its impacts on land, see Johnson, *Order Upon the Land*, pp. 143–148.

18. Hildebrand, *Mapping the Farm*. p. 16.

19. White, *Rectangular Survey System*, p. 237.

20. I am grateful to Robert Nurre, land records manager for the Wisconsin Board of Commissioners of Public Lands, for the metaphor and for sharing his encyclopedic knowledge of the history of the land survey.

21. White, *Rectangular Survey System*, p. 460. See also Linklater, *Measuring America*, p. 162. "Correction lines" are sometimes called "guide meridians" and "standard parallels." The standard interval for inserting correction lines varied in the earlier stages of the survey. In Wisconsin, for example, the lines were drawn every 60 miles. In much of the country, the interval came to be every 24 miles (or four townships) from the base line. The technique also accounted for "correction sections" that deviated from the standard 640 acres. The phenomenon of "short sections" (those containing less than 640 acres) accounts for the now common designation of 35-acre subdivision lots and limits— a way of accommodating landowners whose land falls within short sections.

22. Johnson, *Order Upon the Land*, p. 58. Residents of Correctionville, Iowa, along U.S. Highway 20 in western Iowa, have made a virtue of the curiosity. A plaque and monument mark the correction line that gave the town its name. See Michael Martone's essay, "Correctionville, Iowa" in *The Flatness and Other Landscapes* (Athens, Ga.: University of Georgia Press, 2000), pp. 158–171.

23. C. Meine, *Aldo Leopold: His Life and Work* (Madison: University of Wisconsin Press, 1988), pp. 200–201, 224.

24. Johnson, *Order Upon the Land*, p. 238.

25. R. K. Swihart and N. A. Slade, "Road Crossing in *Sigmodon hispidus* and *Microtus ochrogaster*," *Journal of Mammalogy* 65, no. 2 (1984): 357–360. See also R. F. Noss and B. Csuti, "Habitat Fragmentation," in Meffe et al., *Principles of Conservation Biology*, pp. 269–304; M. L. Hunter, *Fundamentals of Conservation Biology* (Cambridge, Mass.: Blackwell Science, 1996), pp. 158–162; R. T. T. Forman, D. Sperling, J. Bissonette, A. P. Clevenger, C. D. Cutshall, V. H. Dale, L. Fahrig, R. France, C. R. Goldman, K. Heanue, J. A. Jones, F. J. Swanson, T. Turrentine, and T.C. Winter, *Road Ecology: Science and Solutions* (Washington, D.C.: Island Press, 2002). See also the special section on the ecological effects of roads in *Conservation Biology* 14, no. 1 (2000): 16–94.

26. R. P. Thiel, "Relationship Between Road Densities and Wolf Habitat Suitability in Wisconsin," *American Midland Naturalist* 113, no. 2 (1985): 404–407; L. D. Mech, S. H. Fritts, G. L. Radde, and W. J. Paul, "Wolf Distribution and Road Density in Minnesota," *Wildlife Society Bulletin* 16, no. 1 (1988): 85–87.

27. Originally reported in H. L. Whitaker, "Fox Squirrel Utilization of Osage Orange in Kansas," *Journal of Wildlife Management* 3, no. 2 (1939): 117–118.

28. See S. C. Trombulak and C. A. Frissell, "Review of Ecological Effects of Roads on Terrestrial and Aquatic Communities," *Conservation Biology* 14, no. 1 (2000): 18–30.

29. See the anti-coffee-table book *Clearcut: The Tragedy of Industrial Forestry* (San Francisco: Sierra Club Books, 1994), edited by B. Devall.

30. R. F. Noss, E. T. LaRoe III, and J. M. Scott, *Endangered Ecosystems of the United States: A Preliminary Assessment of Loss and Degradation*, Biological Report 28 (Washington, D.C.: National Biological Service, U.S. Department of the Interior, 1995).

31. W. Cronon, *Nature's Metropolis: Chicago and the Great West* (New York: W. W. Norton, 1991), p. 102.

32. W. Romme, "Creating Pseudo-rural Landscapes in the Mountain West," p. 151. For overviews of landscape ecology, see R. T. T. Forman, *Land Mosaics: The Ecology of Landscapes and Regions* (Cambridge: Cambridge University Press, 1995); M. Turner, R. H. Gardner, and R. V. O'Neill, *Landscape Ecology in Theory and Practice: Pattern and Process* (New York: Springer-Verlag, 2001); and K. J. Gutzwiler, *Applying Landscape Ecology in Biological Conservation* (New York: Springer-Verlag, 2002).

33. See chap. 10, n. 26.

34. W. Stegner and R. W. Etulain, *Conversations with Wallace Stegner on Western History and Literature*, rev. ed. (Salt Lake City: University of Utah Press, 1990), p. 151.

35. Vernon Carstensen writes, "Had a system of describing land by metes and bounds been employed, with the almost infinite possibility of odd-shaped parcels and hence overlapping and conflicting claims, lawsuits and neighborhood feuds would have been one certain harvest of [the] vast movement of land-seekers on to new land" (*The Public Lands: Studies in the History of the Public Domain*, p. xvi).

36. Johnson, *Order Upon the Land*, p. 219; Leopold, *Sand County Almanac*, p. viii.

37. Johnson, *Order Upon the Land*, p. 233.

38. Carstensen, *The Public Lands*, p. xvi. See chap. 1, n. 21.

39. Wallace Stegner, *Beyond the Hundredth Meridian*, pp. 214, 227. Powell's original recommendations are in the *Report on the Lands of the Arid Region of the United States, With a More Detailed Account of the Lands of Utah* (1878, 45th Congress, 2nd Session, H. R. Exec. Doc. 73; reprint, Boston: Harvard Common Press, 1983). Powell's life is reexamined in D. Worster, *A River Running West: The Life of John Wesley Powell* (New York: Oxford University Press, 2001). Selected

writings of Powell are collected in W. DuBuys, ed., *Seeing Things Whole: The Essential John Wesley Powell* (Washington, D.C.: Island Press, 2001).

40. See Johnson, *Order Upon the Land*, p. 200; chap. 2 in this volume.

41. Johnson, *Order Upon the Land*, p. 178.

42. The phrase comes from the roadside historical marker at Coon Valley, Wisconsin. See Johnson, *Order Upon the Land*, pp. 193–194; R. Anderson, "Coon Valley Days," *Wisconsin Academy Review* 48, no. 2 (2002): 42–48.

43. A. Leopold, "Coon Valley: An Adventure in Cooperative Conservation," *American Forests* 41, no. 5 (1935): 205; S. L. Flader and J. B. Callicott, eds., *The River of the Mother of God and Other Essays by Aldo Leopold* (Madison: University of Wisconsin Press, 1991), p. 219.

44. A. Leopold, *Game Management* (New York: Charles Scribner's Sons, 1933), p. 132.

45. Johnson, *Order Upon the Land*, p. 223.

46. I. McHarg, *Design with Nature* (Garden City, N. Y.: Doubleday Natural History Press, 1969). See also I. McHarg, *A Quest for Life: An Autobiography* (New York: John Wiley and Sons, 1996).

47. See, for example, W. Hudson, ed., *Landscape Linkages and Biodiversity* (Washington, D.C.: Island Press, 1991); D. A. Saunders and R. J. Hobbs, *Nature Conservation 2: The Role of Corridors* (Minneapolis: University of Minnesota Press, 1991); D. S. Smith and P. C. Hellmund, *Ecology of Greenways: Design and Function of Linear Conservation Areas* (Minneapolis: University of Minnesota Press, 1993); R. H. Platt, R. A. Rowntree, and P. C. Muick, eds., *The Ecological City: Preserving and Restoring Urban Biodiversity* (Amherst: University of Massachusetts Press, 1994); W. E. Dramstad, J. D. Olsen, and R. T. T. Forman, *Landscape Ecology Principles in Landscape Architecture and Planning* (Washington, D.C.: Island Press, 1996); R. L Knight and P. B. Landres, eds., *Stewardship Across Boundaries* (Washington, D.C.: Island Press, 1998).

48. See chap. 4 in this volume; J. I. Nassauer, "Cultural Sustainability: Aligning Aesthetics and Ecology" and M. M. Eaton, "The Beauty That Requires Health," in Nassauer, *Placing Nature*, pp. 65–106; J. B. Callicott, "Leopold's Land Aesthetic," in *In Defense of the Land Ethic: Essays in Environmental Philosophy* (Albany: State University of New York Press, 1989), pp. 239–247.

49. K. Yeang, *Designing with Nature: The Ecological Basis for Architectural Design* (New York: Mac-Graw-Hill, 1995), pp. 4–5. See also S. van der Ryn and S. Cowan, *Ecological Design* (Washington, D.C.: Island Press, 1995).

50. See n. 32 and n. 47 above; R. T. T. Forman and M. Godron, *Landscape Ecology* (New York: John Wiley and Sons, 1986); R. T. T. Forman, "Designing Landscapes and Regions to Conserve Nature," in Meffe et al., *Principles of Conservation Biology*, pp. 331–332.

51. See chap. 10, n. 26.

52. See M. Soulé and J. Terborgh, *Continental Conservation: Scientific Foundations of Regional Reserve Networks* (Washington, D.C.: Island Press, 1999).

53. Snyder, *Practice of the Wild*, p. 24.

10. The Once and Future Land Ethic

Leopold's statement is from "The Land Ethic," in *A Sand County Almanac and Sketches Here and There* (New York: Oxford University Press, 1949), p. 225. It is among the parts of the essay that were newly written in the summer of 1947 as Leopold was completing the manuscript. Roderick Nash surveyed the evolution of conservation philosophy in *The Rights of Nature: A History of Environmental Ethics* (Madison: University of Wisconsin Press, 1989). A. Carl Leopold commented on his father's philosophy and the continuing "elaboration of ethical concepts in relation to biology and conservation" in "Living With the Land Ethic," *BioScience* 54, no. 2 (2004): pp. 149–154.

1. Leopold, *A Sand County Almanac*, p. 225.
2. See C. Meine, "Building 'The Land Ethic'," in *Companion to* A Sand County Almanac: *Interpretive and Critical Essays*, edited by J. B. Callicott (Madison: University of Wisconsin Press, 1987), pp. 172–185.
3. See chap. 2, n. 16.
4. A. H. Deming and L. E. Savoy, eds., *The Colors of Nature: Culture, Identity, and the Natural World* (Minneapolis, Minn.: Milkweed Editions, 2002), pp. 7, 11.
5. See P. S. Martin and R. G. Klein, *Quaternary Extinctions: A Prehistoric Revolution* (Tucson: University of Arizona Press, 1989); D. H. Raup, *Extinction: Bad Genes or Bad Luck?* (New York: W. W. Norton, 1991); N. Eldredge, *The Miner's Canary: Unraveling the Mysteries of Extinction* (New York: Prentice Hall Press, 1991); T. E. Flannery, *The Future Eaters: An Ecological History of the Australasian Lands and People* (Port Melbourne, Australia: Reed Books, 1994); C. Tudge, *The Time Before History: Five Million Years of Human Impact* (New York: Simon and Schuster, 1997); R. D. E. MacPhee, *Extinctions in Near Time: Contexts, Causes, and Consequences* (New York: Plenum Press, 1999); T. E. Flannery, *The Eternal Frontier: An Ecological History of North America and Its People* (New York: Grove Press, 2001); P. D. Ward, *Rivers in Time: The Search for Clues to Earth's Mass Extinctions* (New York: Columbia University Press, 2002). For an overview, see C. Meine, *Humans and Other Catastrophes: Perspectives on Extinction* (New York: Center for Biodiversity Conservation, American Museum of Natural History, 1999).
6. See W. Cronon, *Changes in the Land: Indians, Colonists, and the Ecology of New England* (1983; reissued, New York: Hill and Wang, 2003); A. W. Crosby, *Ecological Imperialism: The Biological Expansion of Europe, 900–1900* (Cambridge: Cambridge University Press, 1986); G. G. Whitney, *From Coastal Wilderness to Fruited Plain: A History of Environmental Change in Temperate North America from 1500 to the Present* (Cambridge: Cambridge University Press, 1994); D. Quammen, *The Song of the Dodo: Island Biogeography in an Age of Extinctions* (New York: Simon and Schuster, 1996); J. Diamond, *Guns, Germs, and Steel: The Fates of Human Societies* (New York: W. W. Norton, 1997).
7. See chap. 5, n. 42 and chap. 9, n. 4.
8. A. Leopold, "The Meaning of Conservation," unpublished lecture notes (Aldo Leopold Papers 6B16). Leopold probably gave the lecture in the last few years of his life. The manuscript indicates that it was delivered in Milwaukee on September 10, but the year is not noted.
9. W. Jackson, "Preparing for a Sustainable Agriculture," in C. Meine and R. L. Knight, eds., *The Essential Aldo Leopold: Quotations and Commentaries* (Madison: University of Wisconsin Press, 1999), p. 89. See also, in this context, K. K. Smith, *Wendell Berry and the Agrarian Tradition: A Common Grace* (Lawrence: University Press of Kansas, 2003); and E. T. Freyfogle, ed., *The New Agrarianism: Land, Culture, and the Community of Life* (Washington, D.C.: Island Press, 2001).
10. Leopold's early interest in watershed functions in the Southwest in the late 1910s and early 1920s is described in C. Meine, *Aldo Leopold: His Life and Work* (Madison: University of Wisconsin Press, 1988), pp. 175–228. His interest remained strong throughout his years in the Midwest. His most explicit article on the theme of aquatic ecosystems was "Lakes in Relation to Terrestrial Life Patterns," in *A Symposium on Hydrobiology*, edited by J. G. Needham, P. B. Sears, and A. Leopold (Madison: University of Wisconsin Press, 1941), pp. 17–22, which begins: "Mechanized man, having rebuilt the landscape, is now rebuilding the waters. The sober citizen who would never submit his watch or his motor to amateur tamperings freely submits his lakes to drainings, fillings, dredgings, pollutions, stabilizations, mosquito control, algae control, swimmer's itch control, and the planting of any fish able to swim. So also with rivers. We constrict them with levees and dams, and then . . . flush them with dredgings, channelizations, and the floods and silt of bad farming. . . . Thus men too wise to tolerate hasty tinkerings with our political constitution accept without a qualm the most radical amendments to our biotic constitu-

tion." See also M. Nelson, "Earth, Air, Water . . . Ethics," in C. Meine, ed., *Wisconsin's Waters: A Confluence of Perspectives, Transactions of the Wisconsin Academy of Sciences, Arts and Letters* 90 (2003): 163–172.

11. The original source of Luna's quotation is unclear. But see L. B. Leopold, "Ethos, Equity and the Water Resource," *Environment* 32, no. 2 (1990): 16–20, 37–42; and *A View of the River* (Cambridge, Mass.: Harvard University Press, 1994).

12. For surveys of current water information and issues, see P. Simon, *Tapped Out* (New York: Welcome Rain Publishers, 1998); M. De Villiers, *Water: The Fate of Our Most Precious Resource* (New York: Houghton Mifflin, 1999); M. Barlow and T. Clarke, *Blue Gold: The Fight to Stop Corporate Theft of the World's Water* (New York: New Press, 2002); P. Gleick, *The World's Water, 2002–2003: The Biennial Report on Freshwater Resources* (Washington, D.C.: Island Press, 2002); R. Glennon, *Water Follies: Groundwater Pumping and the Fate of America's Fresh Waters* (Washington, D.C.: Island Press, 2002); Wisconsin Academy of Sciences, Arts and Letters, *Waters of Wisconsin: The Future of Our Aquatic Ecosystems and Resources* (Madison: Wisconsin Academy of Sciences, Arts and Letters, 2003).

13. See E. A. Norse, "Uncharted Waters: Conserving Marine Biological Diversity," in G. K. Meffe, C. R. Carroll, and contributors, *Principles of Conservation Biology*, 2nd ed. (Sunderland, Mass.: Sinauer Associates, 1997), pp. 94–97; T. S. Agardy, *Marine Protected Areas and Ocean Conservation* (Washington, D.C.: Academic Press, 1997); National Marine Fisheries Service (NMFS), Ecosystem Principles Advisory Panel, "Ecosystem-based Fishery Management: A Report to Congress" (Washington, D.C.: NMFS, 1998); B. Thorne-Miller, *The Living Ocean: Understanding and Protecting Marine Biodiversity*, 2nd ed. (Washington, D.C.: Island Press, 1999); National Research Council, *Marine Protected Areas: Tools for Sustaining Ocean Ecosystems* (Washington, D.C.: National Academy Press, 2001).

14. The song was written by Sheldon Posen and John Goss, and recorded by Finest Kind, *Heart's Delight* (Ottawa, Ontario: Fallen Angel Music, 1999). For recent overviews of sustainable fisheries, see D. Pauly, V. Christensen, S. Guenette, T. J. Pitcher, U. R. Sumaila, C. J. Walters, R. Watson, and D. Zeller, "Towards Sustainability in World Fisheries," *Nature* 418, no. 6898 (2002): 689–695. See also: D. Dobbs, *The Great Gulf: Fishermen, Scientists, and the Struggle to Revive the World's Greatest Fishery* (Washington, D.C.: Island Press, 2000); and R. Ellis, *The Empty Ocean* (Washington, D.C.: Island Press, 2003).

15. C. Safina, "Launching a Sea Ethic," *Wild Earth* 12, no. 4 (2002–2003), p. 5. See also the other articles in the "Freedom of the Seas" issue of *Wild Earth* 12, no. 4 (2002–2003); C. Safina, *Song for the Blue Ocean: Encounters Along the World's Coasts and Beneath the Seas* (New York: Henry Holt, 1998); J. Bohnsack, "Shifting Baselines, Marine Reserves, and Leopold's Land Ethic," *Gulf and Caribbean Research* 14, no. 2 (2003): 1–7; the report of the Pew Oceans Commission, *America's Living Oceans: Charting a Course for Sea Change* (Arlington, Va.: Pew Oceans Commission, 2003); and the U.S. Commission on Ocean Policy's *Preliminary Report* (Washington, D.C.: U.S. Commission on Ocean Policy, 2004).

16. A. Leopold, "The Home Builder Conserves" *American Forests and Forest Life* 34, no. 413 (1928): 276, 277. S. L. Flader and J. B. Callicott, eds., *The River of the Mother of God and Other Essays by Aldo Leopold* (Madison: University of Wisconsin Press, 1991), pp. 144, 145.

17. D. MacCleery, "Aldo Leopold's Land Ethic: Is It Only Half a Loaf Unless a Consumption Ethic Accompanies It?" *Forest History Today* (Spring 2000): 39–41. See M. Strigel and C. Meine, eds., *Report of the Intelligent Consumption Project* (Madison: Wisconsin Academy of Sciences, Arts and Letters and USDA Forest Service, Forest Products Laboratory, 2001); T. Knudson, "State of Denial: World's Other Forests Feed State's Appetite for Timber," *Sacramento Bee* (California), 5 October 2003.

18. Leopold, *Sand County Almanac*, pp. viii, ix.

19. The literature of alternative ecological economics has grown prodigiously in recent years. Helpful background discussions include H. E. Daly and J. B. Cobb, *For the Common Good: Redirecting the Economy Toward Community, the Environment, and a Sustainable Future* (Boston: Beacon Press, 1989); P. Christensen, "Historical Roots for Ecological Economics," *Ecological Economics* 1, no. 1 (1989): 17–36; C. A. Tisdell, "Environmental Conservation: Economics, Ecology, and Ethics," *Environmental Conservation* 16, no. 2 (1989): 107–162; D. Worster, *The Wealth of Nature: Environmental History and the Ecological Imagination* (New York: Oxford University Press, 1993); R. Krishnan, J. M. Harris, and N. R. Goodwin, eds., *A Survey of Ecological Economics* (Washington, D.C.: Island Press, 1995); H. Hannum, ed., *People, Land, and Community: Collected E. F. Schumacher Society Lectures* (New Haven, Conn.: Yale University Press, 1997).

20. See, for example, G. C. Daily, ed., *Nature's Services: Societal Dependence on Natural Ecosystems* (Washington, D.C.: Island Press, 1997); P. Hawken, A. Lovins, and L. H. Lovins, *Natural Capital: Creating the Next Industrial Revolution* (New York: Little, Brown, 1999); G. C. Daily and K. Ellison, *The New Economy of Nature: The Quest to Make Conservation Profitable* (Washington, D.C.: Island Press, 2002); D. N. Bengston and D. C. Iverson, "Reconstructing Conservation in an Age of Limits: An Ecological Economics Perspective," in *Reconstructing Conservation: Finding Common Ground*, edited by B. A. Minteer and R. E. Manning (Washington, D.C.: Island Press, 2003), pp. 223–238.

21. A. Leopold, "The Role of Wildlife in a Liberal Education," in *Transactions of the Seventh North American Wildlife Conference* (Washington, D.C.: American Wildlife Institute, 1942), p. 487; Flader and Callicott, *River*, p. 303.

22. Leopold, *Sand County Almanac*, p. 207. Emphases in original.

23. Leopold, *Sand County Almanac*, p. 224.

24. D. Orr, "What Is Education For?," in Meine and Knight, *Essential Aldo Leopold*, p. 257.

25. Leopold, *Sand County Almanac*, p. 221.

26. For discussions of the rise of decentralized and community-based approaches in conservation, see D. Western and M. C. Pearl, eds., *Conservation for the Twenty-First Century* (New York: Oxford University Press, 1989); D. Kemmis, *Community and the Politics of Place* (Norman: University of Oklahoma Press, 1990); R. M. Wright, D. Western, and S. C. Strum, eds., *Natural Connections: Perspectives on Community-Based Conservation* (Washington D.C.: Island Press, 1994); W. Jackson, *Becoming Native to This Place* (Lexington: University Press of Kentucky, 1994); W. K. Stevens, *Miracle Under the Oaks: The Revival of Nature in America* (New York: Pocket Books, 1995); W. Vitek and W. Jackson, eds., *Rooted in the Land: Essays on Community and Place* (New Haven, Conn.: Yale University Press, 1996); S. L. Yaffee, A. F. Phillips, I. C. Frentz, P. W. Hardy, S. M. Maleki, and B. E. Thorpe, *Ecosystem Management in the United States: An Assessment of Current Conditions* (Washington D.C.: Island Press, 1996); T. Bernard and J. Young, *The Ecology of Hope: Communities Collaborate for Sustainability* (Gabriola Island, British Columbia: New Society Publishers, 1997); J. E. Williams, C. A. Wood, and M. P. Dombeck, *Watershed Restoration: Principles and Practices* (Bethesda, Md.: American Fisheries Society, 1997); R. Keiter, *Reclaiming the Native Home of Hope: Community, Ecology, and the American West* (Salt Lake City: University of Utah Press, 1998); R. L. Knight and P. B. Landres, eds., *Stewardship Across Boundaries* (Washington D.C.: Island Press, 1998); E. T. Freyfogle, *Bounded People, Boundless Lands: Envisioning a New Land Ethic* (Washington D.C.: Island Press, 1998); J. M. Wondolleck and S. L. Yaffee, *Making Collaboration Work: Lessons from Innovation in Natural Resource Management* (Washington D.C.: Island Press, 2000); P. Brick, D. Snow, and S. Van de Wetering, eds., *Across the Great Divide: Explorations in Collaborative Conservation and the American West* (Washington, D.C.: Island Press, 2000); P. Forbes, *The Great Remembering: Further Thoughts on Land, Soul, and Society* (San Francisco: The Trust for Public Land, 2001); G.

K. Meffe, L. A. Nielsen, R. L. Knight, and D. A. Schenborn, *Ecosystem Management: Adaptive, Community-Based Conservation* (Washington D.C.: Island Press, 2002).

27. R. Diament, J. G. Eugster, and N. J. Mitchell, "Reinventing Conservation: A Practitioner's View," in Minteer and Manning, *Reconstructing Conservation*, pp. 313–326.

28. Worster, *Wealth of Nature*, p. 219.

29. See J. R. Engel and J. G. Engel, eds., *Ethics of Environment and Development: Global Challenge, International Response* (Tucson: University of Arizona Press, 1993); R. Guha and J. Martinez-Alier, *Varieties of Environmentalism: Essays North and South* (London: Earthscan, 1997).

30. Leopold, *Sand County Almanac*, pp. 221, 224–225.

11. Home, Land, Security

Walt Whitman's lines are from "For You O Democracy" in *Leaves of Grass* (1892; reprint, New York: New American Library, 1980), p. 115. Aldo Leopold cited this passage in his essay "The Conservation Ethic," *Journal of Forestry* 31, no. 6 (1933): 642; S. L. Flader and J. B. Callicott, eds., *The River of the Mother of God and Other Essays by Aldo Leopold* (Madison: University of Wisconsin Press, 1991), p. 191.

1. Whitman, *Leaves of Grass*, pp. 145, 146.

2. Whitman, *Leaves of Grass*, p. 112.

3. Whitman, *Leaves of Grass*, pp. 180, 182, 183.

4. See E. Folsom, "Walt Whitman's Prairie Paradise," in *Recovering the Prairie*, edited by R. Sayre (Madison: University of Wisconsin Press, 1999), pp. 47–60.

5. A. Leopold, "The Farmer as a Conservationist," *American Forests* 45, no. 6 (1939): 316; Flader and Callicott, *River*, p. 263.

6. E. Porter, W. Stegner, and P. Stegner, *American Places*, edited by John Macrae III (New York: E. P. Dutton, 1981), p. 10.

7. C. T. Onions, ed., *The Shorter Oxford English Dictionary*, 3rd ed., Vol. 2. (Oxford: Oxford University Press, 1973), pp. 1507–1508. The Greek term is παράδεισος.

8. D. Worster, *The Wealth of Nature: Environmental History and the Ecological Imagination* (New York: Oxford University Press, 1993), pp. 9, 10, 11.

9. See chap. 9 in this volume.

10. Worster, *Wealth of Nature*, p. 15.

11. See E. J. Blakely and M. G. Snyder, *Fortress America: Gated Communities in the United States* (Washington, D.C.: Brookings Institution Press / Lincoln Institute of Land Policy, 1997); S. Low, *Behind the Gates: Life, Security, and the Pursuit of Happiness in Fortress America* (New York: Routledge, 2003); R. Moe and C. Wilkie, *Changing Places: Rebuilding Community in the Age of Sprawl* (New York: Henry Holt, 1999); R. Rymer, "Back to the Future: Disney Reinvents the Company Town," *Harper's Magazine* (1996): 65–71, 75–78; R. Atkin, "Please Fence Me In," *Christian Science Monitor*, 6 August 2003.

12. See R. L. Knight and P. B. Landres, eds., *Stewardship Across Boundaries* (Washington D.C.: Island Press, 1998); E. T. Freyfogle, *Bounded People, Boundless Lands: Envisioning a New Land Ethic* (Washington D.C.: Island Press, 1998).

13. A. Leopold, *A Sand County Almanac and Sketches Here and There* (New York: Oxford University Press, 1949), p. 198. Key modern studies of protected areas and the loss of wildlife include W. D. Newmark, "Legal and Biotic Boundaries of Western North American Parks: A Problem of Congruence," *Biological Conservation* 33, no. 3 (1985): 197–208; W. D. Newmark, "A Land-Bridge Island Perspective on Mammalian Extinctions in Western North American Parks," *Nature* 325, no. 6103 (1987): 430–432; W. D. Newmark, "Extinction of Mammal Populations in Western

North American Parks," *Conservation Biology* 9, no. 3 (1995): 512–526; W. D. Newmark, "Insularization of Tanzanian Parks and Local Extinctions of Large Mammals," *Conservation Biology* 10, no. 6 (1996): 1549–1556; D. B. Gurd and T. D. Nudds, "Insular Biogeography of Mammals in Canadian National Parks: A Re-analysis," *Journal of Biogeography* 26, no. 5 (1999): 973–982; D. H. Rivard, J. Poitevin, D. Plasse, M. Carleton, and D. J. Currie, "Changing Species Richness and Composition in Canadian National Parks," *Conservation Biology* 14, no. 4 (2000): 1099–1109; S. A. Parks and H. A. Harcourt, "Reserve Size, Local Human Density, and Mammalian Extinctions in U.S. Protected Areas," *Conservation Biology* 16, no. 3 (2002): 800–808.

14. For general background, see R. F. Noss and A. Y. Cooperrider, *Saving Nature's Legacy: Protecting and Restoring Biodiversity* (Washington, D.C.: Island Press, 1994); D. Quammen, *The Song of the Dodo: Island Biogeography in an Age of Extinction* (New York: Simon and Schuster, 1996); G. K. Meffe, C. R. Carroll and contributors, *Principles of Conservation Biology*, 2nd ed. (Sunderland, Mass.: Sinauer Associates, 1997).

15. W. Berry, *The Hidden Wound* (San Francisco: North Point Press, 1989), pp. 124, 129.

16. P. Johnson, statement at the symposium "Preventing Extinction: Advances in Biodiversity Conservation," American Museum of Natural History, New York City, 18 April 1997. Johnson was chief of the Natural Resources Conservation Service at the time. See *America's Private Land: A Geography of Hope* (Washington, D.C.: USDA Natural Resources Conservation Service, 1996). These realizations are increasingly evident at the international level as well. The theme of the 5th IUCN (The World Conservation Union) World Parks Congress in Durban, South Africa (8–17 September 2003) was "Benefits Beyond Boundaries." The Durban Accord, the main product of the meeting, stressed the value of the ecosystems services provided by protected areas, and presented "a new paradigm for protected areas . . . emphasizing the role of local communities to share in protected area benefits and decision-making" (IUCN press release, "5th IUCN World Parks Congress Sets Agenda for Next Decade, Spurs Conservation Initiatives for Africa," 17 September 2003).

17. Worster, *Wealth of Nature*, p. 103.

18. Leopold, *Sand County Almanac*, pp. 203–204.

19. T. Jefferson, *The Life and Selected Writings of Thomas Jefferson*, edited by A. Koch and W. Peden (New York: Modern Library, 1998), p. 299. See P. S. Onuf, "'The Strongest Government on Earth'": Jefferson's Republicanism, the Expansion of the Union, and the New Nation's Destiny," in *The Louisiana Purchase and American Expansion*, edited by B. Sparrow and S. Levinson (Durham, N.C.: Duke University Press, in press).

20. Onuf, "'Strongest Government on Earth.'" The emphasis is Onuf's.

21. M. Lewis and W. Clark, G. E. Moulton and T. W. Dunlay, eds., *The Definitive Journals of Lewis and Clark* (Lincoln: University of Nebraska Press, 1986), vol. 2, p. 227 and vol. 8, pp. 370–371.

22. Quoted in Onuf, "'Strongest Government on Earth.'" The words are those of Jefferson's correspondent Antoine Claude Destutt de Tracy in *A Commentary and Review of Montesquieu's Spirit of the Laws* (1811; reprint, New York: Burt Franklin, 1969), p. 181.

23. Quoted in Onuf, "'Strongest Government on Earth.'" The passage is from a 27 April 1809 letter to Madison.

24. Quoted in Onuf, "'Strongest Government on Earth.'" The phrase is from a 26 February 1810 letter to Jefferson's Polish revolutionary comrade Gen. Thaddeus Kosciusko.

25. K. R. Robertson, *Corridors for Tomorrow*, Illinois Natural History Survey Reports No. 320 (Champaign: Illinois Natural History Survey, 1993). I thank Kenneth Robertson for his assistance in providing details on the history of the Corridors for Tomorrow program.

26. Leopold, *Sand County Almanac*, p. 119.

27. A. Lincoln, *The Life and Writings of Abraham Lincoln*, edited by P. Van Doren Stern (1940; reprint, New York: Modern Library, 2000), p. 429.

28. Roosevelt's statement was made in a speech on 19 May 1903 in Sacramento. See E. Morris, *Theodore Rex* (New York: Random House, 2001), p. 231.

29. Leopold, *Sand County Almanac*, p. 204. For a prescient discussion, see David Brower's 1981 lecture "Conservation and National Security," (Berkeley: University of California, College of Natural Resources, Department of Forestry and Natural Resources, 1981; available at www.cnr.berkeley.edu/forestry/lecture.html). Brower's lecture was presented as part of the Horace M. Albright Lectureship in Conservation series.

30. The statement by Vice President Richard Cheney, from a speech in Toronto, was widely reported. See "Quotation of the Day," *New York Times*, 1 May 2001, p. A2.

31. G. Rabb, statement of the IUCN in response to the terrorist attacks of September 11, 24 September 2001.

ACKNOWLEDGMENT OF SOURCES

The essays in this volume have been adapted and updated from the original versions that appeared in the following books and journals. I thank the publishers for their permissions, and am pleased to acknowledge the original publications.

"The Oldest Task in Human History" was originally published in *A New Century for Natural Resources Management*, edited by Richard L. Knight and Sarah F. Bates. Copyright © 1995 Island Press. Reproduced by permission of Island Press, Washington, D.C.

"Conservation and the Progressive Movement" was originally published as "Conservation and the Progressive Movement: Growing from the Radical Center," in *Reconstructing Conservation: Finding Common Ground*, edited by B. A. Minteer and R. E. Manning. Copyright © 2003 Island Press. Reproduced by permission of Island Press, Washington, D.C.

"Conservation Biology and Sustainable Societies" was originally published as "Conservation Biology and Sustainable Societies: A Historical Perspective," in *After Earth Day: Continuing the Conservation Effort*, edited by M. Oelschlaeger. Copyright © 1992 University of North Texas Press.

"Leopold's Fine Line" was originally published as "The Utility of Preservation and the Preservation of Utility: Leopold's Fine Line," in *The Wilderness Condition: Essays on Environment and Civilization*, edited by M. Oelschlaeger. Copyright © 1992 Max Oelschlaeger. Used by permission of Sierra Club Books.

An earlier version of "Emergence of An Idea" appeared as "Keeper of the Cogs." Reprinted with permission from the Nov/Dec 1992 issue of *Defenders* magazine. Copyright © 1992 Defenders of Wildlife. All rights reserved.

"Giving Voice to Concern" was originally published as "Giving Voice to Concern: Aldo Leopold's 'Marshland Elegy,'" in *Marshland Elegy*, edited by F. B. Miracle. Copyright © 1999 Wisconsin Center for the Book at the Wisconsin Academy of Sciences, Arts and Letters.

"Moving Mountains" was originally published as "Moving Mountains: Aldo Leopold and *A Sand County Almanac*," in the Winter 1998 issue of the *Wildlife Society Bulletin* Copyright © 1998 The Wildlife Society.

"The *Secret* Leopold" was originally published as "The *Secret* Leopold, or Who Really Wrote *A Sand County Almanac?*" in *Transactions of the Wisconsin Academy of Sciences, Arts and Letters*, Volume 88. Copyright © 2000 The Wisconsin Academy of Sciences, Arts and Letters.

"Inherit the Grid" was originally published in *Placing Nature: Culture and Landscape Ecology*, edited by J. I. Nassauer. Copyright © 1997 Island Press. Reproduced by permission of Island Press, Washington, D.C.

An abridged version of "The Once and Future Land Ethic," coauthored with Nina Leopold Bradley, appeared in *From Conquest to Conservation: Our Public Lands Legacy*, edited by M. P. Dombeck, C. A. Wood, and J. E. Williams. Copyright © 2003 Michael P. Dombeck and Christopher A. Wood. Reproduced by permission of Island Press, Washington, D.C.

"Home, Land, Security" includes materials from two previously published essays as well as previously unpublished material. Parts of this essay were originally published as "The Continent Indissoluble," in *Stewardship Across Boundaries*, edited by R. L. Knight and P. B. Landres. Copyright © 1998 Island Press. Reproduced by permission of Island Press, Washington, D.C. Another part of this essay was adapted from material in "Leave No Acre Behind: Renewing the Conservation Consensus" in *Wingspread Journal*, copyright © 2004 The Johnson Foundation.

ABOUT THE AUTHOR

Curt Meine is a writer and conservation biologist. He is author of the biography *Aldo Leopold: His Life and Work*, editor of the collection *Wallace Stegner and the Continental Vision: Essays on Literature, History, and Landscape*, and coeditor with Richard L. Knight of *The Essential Aldo Leopold: Quotations and Commentaries*. He has served on the board of governors of the Society for Conservation Biology and on the editorial boards of the journals *Conservation Biology* and *Environmental Ethics*.

ISLAND PRESS BOARD OF DIRECTORS

Victor M. Sher, Esq.
Chair
Sher & Leff
San Francisco, CA

Dane A. Nichols
Vice-Chair
Washington, DC

Carolyn Peachey
Secretary
Campbell, Peachey & Associates
Washington, DC

Drummond Pike
Treasurer
President
The Tides Foundation
San Francisco, CA

Robert E. Baensch
Director, Center for Publishing
New York University
New York, NY

David C. Cole
President
Aquaterra, Inc.
Washington, VA

Catherine M. Conover
Quercus LLC
Washington, DC

William H. Meadows
President
The Wilderness Society
Washington, DC

Henry Reath
Collectors Reprints
Princeton, NJ

Will Rogers
President
The Trust for Public Land
San Francisco, CA

Charles C. Savitt
President
Island Press
Washington, DC

Susan E. Sechler
Senior Advisor
The German Marshall Fund
Washington, DC

Peter R. Stein
General Partner
LTC Conservation Advisory Services
The Lyme Timber Company
Hanover, NH

Diana Wall, Ph.D.
Director and Professor
Natural Resource Ecology Laboratory
Colorado State University
Fort Collins, CO

Wren Wirth
Washington, DC